HEALTH LITERACY

IMPROVING HEALTH, HEALTH SYSTEMS, AND HEALTH POLICY AROUND THE WORLD

WORKSHOP SUMMARY

Lyla M. Hernandez, *Rapporteur*

Roundtable on Health Literacy

Board on Population Health and Public Health Practice

INSTITUTE OF MEDICINE
OF THE NATIONAL ACADEMIES

THE NATIONAL ACADEMIES PRESS
Washington, D.C.
www.nap.edu

THE NATIONAL ACADEMIES PRESS   500 Fifth Street, NW   Washington, DC 20001

NOTICE: The project that is the subject of this report was approved by the Governing Board of the National Research Council, whose members are drawn from the councils of the National Academy of Sciences, the National Academy of Engineering, and the Institute of Medicine.

This study was supported by contracts between the National Academy of Sciences and Aetna; the Agency for Healthcare Research and Quality (HHSP233200900537P); the American College of Physicians Foundation; America's Health Insurance Plans; the Health Resources and Services Administration (HHSH25034004T); the East Bay Community Foundation (Kaiser Permanente); GlaxoSmithKline; Humana; Johnson & Johnson; Merck and Co., Inc.; the Missouri Foundation for Health (09-0290-HL-09); Office of Disease Prevention and Health Promotion; and United Healthcare. Any opinions, findings, conclusions, or recommendations expressed in this publication are those of the author(s) and do not necessarily reflect the view of the organizations or agencies that provided support for this project.

International Standard Book Number-13:   978-0-309-28484-4
International Standard Book Number-10:   0-309-28484-8

Additional copies of this report are available from the National Academies Press, 500 Fifth Street, NW, Keck 360, Washington, DC 20055; (800) 624-6242 or (202) 334-3313; http://www.nap.edu.

For more information about the Institute of Medicine, visit the IOM home page at: **www.iom.edu**.

Printed in the United States of America

The serpent has been a symbol of long life, healing, and knowledge among almost all cultures and religions since the beginning of recorded history. The serpent adopted as a logotype by the Institute of Medicine is a relief carving from ancient Greece, now held by the Staatliche Museen in Berlin.

Suggested citation: IOM (Institute of Medicine). 2013. *Health literacy: Improving health, health systems, and health policy around the world: Workshop summary*. Washington, DC: The National Academies Press.

"Knowing is not enough; we must apply.
Willing is not enough; we must do."
—Goethe

INSTITUTE OF MEDICINE
OF THE NATIONAL ACADEMIES

Advising the Nation. Improving Health.

THE NATIONAL ACADEMIES
Advisers to the Nation on Science, Engineering, and Medicine

The **National Academy of Sciences** is a private, nonprofit, self-perpetuating society of distinguished scholars engaged in scientific and engineering research, dedicated to the furtherance of science and technology and to their use for the general welfare. Upon the authority of the charter granted to it by the Congress in 1863, the Academy has a mandate that requires it to advise the federal government on scientific and technical matters. Dr. Ralph J. Cicerone is president of the National Academy of Sciences.

The **National Academy of Engineering** was established in 1964, under the charter of the National Academy of Sciences, as a parallel organization of outstanding engineers. It is autonomous in its administration and in the selection of its members, sharing with the National Academy of Sciences the responsibility for advising the federal government. The National Academy of Engineering also sponsors engineering programs aimed at meeting national needs, encourages education and research, and recognizes the superior achievements of engineers. Dr. C. D. (Dan) Mote, Jr., is president of the National Academy of Engineering.

The **Institute of Medicine** was established in 1970 by the National Academy of Sciences to secure the services of eminent members of appropriate professions in the examination of policy matters pertaining to the health of the public. The Institute acts under the responsibility given to the National Academy of Sciences by its congressional charter to be an adviser to the federal government and, upon its own initiative, to identify issues of medical care, research, and education. Dr. Harvey V. Fineberg is president of the Institute of Medicine.

The **National Research Council** was organized by the National Academy of Sciences in 1916 to associate the broad community of science and technology with the Academy's purposes of furthering knowledge and advising the federal government. Functioning in accordance with general policies determined by the Academy, the Council has become the principal operating agency of both the National Academy of Sciences and the National Academy of Engineering in providing services to the government, the public, and the scientific and engineering communities. The Council is administered jointly by both Academies and the Institute of Medicine. Dr. Ralph J. Cicerone and Dr. C. D. (Dan) Mote, Jr., are chair and vice chair, respectively, of the National Research Council.

www.national-academies.org

PLANNING COMMITTEE ON HEALTH LITERACY: IMPROVING HEALTH, HEALTH SYSTEMS, AND HEALTH POLICY AROUND THE WORLD[1]

DEBBIE FRITZ, Director for Policy and Standards, Health Management Innovations Division, GlaxoSmithKline

MARGARET LOVELAND, Senior Director of Global Medical Affairs, Merck & Co., Inc.

CLARENCE PEARSON, Global Health Leadership and Management Consultant to Nonprofit Organizations

ANDREW PLEASANT, Health Literacy and Research Director, Canyon Ranch Institute

SCOTT C. RATZAN, Vice President, Global Health, Johnson & Johnson, Editor-in-Chief, *Journal of Health Communication: International Perspectives*

WILL ROSS, Associate Dean for Diversity and Associate Professor of Medicine, Washington University School of Medicine

RIMA RUDD, Department of Society, Human Development, and Health, Harvard School of Public Health

---

[1]Institute of Medicine planning committees are solely responsible for organizing the workshop, identifying topics, and choosing speakers. The responsibility for the published workshop summary rests with the workshop rapporteur and the institution.

v

ROUNDTABLE ON HEALTH LITERACY[1]

GEORGE ISHAM (*Chair*), Medical Director and Chief Health Officer, HealthPartners

WILMA ALVARADO-LITTLE, Director, Community Engagement/Outreach Center for the Elimination of Minority Health Disparities, University of Albany

CINDY BRACH, Senior Health Policy Researcher, Center for Delivery, Organization, and Markets, Agency for Healthcare Research and Quality

DARREN DEWALT, Associate Professor of Medicine, University of North Carolina

BENARD P. DREYER, Professor of Pediatrics, New York University School of Medicine; Chair, American Academy of Pediatrics Health Literacy Program Advisory Committee

LEONARD EPSTEIN, Senior Advisor, Clinical Quality and Culture, Health Resources and Services Administration

LAURIE FRANCIS, Senior Director of Clinic Operations and Quality, Oregon Primary Care Association

DEBBIE FRITZ, Director, Policy and Standards, Health Management Innovations Division, GlaxoSmithKline

MARTHA GRAGG, Vice President of Program, Missouri Foundation for Health

JILL GRIFFITHS, Vice President, Communications, Aetna

LINDA HARRIS, Team Leader, Health Communication and eHealth Team, Office of Disease Prevention and Health Promotion, U.S. Department of Health and Human Services

BETSY L. HUMPHREYS, Deputy Director, National Library of Medicine, National Institutes of Health

JOAN KELLY, Director, Consumer Experience, Humana, Inc.

MARGARET LOVELAND, Global Medical Affairs, Merck & Co., Inc.

PATRICK McGARRY, Assistant Division Director, Scientific Activities Division

RUTH PARKER, Professor of Medicine, Emory University School of Medicine

KAVITA PATEL, Managing Director for Clinical Transformation and Delivery, The Brookings Institution

CLARENCE PEARSON, Consultant, Global Health Leadership and Management

---

[1]Institute of Medicine forums and roundtables do not issue, review, or approve individual documents. The responsibility for the published workshop summary rests with the workshop rapporteur and the institution.

SUSAN PISANO, Vice President of Communications, America's Health Insurance Plans

ANDREW PLEASANT, Health Literacy and Research Director, Canyon Ranch Institute

SCOTT C. RATZAN, Vice President, Global Health, Johnson & Johnson

WILL ROSS, Associate Dean for Diversity, Associate Professor of Medicine, Washington University School of Medicine

RIMA RUDD, Department of Society, Human Development & Health, Harvard School of Public Health

STEVEN RUSH, Director, Health Literacy Innovations Program, United Health Group

PAUL M. SCHYVE, Senior Vice President, The Joint Commission

PATRICK WAYTE, Vice President, Marketing and Health Education, American Heart Association

WINSTON F. WONG, Medical Director, Community Benefit, Disparities Improvement and Quality Initiatives, Kaiser Permanente

IOM Staff

LYLA M. HERNANDEZ, Roundtable Director
ANDREW LEMERISE, Research Associate
ANGELA MARTIN, Senior Program Assistant
ROSE MARIE MARTINEZ, Director, Board on Population Health and Public Health Practice

Reviewers

This workshop summary has been reviewed in draft form by individuals chosen for their diverse perspectives and technical expertise, in accordance with procedures approved by the National Research Council's Report Review Committee. The purpose of this independent review is to provide candid and critical comments that will assist the institution in making its published workshop summary as sound as possible and to ensure that the workshop summary meets institutional standards for objectivity, evidence, and responsiveness to the study charge. The review comments and draft manuscript remain confidential to protect the integrity of the process. We wish to thank the following individuals for their review of this workshop summary:

Cynthia Baur, Centers for Disease Control and Prevention
Yolanda Partida, UCSF Fresno Center for Medical Education & Research
Lee Sanders, Stanford University
Sarah Hudson Scholle, National Committee for Quality Assurance

Although the reviewers listed above have provided many constructive comments and suggestions, they were not asked to endorse the final draft of the workshop summary before its release. The review of this workshop summary was overseen by **Harold J. Fallon,** Medical University of South Carolina. Appointed by the Institute of Medicine, he was responsible for making certain that an independent examination of this workshop summary was carried out in accordance with institutional procedures and that all review comments were carefully considered. Responsibility for the final content of this workshop summary rests entirely with the rapporteur and the institution.

Acknowledgments

The sponsors of the Institute of Medicine Roundtable on Health Literacy made it possible to plan and conduct the workshop Health Literacy: Improving Health, Health Systems, and Health Policy Around the World: Workshop Summary. Sponsors from the U.S. Department of Health and Human Services are the Agency for Healthcare Research and Quality, the Health Resources and Services Administration, and the Office of Disease Prevention and Health Promotion. Nonfederal sponsorship was provided by Aetna; the American College of Physicians Foundation; the America's Health Insurance Plans; the East Bay Community Foundation (Kaiser Permanente); GlaxoSmithKline; Humana; Johnson & Johnson; Merck and Co., Inc.; the Missouri Foundation for Health; and the UnitedHealth Group.

The Roundtable wishes to extend its appreciation to Andrew Pleasant for his excellent paper exploring health literacy practices around the world. The Roundtable also wishes to express its gratitude to the following speakers for their thoughtful and stimulating presentations: Franklin Apfel, Cynthia Baur, Jo Ivey Boufford, Jennifer Cabe, Nicola Dunbar, Federica Gazzotti, Steven Hoffman, Fikry W. Isaac, Ilona Kickbusch, Jacob Kumaresan, Diane Levin-Zamir, Jennifer Lynch, Don Nutbeam, Jürgen M. Pelikan, Scott C. Ratzan, Michael Rosenblatt, Kristine Sørensen, Suzanne Thompson, and Sandra Vamos. The planning committee members are also to be commended for their work in developing an excellent workshop agenda. Members of the planning committee were Debbie Fritz, Margaret Loveland, Clarence Pearson, Andrew Pleasant, Scott C. Ratzan, Will Ross, and Rima Rudd.

Contents

Tables and Figures

TABLES

FIGURES

1

Introduction

Health literacy is the degree to which individuals have the capacity to obtain, process, and understand basic health information and services needed to make appropriate health care decisions.
(Ratzan and Parker, 2000)

The roots of health literacy can be traced back to the national literacy movement in India under Gandhi and to aid groups working in Africa to promote education and health. The term *health literacy* was first used in 1974 and described as "health education meeting minimal standards for all school grade levels" (Ratzan, 2001). From that first use the definition of health literacy evolved during the next 30 years with official definitions promulgated by government agencies and large programs. Despite differences among these definitions, they all hold in common the idea that health literacy involves the need for people to understand information that helps them maintain good health.

With the expansion of health literacy research and programs in the 1990s, health literacy has taken two different approaches, one oriented to clinical care and the other to public health (Pleasant and Kuruvilla, 2008). The clinical approach often involves a patient–provider interaction and is the focus of much of the health literacy efforts in the United States and Europe (Brand and Sørensen, 2010; Pleasant and Kuruvilla, 2008). The public health approach to health literacy is more prominent in developing nations, where organizations not only work to improve health for large groups of people but also provide educational opportunities to the same groups.

Although the United States produces a majority of the research on health literacy (Kondilis et al., 2008), Europe has strong multinational programs as well as research efforts (Brand and Sørensen, 2010), and health literacy experts in developing countries have created successful programs implemented on a community level (UN ECOSOC, 2010). Given these distinct strengths of efforts worldwide, there are many opportunities for collaboration. International collaboration can harness the United States' research power, Europe's multilingual and multinational experience, and developing nations' community-based programs to create robust programs and research that reach people—not based on language or nationality but on need and value.

The Institute of Medicine Roundtable on Health Literacy decided to hold a workshop focused on international health literacy efforts that would feature presentations and discussion about health literacy interventions from various countries as well as other topics related to international health literacy. As background for the workshop, a paper was commissioned to explore and report on health literacy policies and practices outside the United States (see Appendix A). The workshop was organized by an independent planning committee in accordance with the procedures of the National Academy of Sciences. The planning committee members were Debbie Fritz, Margaret Loveland, Clarence Pearson, Andrew Pleasant, Scott C. Ratzan, Will Ross, and Rima Rudd. The role of the workshop planning committee was limited to planning the workshop. Unlike a consensus committee report, a workshop summary may not contain conclusions and recommendations, except as expressed by and attributed to individual presenters and participants. Therefore, this summary has been prepared by the workshop rapporteur as a factual summary of what occurred at the workshop.

The workshop was moderated by Roundtable chair George Isham and featured presentations from invited speakers. These presentations make up the chapters that follow. Each topic (chapter) includes one or more presentations that are followed by a group discussion. Chapter 2 includes two presentations that set the stage for a discussion of international health literacy efforts. The presentations in Chapter 3 detail different health literacy perspectives and a discussion of public–private partnerships for health literacy. Chapter 4 presentations address national policies and programs promoting health literacy. Chapter 5 presentations focus on local innovations in health literacy. Chapter 6 discusses future directions, including conceptualizing health literacy, research and measures, and translating what is known in order to improve health literacy programs and policies.

REFERENCES

Brand, H., and K. Sørensen. 2011. *Measuring health literacy in Europe: The development of the HLS-EU tool.* http://inthealth.eu/app/download/3310881502/Measuring+Health+Literacy+in+Europe+-+Stockholm+9+3+2010.pdf (accessed October 19, 2011).

Kondilis, B. K., I. J. Kiriaze, A. P. Athanasoulia, and M. E. Falagas. 2008. Mapping health literacy research in the European Union: A bibliometric analysis. *PLoS ONE* 3(6):e2519.

Pleasant, A., and S. Kuruvilla. 2008. A tale of two health literacies: Public health and clinical approaches to health literacy. *Health Promotion International* 23(2):152-159.

Ratzan, S. C. 2001. Health literacy: Communication for the public good. *Health Promotion International* 16(2):207-214.

Ratzan, S. C., and R. M. Parker. 2000. Introduction. In *National Library of Medicine current bibliographies in medicine: Health literacy,* edited by C. R. Selden, M. Zorn, S. C. Ratzan, and R. M. Parker. NLM Pub. No. CBM 2000-1. Bethesda, MD: National Institutes of Health.

UN ECOSOC (United Nations Economic and Social Council). 2010. Health literacy and the Millennium Development Goals: United Nations Economic and Social Council (ECOSOC) regional meeting background paper (abstracted). *Journal of Health Communication* 15(Supp 2):211-223.

2

Welcome

THE NEW YORK ACADEMY OF MEDICINE

Jo Ivey Boufford, M.D.
President, New York Academy of Medicine
Foreign Secretary, Institute of Medicine

The New York Academy of Medicine was established in 1847 by a group of physicians in New York who wanted to improve the quality of health care, Boufford said. The academy then moved to address public health issues (e.g., infant immunization and feeding practices) and was instrumental in establishing the Board of Health in New York City at the end of the 19th century. Following the events of September 11, 2001, the academy became involved in working with schoolchildren suffering from posttraumatic stress syndrome. Current priorities are urban health and healthy aging, prevention, and eliminating health disparities.

The New York Academy of Medicine works on the kind of continuum represented by this meeting, Boufford said—the continuum of local to global. For example, using the World Health Organization (WHO) model for an age-friendly city,[1] the academy has been working with the East

---

[1]"The WHO Age-friendly Environments Programme is an international effort to address the environmental and social factors that contribute to active and healthy ageing. The Programme helps cities and communities become more supportive of older people by addressing their needs across eight dimensions: the built environment, transport, housing, social participation, respect and social inclusion, civic participation and employment,

Harlem community as well as four other parts of the city to develop aging-improvement districts. It is also working with colleagues in Philadelphia, Chicago, and Oakland and has presented the New York experience with those age-friendly cities to Tokyo and Taiwan. There is a global network of cities learning from each other how to apply the principles for the development of age-friendly cities and communities in their own contexts.

Health literacy is fundamental to age-friendly cities, Boufford said. It involves starting with the voices of older persons, asking simple questions such as "What makes it harder or easier for you to live an active and engaged life in your community?" This approach has led to major policy changes in New York City over the last 2 to 3 years: things such as benches on sidewalks, traffic lights with slower timers so older persons can get across the street before the light changes, and senior hours at city pools. Asking people what they want and need is fundamental to the Affordable Care Act, both at the patient level and at the community-based prevention level.

Boufford also described efforts at the Institute of Medicine (IOM) to include a more global perspective. Recently, the IOM council voted to increase the number of new foreign associate members from 5 per year to 10 per year. There will also be increased effort to add international scholars as presenters at workshops and members of roundtables and peer-reviewed studies. The IOM is also working with academies in other countries to apply the reports and other products of the IOM in their own contexts.

The New York Academy of Medicine is pleased to be the venue selected for the beginning of efforts on the part of the IOM Roundtable on Health Literacy to develop a global health literacy community, Boufford said. Such a community can provide the opportunity to learn from each other and to move health literacy forward.

UNITED NATIONS

Steven J. Hoffman
Executive Office of the United Nations Secretary-General

Hoffman said that it is an exciting moment in New York City with the United Nations General Assembly beginning the next day and world leaders arriving to debate some of the greatest issues facing the United Nations. There is no better time or place for the IOM Roundtable on Health Literacy, he said, because health literacy is fundamental to attain-

communication, and community support and health services" (http://www.who.int/ageing/age_friendly_cities/en [accessed November 15, 2012]).

ing the best possible health status and mitigating health inequalities around the world.

From a global perspective, improving health literacy is essential for making progress on the Millennium Development Goals (MDGs),[2] Hoffman said. The manner in which health literacy affects the three health-related MDGs is clear, he continued, because it is known that health literate people are healthier people, especially when they are empowered to act upon the social determinants of health and to demand the fulfillments of their health rights.

But health literacy also affects the other MDGs—for without a sufficient level of health literacy it will be impossible to fully eradicate poverty, to achieve universal primary education, and to promote gender equality, Hoffman said. Given increases in cross-border trade and travel that exposes people to new threats and diseases, health literacy becomes more important than ever before. In addition, he said, noncommunicable diseases are increasingly taking the spotlight on the global agenda, with the top six causes of mortality worldwide being high blood pressure, tobacco use, high blood glucose, physical inactivity, obesity, and high cholesterol.

The United Nations is serious about promoting health literacy, Hoffman said. For example, the Joint United Nations Programme on HIV/AIDS (UNAIDS); United Nations Educational, Scientific and Cultural Organization (UNESCO); and other key stakeholders launched EDU-KIDS in 2004 This is an initiative focusing on preventing the spread of HIV through education. Another example is the United Nations Children's Fund (UNICEF)-supported skills-based health education efforts that focus on the development of knowledge, attitudes, values, and life skills that children need to make the best health decisions possible. The WHO is helping member states use new e-health technologies, and the Pan American Health Organization is implementing a regional e-health strategy and plan for action for all countries in its region.

The Secretary-General is also serious about health literacy, Hoffman said. For example, last week, instead of meeting prime ministers or presidents for his first bilateral meeting of this General Assembly session, the Secretary-General chose to meet Kami, an HIV-positive Muppet from *Sesame Street*. He did this to raise global awareness of HIV among children and the challenges facing people who live with HIV, Hoffman said.

Improving health literacy among women and children is particu-

---

[2]"The eight Millennium Development Goals (MDGs)—which range from halving extreme poverty to halting the spread of HIV/AIDS and providing universal primary education, all by the target date of 2015—form a blueprint agreed to by all the world's countries and all the world's leading development institutions. They have galvanized unprecedented efforts to meet the needs of the world's poorest" (http://www.un.org/millenniumgoals/bkgd.shtml [accessed November 15, 2012]).

larly important, Hoffman said, and the Secretary-General, guided by the MDGs, has focused a great deal of his efforts on the Every Woman Every Child initiative.[3] Women and children are the most vulnerable members of society, face the greatest levels of poverty and discrimination, have the fewest opportunities, have the most to gain from health literacy initiatives, and are where the greatest successes for health and other goals might be achieved, Hoffman said. He then quoted the Secretary-General as often saying: "Where women and children are empowered and educated, economies are productive and strong. Where women and children are more fully represented, societies are more peaceful and stable." And, Hoffman added, women and children probably represent our world's greatest untapped resource.

But, Hoffman said, one cannot think only about how health literacy may change the world. One must also think about what the changes in our world mean for how we deliver health literacy initiatives. For example, with the largest proportion of young people ever on the face of the planet, it is important to think creatively about how to reach this group, to appeal to their tech-savvy ways, and to empower them with choice. Technology will no doubt be a key facilitator of health literacy, Hoffman said, since three-quarters of the world's inhabitants have access to a mobile phone, a greater proportion than that of people with access to essential medicines (World Bank, 2012).

Concluding his presentation, Hoffman said that bridging the gap between what is known about health issues and how the media reports them is important. He advocated for the potential of Web 2.0, the blogosphere, Twitter, and other online spaces for the promotion of health. It is important to think about how these technologies and platforms can be used to improve health literacy and accelerate progress in global health, Hoffman said.

REFERENCE

World Bank. 2012. *Information and communications for development: Maximizing mobile.* http://siteresources.worldbank.org/EXTINFORMATIONANDCOMMUNICATION ANDTECHNOLOGIES/Resources/IC4D-2012-Report.pdf (accessed November 15, 2012).

---

[3]Every Woman Every Child, led by UN Secretary-General Ban Ki-moon, aims "to mobilize and intensify global action to improve the health of women and children around the world. Working with leaders from governments, multilateral organizations, the private sector and civil society, *Every Woman Every Child* aims to save the lives of 16 million women and children and improve the lives of millions more" (http://www.everywomaneverychild.org/ [accessed November 15, 2012]).

3

Health Literacy Perspectives

HEALTH LITERACY WORK OF THE
WORLD HEALTH ORGANIZATION

Jacob Kumaresan, M.D., Dr.P.H.
Executive Director, World Health Organization
Office at the United Nations in New York

This is a great time to celebrate the United Nations (UN) Literacy Decade of 2003 to 2012, Kumaresan said, and an opportune moment to convene this roundtable on health literacy. Health literacy is the cognitive and social skills that determine the motivation and ability of individuals to gain access to, to understand, and to use information in ways that promote and maintain good health. Health literacy implies achievement of a level of knowledge, personal skills, and confidence to take action to improve personal and community health by changing personal lifestyles and living conditions, Kumaresan said.

Kumaresan said that health education aims to influence individual lifestyle decisions and raise awareness of the determinants of health. This is achieved through methods that go beyond information diffusion; it entails interaction, participation, and critical analysis. Health education leads to health literacy, he said, which then empowers individuals, families, and the community. Health literacy goes beyond a narrow concept of health education and individual behavior-oriented communications to address social, environmental, and political issues.

Health literacy is a tool for empowering people to take control of their

9

health by helping them properly use information, leading to personal and social benefit and thereby enabling community action and the building of social capital, Kumaresan said. It is a means to social and human development. Because it improves people's access to health information and their capacity to use it, health literacy is critical to empowerment.

Major challenges exist, however. Worldwide the level of health literacy is low. Kumaresan noted that people with low levels of health literacy are more likely to

- have a low level of information and communication technology literacy and less access to the Internet and online health information,
- not be able to evaluate the quality of information from different sources, and
- have lower use of preventive services and higher use of treatment services resulting in higher health care costs.

Although there is a plethora of health information on the Internet, there is a lack of evidence-based information that is easily available to the general public. There is no standard quality check, and it is difficult for consumers to understand and evaluate the accuracy of the information they do have, Kumaresan said. Furthermore, the level of health literacy in many developing countries is unknown. Cultural issues and language barriers also exist.

Kumaresan described several strategies for improving health literacy. First, community action for health should be a key component of health literacy. And, in order for that to be helpful, Kumaresan added, one needs a well-functioning, rights-based, patient-centered health care system. Finally, there must be multisector collaboration at the national, regional, and international levels to provide all people with access and to overcome inequities.

Inequalities in health are a major problem, Kumaresan noted. For example, in New Zealand the gap between non-Māori and Māori life expectancies was 16 years for males and 14 years for females in 1951. With strong government action that gap decreased to about 7 years for both in 2006. But this decrease required major action by the government and strong leadership from the Ministry of Health, Kumaresan said. Strategies and actions included providing universal access to health care services, appropriate education materials, community empowerment programs, and educational programs to help increase the literacy levels of consumers. Education needs to be provided not only by the clinics and hospitals but also by other institutions that can increase public health literacy rates such as schools, colleges, workplaces, and libraries.

Also important is the use of innovative and appropriate information and communication technologies to bridge the health literacy gap and pass on information using traditional media, mobile devices, and the Internet, Kumaresan said. The term *mobile health* is used to describe the use of mobile and wireless devices to improve health outcomes, health care services, and health services. The mobile health tobacco cessation project, a program of the World Health Organization (WHO) and the International Telecommunications Union, is an example of success with new technologies. The project used mobile phones to send messages aimed at raising awareness of risk factors, screening, and citizen reporting. The Short Message Service (SMS)-based cessation programs are low-cost, personalized, and interactive, and they provide information on medication and support tools, as well as encouragement, Kumaresan said. Successful programs have been implemented in the United Kingdom, the United States, and New Zealand.

Kumaresan said that noncommunicable diseases are responsible for the highest proportion of deaths globally (see Figure 3-1). This is also a critical issue for low- and middle-income countries. Hence, for only the second time in the history of the United Nations, a health issue was discussed at the high-level meeting in September 2011, attended by heads of state. World leaders adopted a political declaration on prevention and control of noncommunicable diseases (NCDs) that requests the UN Secretary-General, in cooperation with the Director-General of the WHO, to prepare a report on strengthening multisectoral preventive action and to report on progress made in combating NCDs (UN General Assembly, 2011a).

One approach to addressing NCDs is through the use of mobile health, which has been used to train health workers and trainee nurses about prevention of noncommunicable disease risk factors. Text messages, Kumaresan said, can be used to improve diabetes management compliance and encourage the use of condoms. Mobile technology can also use sensors to track and map use of inhalers by asthmatics. Mobile health technologies are important because their reach in developing countries is so much greater than other technology or health infrastructures. He said that in developing countries 11 million people have access to hospital beds and 305 million people have access to computers, but 2.2 billion people use mobile phones, and 40 percent of those users are in rural areas. The global coverage for mobile phones is 7.4 billion today and is projected to be 10 billion by 2017 (BBC, 2012).

Use of mobile health technologies overcomes structural barriers to health by allowing for more personal forms of communication and community-based educational outreach, Kumaresan said. One example is the CommCare program in the state of Bihar in India. This program uses a mobile phone application as a tool for "counseling adolescent girls and women on menstrual hygiene, sexually transmitted diseases and family planning methods" (Treatman et al., 2012). This is a rural develop-

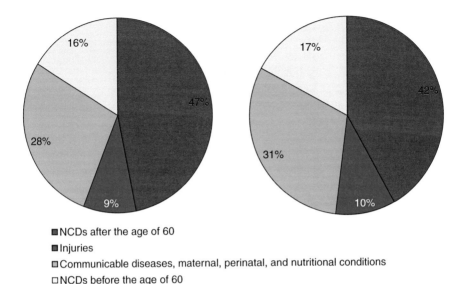

■ NCDs after the age of 60
■ Injuries
□ Communicable diseases, maternal, perinatal, and nutritional conditions
□ NCDs before the age of 60

FIGURE 3-1 The rapidly increasing burden of noncommunicable diseases in the developing world.
NOTE: NCDs = noncommunicable diseases.
SOURCE: WHO, 2011.

ment program supported by the Ministry of Health, and it is helping to empower young women.

Examples of health literacy in action can be found in many parts of the world. In the Philippines, for example, there is a national plan for a campaign to promote breastfeeding and infant nutrition. This program resulted in not only an increase in breastfeeding but also a decrease in the infant mortality rate, Kumaresan said. Another example is a malaria program in eight countries in Central America. The program consists of an environmental campaign focused on community cleaning of neighborhoods without the use of DDT pesticide. People were encouraged to cover water storage containers and drain standing water. They organized community cleanings in streets, forest areas, and swamps. In 2 years, there was a reduction in vector density and a 63 percent reduction in malaria cases, Kumaresan said.

The WHO partners with UN agencies to promote health literacy work. In February 2012, the WHO, in collaboration with the International Telecommunication Union (ITU), launched the National eHealth Strategy Toolkit[1] to help individual governments develop an e-health strategy,

---

[1] The toolkit can be found at http://www.itu.int/pub/D-STR-E_HEALTH.05-2012 (accessed November 15, 2012).

action plan, and monitoring framework at the national level. An e-health infrastructure (see Figure 3-2) can help manage health and well-being by monitoring and managing medications. It can access records—either personal or medical records—and it can have automated dispensing of medication. There can also be interaction with care providers and remote monitoring.

WHO regional offices are closely involved in building health literacy, mobile health, and e-health efforts. For example, according to Kumaresan, the European region has initiated various programs that are empowerment focused. First is the NCDs prevention program that supplies information and tools to prevent and manage such diseases. A second program is focused on mental health, and the third is focused on patients' rights and safety around the theme of blood transfusion and hospital infections.

Kumaresan concluded by saying that the way information is provided to people should increase understanding, not baffle the recipient.

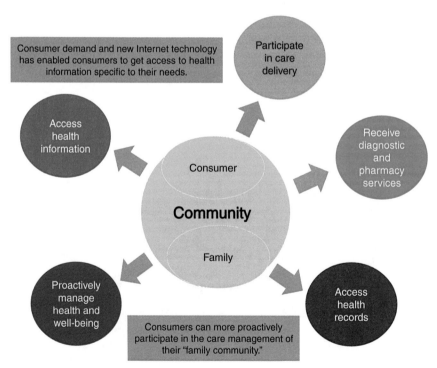

FIGURE 3-2 E-health architecture model.
SOURCE: Kumaresan, 2012.

POLICIES AND PROGRAMS PROMOTING
HEALTH LITERACY GLOBALLY

Scott C. Ratzan, M.D., M.P.A.
Vice President, Global Health
Johnson & Johnson

Ratzan begin by quoting the preamble of the constitution of the WHO that states, "Informed opinion and active cooperation on the part of the public are of the utmost importance in the improvement of health of the people" (WHO, 2006). Much of health literacy is focused on the public good, that is, on helping to create the conditions under which people can be informed and actively participate in their health management. It will take time to marshal the necessary forces to achieve health literacy for the world's population, Ratzan said.

"Health literacy is the degree to which individuals have the capacity to obtain, process, and understand basic health information and services needed to make appropriate health decisions" (Ratzan and Parker, 2000). This definition can encompass mobile health information and e-health technologies. It also addresses health services, which is important because much of what needs to be addressed is how health care is delivered. The framework for health literacy involves both individual skills and abilities as well as system complexities (see Figure 3-3).

Ratzan said this framework fits well with Kumaresan's discussion of health promotion and quality. In the figure, on the left in yellow, is what many people think of as health education for individuals. On the right

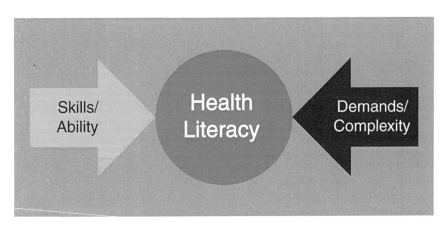

FIGURE 3-3 Health literacy framework.
SOURCE: Parker, 2009.

in red is a component of the health care quality discussion—how can the demands and complexities of the system be simplified? And in the middle is health literacy.

Fortunately, there are a number of discussions on health literacy going on around the world. In October 2008, Ratzan said he participated in an European Union (EU) high-level pharmaceutical forum. Emerging from that forum was an EU declaration that stresses the need to enhance health literacy as a policy at EU and member-state levels. He recommends that future EU policy on information to patients on diseases and treatments should move toward new approaches in a coordinated manner and build on a dialogue with stakeholders, promoting health literacy and health information in the broadest sense (European Communities, 2008).

At a July 2009 meeting of the UN Economic and Social Council (ECOSOC) in Beijing, the ECOSOC issued a ministerial declaration stating, "We stress that health literacy is an important factor in ensuring significant health outcomes and in this regard, call for the development of appropriate action plans to promote health literacy."[2] Several months later, Ratzan said, the Chinese health minister, during a speech in Geneva, Switzerland, said that health literacy is an important factor in ensuring positive health outcomes and called for the development of appropriate action plans to promote health literacy.

In September 2011, a political declaration of the high-level meeting of the UN General Assembly on the prevention and control of NCDs was issued. One of the recommendations reads,

> Develop, strengthen and implement as appropriate, multisectoral public policies and action plans to promote health education and health literacy, including through evidence-based education and information strategies and programmes in and out of schools, and through public awareness campaigns. (UN General Assembly, 2011b)

It was specifically decided and widely supported to view health literacy as different from health education and to state that health literacy programs occur in more places than just schools. The focus now is how to implement this NCD action plan.

Health literacy is also a priority in the United States. In May 2010, the National Action Plan to Improve Health Literacy was released. It has seven goals and during the release of the plan Secretary Kathleen Sebelius of the Department of Health and Human Services stated, "Health literacy is needed to make health reform a reality. Without health information that

---

[2]See http://www.un.org/en/ecosoc/julyhls/pdf09/ministerial_declaration-2009.pdf (accessed November 16, 2012).

makes sense to them, people can't access cost-effective, safe, and high-quality health services" (HHS, 2010).

Twenty-one states have ongoing health literacy activities,[3] and more are developing programs at the city, county, state, and regional levels, Ratzan said. Health communication and health literacy is also integrated into health professional training. For example, the University of Minnesota School of Public Health has a course that addresses health literacy and its relationship to health disparities. Evolving competencies for 21st-century medical training provide an opportunity for increasing knowledge about health literacy, Ratzan said. Use of health checklists or scorecards and mobile health applications in the private sector are other avenues to improve health literacy.

Ratzan said that for the past 2.5 years he has been working with the WHO Innovation Working Group (IWG) Task Force that is focused on creating innovative ways to improve the delivery of health care. One approach related to health literacy is the use of checklists and scorecards. Atul Gawande made groundbreaking strides in the idea of the checklist with his book *The Checklist Manifesto: How to Get Things Right*. A *New York Times* article by Ezekiel Emanuel (2012), cited a 2006 study (Pronovost et al., 2006)[4] that found a five-item checklist could be used to reduce infection rates from intravenous catheters to zero, thereby saving $45,000 per patient and avoiding 28,000 deaths in intensive care units. An editorial in the *Lancet* (Editorial, 2012) stated: "new frugal technologies do not have to be sophisticated gadgets, but can be as simple as a checklist. A 29-item Safe Childbirth Checklist has been developed and successfully piloted in India, with a draft version available by the end of 2012." Examples of checklists for improving health outcomes can be found in Table 3-1.

Although the examples provided are checklists for improving the quality of provider activity, other areas are ripe for health literacy checklists, Ratzan said, including a checklist for the last 30 days of pregnancy. A yet-to-be released report of the IWG, edited by Ratzan and Jonathan Spector, highlights the potential of checklists for improving health literacy, including the following:

- Checklists are a low-cost innovation with an increasingly large evidence base to address management of complex or neglected tasks.

---

[3]See http://www.cdc.gov/healthliteracy/StateData/index.html (accessed November 26, 2012).

[4]The study title is An Intervention to Decrease Catheter-Related Bloodstream Infections in the ICU.

- Effective checklist programs bundle vital elements of existing guidelines into a simple, user-friendly format comprised of actionable items.
- Prior health-related checklist programs have been shown to reduce complications and save lives (e.g., surgery, childbirth, and other fields).

Ratzan said that multiple stakeholders continue to advance health literacy at many levels. There are unparalleled scaling opportunities with online and mobile communication technologies that provide new promise and opportunities for advancing health literacy. Future options may include checklist tools that provide easily accessible, understandable, and actionable health information to patients and consumers of varying lev-

TABLE 3-1 Examples of Health Checklists

Initiative	Description	Current Stage
Central Line ICU Checklist	Simple five-point checklist to ensure safe insertion of central-venous catheters; proven to significantly reduce central line infections	Global rollout
WHO Surgical Safety Checklist (2007–)	Universally applicable tool to systematically ensure that all conditions are optimum for patient safety during surgery; proven to reduce severe morbidity and mortality	Global rollout; in use in >4,000 hospitals and national policy in several countries
WHO Safe Childbirth Checklist Program (2008–)	Checklist-based program for reducing childbirth-related mortality in institutional births in lower-income settings; shown to significantly improve adherence to essential clinical practices	Development and pilot testing successfully completed; currently in large-scale rollout and evaluation phase
mCheck "7-day" Tool (2010–)	WHO Patient Safety Programme project aimed at empowering women with a simple checklist complemented by a mobile phone component	Development completed; currently in evaluation phase (Kamataka State, India)

SOURCE: Ratzan, 2012.

els of economic status and health literacy. Checklists and scorecards are, Ratzan said, becoming widely acceptable tools that can advance health literacy and make improvements in other areas such as NCDs.

The book *Just Six Numbers* by Martin Rees (2000) explored the idea that six factors are necessary to shape the universe, and if one of these numbers were not in place, there would be no universe. This concept triggered Ratzan to think about whether something like this could be developed for health, that is, could there be a simple, digitized scorecard of six or more factors necessary for health? Ratzan (2000) proposed a scorecard of the following six factors:

1. Blood pressure/heart rate
2. Body mass index
3. Cholesterol levels
4. Immunizations
5. Appropriate preventive measures (e.g., smoking cessation, sigmoidoscopy, mammograms)
6. Self-reported health status

At an Institute of Medicine (IOM) Roundtable on Health Literacy workshop on promoting health literacy to encourage prevention and wellness (September 2009), Ratzan presented a paper that developed the theme of using scorecards to improve health and health literacy. Numerous organizations and individuals have pursued the development of scorecards for health, Ratzan said. For example, the World Health Professions Alliance is using an adapted version of the scorecard presented at the IOM meeting.

As the evolution in scorecards continues, Ratzan said, people are beginning to look at how they can be used online and with mobile technology. Perhaps there could be a digital health score to keep track of one's health, similar to one's credit score, Ratzan said (see Figure 3-4). The scorecard could educate people about simple goal ranges enabling them to see how they rate and how they can improve. It could also provide a range of medical and health indicators and behaviors, thereby helping people understand how lifestyle choices and NCDs are connected. Such a scorecard could, Ratzan said, motivate action by accurately portraying risk and preventability. Finally, the scorecard would provide the ability to track ratings over time to show trends and incentivize improvement.

Another mobile application that helps people make appropriate deci-

FIGURE 3-4 A scorecard for health.
SOURCE: Johnson & Johnson, 2012.

sions is Text4baby.[5] This is a U.S.-based text service for women who signed up to receive stage-based messages during pregnancy. The Centers for Disease Control and Prevention (CDC) (2012) reports that 96 percent of the 281,000 enrollees said they would recommend the service to a friend. Preliminary data indicate that this is an effective approach for increasing knowledge and changing behavior, Ratzan said. The Mobile Alliance for Maternal Action (MAMA) is a similar program run on a global level. It was found that in Bangladesh people needed to hear the message rather than just read it, so it is now sent in the local language, Ratzan said.

All of these different approaches are helping people make better health decisions, Ratzan said. For the future, checklists and scorecards can have major global impacts for patients and consumers, Ratzan said, including reduction of chronic, NCDs, maternal and child mortality, and infectious diseases. New technologies provide better access and use of information, contributing to expanded health literacy globally and helping to relieve the burden on already strained health workers, Ratzan said. Mobile health or mobile health communication holds great promise as efforts at providing information are scaled up.

Ratzan concluded by saying there are many opportunities to share innovations and programs aimed at health literacy and improving health.

UNITED STATES:
HEALTH LITERACY AND RECENT FEDERAL INITIATIVES

Cynthia Baur, Ph.D.
Senior Advisor for Health Literacy
Centers for Disease Control and Prevention

Baur said that it is time to commit to measurable organizational change in health literacy. A very large and robust infrastructure has been put in place to support that change, she said, and there is a large network of individuals throughout the U.S. Department of Health and Human Services (HHS) committed to making sure that health literacy becomes part of all types of health action. The United States has taken the approach of putting many key pieces in place, and the challenge now is to move from the abstract to the concrete, to commit to measurable organizational

---

[5]"Text4baby is a free cell phone text messaging service for pregnant women and new moms. Text messages are sent three times a week with information on how to have a healthy pregnancy and a healthy baby. The text messages are timed to the pregnant woman's due date or the baby's date of birth" (http://www.cdc.gov/women/text4baby [accessed November 26, 2012]).

change in a concrete way. Three key questions will be answered in this presentation, Baur said. They are

1. What are the key developments in health literacy in the United States?
2. How has the HHS contributed to health literacy improvement?
3. Where can we go from here?

Despite the fact that there is a great deal of information, communication, and education, there is still a gap between the public and health professionals. The professional community has not changed its practices enough to communicate effectively with the public, Baur said. And in some places, for some populations, under some circumstances, this gap can be quite large. Health literacy research and evaluation brings knowledge about how to communicate, how to educate, and how to obtain the maximum effectiveness from these efforts, Baur said. We do not need more communication, we need different kinds of communication and different kinds of education that pay attention to the health literacy insights that are available in the literature. One of the most obvious gaps is the education sector's lack of support for health literacy activities, Baur said.

There are several key developments in health literacy in the United States. Many of the activities are being conducted by private-sector organizations. But the federal government is also active in health literacy. The Patient Protection and Affordable Care Act, while not a health literacy law, does contain important provisions for addressing health literacy. The Plain Writing Act of 2010 is another development. That law directs federal agencies to use plain language in all public communications. Although the law is not health specific, it can be used to address health literacy in public health information. There is also a law related to the use of health information technology that, while not health literacy specific, is fundamentally changing the way that technology is being used to deliver health care in the United States, Baur said. These laws have laid a foundation for health literacy work in the United States.

Baur said that since 2004 the National Institutes for Health have funded $95 million in research under the Health Literacy Program Announcement. While this is a fairly large amount, it does not reflect the total support for health literacy research because other research has been funded through other mechanisms and agencies. For example, the CDC uses contracts to support health literacy work and the Agency for Healthcare Research and Quality (AHRQ) uses cooperative agreements.

The *Journal of Health Communication* has supported a number of special issues related to health literacy, and in January 2012 *Health Affairs* published an article by Koh[6] and colleagues on policy initiatives and health literacy. It was, Baur said, the second-most-read article in *Health Affairs* between January and June 2012. A number of bibliographies have also been published. The growing literature that people can draw on and build on for implementation and research is, Baur said, part of the infrastructure to support health literacy work.

Health Literacy Online, provided by the HHS Office of Disease Prevention and Health Promotion (available at http://www.health.gov/health-literacyonline), is an example of some of the research-based guidance that is available to organizations. This is a practical, hands-on guide that helps people apply health literacy principles to the design of health websites. Other aids include the toolkit on clear communication strategies developed by the Centers for Medicare & Medicaid Services (CMS) and plain language manuals. And for *Healthy People 2020* (U.S. national objectives for health), health literacy objectives were expanded to include health information technology objectives as well as being included under some of the more traditional health topics, Baur said.

There are also a number of state-based activities in health literacy. On the CDC Health Literacy website,[7] there is a map that highlights the states with verifiable health literacy coalitions or collaborations. More states that will be added to the map soon because they are having inaugural health literacy conferences in 2013. States are working to build their own infrastructures at the state level to support a more collaborative approach to health literacy improvement, Baur said.

Many publicly available tools can be used to assess the quality of health care services, and there is a health literacy module to assess providers' use of different health literacy and health communication strategies, Baur said. There are also a number of robust health information services. Healthcare.gov, sponsored by CMS, provides information about access to health insurance. MedlinePlus, sponsored by the National Library of Medicine, and healthfinder.gov, sponsored by the HHS, provide health information built on plain language principles in order to make information more accessible to all segments of the public, Baur said.

All these activities support the National Action Plan to Improve Health Literacy, a comprehensive framework organizations can use to identify priorities, strategies, and activities for health literacy. There are seven goals within the National Action Plan (NAP). They focus on

---

[6]Dr. Howard Koh is U.S. Assistant Secretary for Health.
[7]*Health literacy: Accurate, accessible, and actionable health information for all* (http://www.cdc.gov/healthliteracy [accessed November 28, 2012]).

1. Creating and disseminating information,
2. Providing health care services,
3. Educating people,
4. Delivering services through community-based organizations and nonprofit organizations,
5. Working together across organizations and across sectors,
6. Conducting research and evaluation, and
7. Telling others about the research and evaluations completed.

The NAP has put health literacy on the national agenda, Baur said. It allows local organizations to link their work to the national agenda and confirms the importance of health literacy as a policy topic. The NAP also provides talking points, benchmarks, project ideas, and conference themes. It provides the "glue" for local coalitions, Baur said. Organizations that might not think they have much in common can use the NAP as a framework for identifying common interests in health literacy.

Baur provided quotes from some organizations in the field that use the NAP. Beth Rueland, from Health Literacy San Diego, said,

> We use the NAP as a benchmark to align with national best practices and recommendations. In addition, the NAP helps health and literacy efforts across the nation compare and share best practices, as well as understand how they can align their efforts to take full advantage of recent policy and legislation changes.

Dr. Suad Ghaddar of the South Texas Border Health Disparities Center said,

> The NAP has helped identify key strategies that we feel the Center can be involved in at the community level. We have identified potential partners and initiated outreach activities to improve health literacy.

Where do we go from here? Baur asked. As stated earlier, the key message is about organizational change. How can we promote organizational change to incorporate health literacy in our everyday practices? Organizational change must happen at the individual organization level but also in the broader sectors of industry, government, education, and nonprofit organizations. The NAP is relevant here because it talks about groups of organizations as sectors, and change must occur within these sectors, Baur said.

Baur said that organizational change requires us to examine research for insights in practical applications, create and implement easily usable products, and track and report progress in changing our organizations. There is a need to document what health-literate organizations are doing differently from other health organizations. There is a need to document impact on policy-relevant outcomes, Baur concluded.

FROM POLICY TO IMPLEMENTATION

Jennifer Cabe, M.A.
Executive Director
Canyon Ranch Institute
and
Suzanne Thompson, M.S.
Vice President, Research & Development
The Clorox Company

Thompson said that Clorox and Canyon Ranch Institute (CRI), in a public–private partnership, are jointly working on a program to improve hygiene in very poor communities in Peru by combining health literacy, microbiology, and public health science. Clorox was founded in 1913, making Clorox liquid bleach. Today the company has a broad range of products, with 8,400 employees and sales of $5.5 billion. Clorox is headquartered in Oakland, California; it has 24 plants in the United States and manufactures products in 25 countries. It markets products in 100 countries and has 6 facilities for research and development.

Cabe said that CRI is small when compared to Clorox. It was founded in 2002 and is a 501(c)3 nonprofit public charity with a 7-member board, 8 employees, 40 volunteers, and more than 90 funding sources. It seeks to deliver the best practices of the institute and its partners to health-disparate communities; to inform health policies in all sectors; and to partner with universities, grassroots organizations, corporations, and foundations. Cabe said that CRI has a global reach because of collaborations with its partners. Through an integrative approach to advancing health literacy, CRI is able to address challenging problems in public health, working with partners and looking beyond causes of problems to the causes of the causes.

An individual who sits on both the Clorox and CRI boards suggested the two organizations should be working togther. While Clorox is a for-profit company and CRI is a nonprofit public charity, their fundamental guiding principles, missions, visions, and values are complementary. Both organizations are interested in improving lives, both value working in partnership with others, and both are principled in all approaches, Cabe said.

Improving health is a priority for both companies, Thompson said. Clorox has a disinfecting heritage and focus on improving health through hygiene, both in water disinfection and in hard-surface disinfection. The company also has a number of programs to educate people on how to improve their own and their families' health through hygiene and disinfecting products. CRI, with its strong health literacy focus and great skill at educating people, was a great fit for Clorox, Thompson said. With these backgrounds, collaboration on the program in Peru was a perfect place to start a partnership, Thompson said.

There are some major factors necessary for a successful partnership. First is to make clear each organization's role and responsibilities. Second, ongoing communication and collaboration is needed. The working team had regular conference calls and occasional face-to-face meetings. The two project leaders talked regularly to make sure they were giving consistent direction and messages.

Most importantly, Thompson said, they leveraged the strengths of both organizations. Clorox provided the funding, public health experience, and business experience in Peru. It also identified the University of Arizona as a partner for conducting the microbiology research. CRI brought overall program leadership and a strong expertise in the social sciences and health literacy. It identified Boston University's College of Fine Arts as an arts partner. It also identified Peruvian arts and social science partners.

The program is called Arts for Behavior Change. It is a pilot program that uses the arts to help people understand what needs to be done to improve personal and household hygiene behaviors as well as how to use different disinfecting products. Importantly, this is an unbranded program, so it did not promote Clorox products, Thompson said.

Cabe said there were several measurable key outcomes. One of the areas in which the program greatly exceeded expectations was attendance by community members and participation in the 12 performances. There was increased knowledge and understanding about hygiene, and there were actual improved personal and household hygiene behaviors in the areas targeted by the intervention. There was also reduced microbiological burden in areas targeted by the intervention.

The decision was made to work in shantytowns in Peru. It is important to note, Cabe said, that the term *shantytown* is not a pejorative—it is the term Peruvians themselves use to describe the communities. In November 2010, a team from CRI, Boston University, and The Clorox Company conducted site visits at numerous shantytowns around Lima, and two were chosen for the program (see Figure 3-5). There is tremendous need in these communities. There is no plumbing. If one can afford to purchase water it is delivered through blue barrels placed alongside the road. The barrels are not clean and the buckets used to obtain the water are not clean either. So the water comes dirty and that is how it is used.

All work in the Peruvian shantytowns was conducted in the Spanish dialect spoken there, Cabe said. A formative assessment was conducted in the two shantytowns to inform program design, including the stories and characters that would be used. In-depth interviews were conducted with

FIGURE 3-5 Program site in shantytowns of Lima, Peru.
SOURCE: Cabe and Thompson, 2012.

250 households before the start of the performances and with 249 house-holds after the final performance. Observations were also conducted with 50 households before the start of the performances and after the final performance. Following each performance 20 individual interviews were conducted immediately. The performances were structured as a *telenove-la*.[8] Microbiological studies were conducted in 30 households both before and after the performances. There was intensive and diverse community engagement throughout, Cabe said.

One of the most interesting aspects of this arts program that used health literacy to improve household hygiene was the opportunity to work with a community of actors, singers, puppeteers, and dancers, Cabe said. During a 2-week workshop in Lima, these individuals were trained in health literacy principles and the science of personal and household hygiene. Microbiologists from Clorox and the University of Arizona also taught everyone some basics of microbiology.

Also during this 2-week period, the first four episodes of the *telenovela* were outlined. There was, however, constant change in all of the episodes

---

[8]"The telenovela is a form of melodramatic serialized fiction produced and aired in most Latin American countries" (http://www.museum.tv/eotvsection.php?entrycode=telenovela [accessed November 29, 2012]).

because of the interaction of the community. The key thing to emphasize when talking about this kind of partnership, Cabe said, is the importance of engaging and honoring the existing leadership structures in the communities. This was critical, she said.

The play was called *Siempre*, which translates in English to *Always*, as in "always sick." Two families made up the characters portrayed on the stage—the Maranas and the Buendias. *Maranas* means disorganized or messy. *Buendias* means the good days. The basic plot is that the father is missing, the mother says he is dead, but the father is seen with a younger woman. Both families have ongoing health problems related to poor hygiene. The onstage presence of the "Joker"—a physician and public health practitioner—kept the performance grounded in science.

Throughout all 12 performances, the community was extremely engaged, Cabe said, coming up on stage, asking questions, even replacing the actors up on the stage when they wanted to say, "Here's how I think something really should go." For example, around episode seven, one of the beloved characters—a little girl—died. The community did not like that. So the Joker (the public health physician) said, "All right. You know enough now. Maybe we could have prevented the death of this child. How would that occur?" And people in the audience stood up and explained how the death could have been avoided. So the little girl was brought back into the performance, which meant a lot of rewriting for the writing team, but that was fine because the community was really engaged.

In terms of outcomes, overall, there was strong diffusion of information throughout the community and behavior changes based on the performances:

- 97.5 percent of respondents were aware of the performances.
- 69.6 percent of respondents attended the performances.
- 91.3 percent of respondents said they learned something from the performances.
- 77.2 percent of respondents said the performances were important or very important to their lives.
- 54.4 percent of respondents said that there have been changes in household hygiene behaviors during the past 3 months. Of those, the majority said it was because of the performances (means of 3.15 on a 4-point scale).

The microbiological outcomes were more mixed, Thompson said. The overall microbiological load was very high both before and after the performances. This is largely due to the high poverty level of the community and the openness of the water and waste. For example, Figure 3-6 shows a

FIGURE 3-6 A community toilet.
SOURCE: Cabe and Thompson, 2012.

community toilet. One thing learned is that the microbiology team needed to be much more closely linked to the performance messages to make sure the testing before and after was related to the areas the performances were highlighting. Despite these challenges, there was great improvement in food preparation areas, with a 34.4 percent overall decrease in positive results when testing for *E. coli* and listeria. The change correlates with the performance messages, which featured why and how to clean food preparation areas, Thompson said.

The Arts for Behavior Change pilot project demonstrated the effectiveness of community engagement and using performance arts to advance health literacy and improve health-related behaviors, Thompson said. The project also demonstrated the ability of a public–private partnership to achieve meaningful community health benefits. Finally, Thompson said, there is great opportunity to improve public health by replicating the program in different communities and cultures.

In terms of their next steps, Clorox and the CRI are identifying and implementing the lessons learned from the pilot program in order to improve overall outcomes of future programs. They are also communicating the processes and findings of this pilot through publications and presentations. Finally, they hope to expand the program by identifying additional funding sources and partners, Thompson said.

DISCUSSION

One audience member asked Baur what the grade level is for producing plain language and understandable materials. Baur responded that, in general, grade levels are not used as targets because communication is a far more complex process than a grade level can represent.

A different audience member asked Ratzan whether there were any data about the effectiveness of mobile health text messages. Ratzan responded that an article in *JAMA* on text messaging for vaccination among adolescents showed uptake. Kumaresan said an article in the *Lancet* showed a doubling in smoking quit rates within a period of 6 months for the 5,000 participants in mobile health messaging as compared to the control group. Also, Kumaresan said, mobile health is a wonderful way to conduct outreach. For example, in 2010, for the World Health Day on urban health, the only way to reach people in Somalia was with text messages (1 million were sent to Somalia residents) sent by the water and telephone companies. That was an amazing public–private partnership, he said.

Research in this area is important, Ratzan said. The WHO IWG Task Force has research members who are interested in outcomes of use of mobile health messaging. Kumaresan added that measures are needed in order to better understand the effect of mobile health messaging.

Will Ross, a Roundtable member, said he appreciated Kumaresan's comments about using a rights-based approach to coordinate health literacy interventions globally. He asked if it were possible to codify what needs to be done yet still use such an approach and make sure programs are conducted in a manner that allows countries to determine important outcomes. Kumaresan responded that one of the best examples is a program in tobacco control.[9] The program was begun in 2005 and within

---

[9]"The WHO Framework Convention on Tobacco Control (WHO FCTC) is the pre-eminent global tobacco control instrument, containing legally binding obligations for its Parties, set-

a period of 6 years, 175 countries signed on to conduct it. Application, however, is different. Every year, WHO monitors how much of the framework and the articles have been implemented. It takes a long time. In Australia, for example, it took 3 or 4 years of effort to get plain packaging implemented. But other countries will follow suit. Mechanisms are needed, Kumaresan said, to ensure that countries can adapt to their own circumstances yet still be held accountable. Successful models are needed to ensure that UN resolutions and WHO resolutions can be implemented. This takes a long time.

Allison MacEachron from the business council for the United Nation said that the panel provided a number of great examples of collaboration between the public and private sectors. She asked, "Where are the gaps and the biggest opportunities for the private sector to collaborate with the UN and UN agencies in ways to help meet the goals of health literacy?" Ratzan responded that the IWG is a good place to start. This group is a network of leading stakeholders from government and both the for-profit and the nonprofit sector, including health foundations, academic institutions, and businesses. One piece that is missing is the media. The media is not just a conduit, but an ongoing purveyor of health information, Ratzan said. Another possible resource is the CTIA, a cellular telephone group that is working to scale up some mobile health pieces. Although public–private partnerships are growing, Ratzan said, not all governments are open to working with the private sector and not all private-sector companies are the same in terms of being ethically based and trustworthy. There needs to be a good fit among partners in a public–private partnership, Ratzan said.

Baur said that because of competition and different business models the private-sector organizations may not be as open as other organizations in terms of sharing information. However, one possible outcome of a public–private partnership might be increased transparency across all kinds of activities and projects.

Cabe said the real key is to maintain a balance between pushing commercial interests and doing the right thing. Is the private-sector company involved just to make money or because it has a goal of improving

---

ting the foundation for reducing both demand for and supply of tobacco products and providing a comprehensive direction for tobacco control policy at all levels. To assist countries to implement effective strategies for selected demand reduction related articles of the WHO FCTC, WHO introduced a package of measures under the acronym of MPOWER. WHO recently reported the progress Member States are making against the MPOWER measures in the WHO Report on the Global Tobacco Epidemic 2011" (http://www.who.int/gho/tobacco/en/index.html [accessed November 29, 2012]).

people's lives? With companies that have a strong foundation in pursuing high-integrity activities, Cabe said, partnership activities can succeed.

Isham asked whether it could be assumed that the nature of public–private partnerships is the same for different countries around the world. Ratzan responded that it is not the same. There are different models for how companies approach a partnership, and each partnership needs to be culturally sensitive and address local needs and resources.

Winston Wong, a Roundtable member, asked about scalability of projects. Ultimately health literacy efforts get the most traction at the local level. What needs to be considered in, for example, performance metrics, infrastructure, and resource deployment to move a program from a local level to one that has a global impact? Cabe responded that this is a very important question that CRI and Clorox have been asking about the Arts for Behavior Change program that was piloted in Peru. Of major importance in that program was community interaction with the social scientists and the microbiological researchers in order to empower the community. Greater empowerment drives improved outcomes, Cabe said. Can technology—in this case, radio, television, and videos—be used to scale up efforts? How can the stories be told in a health literate, engaging manner that is going to reach a lot more people than were reached in the two shantytowns in Peru?, she asked.

Baur said she thinks about scalability differently. There is scalability in terms of the number of people touched by a project or intervention. Then there is scalability in the context of large organizations. How does one get an entire organization to move? One can go team by team, branch by branch, and division by division. But that is very slow, she said. What other options are there? Baur pointed out that both the CDC and the Health Resources and Services Administration could use funding mechanisms to scale up health literacy efforts. If one inserts health literacy, plain language, cultural competence, and limited English proficiency into the funding announcement template, one has immediately affected every single program that uses the template to request proposals, she said.

Ratzan said that what Baur has alluded to is the idea of moving from local to social change. That is what is needed for health literacy, he said. He asked, "How can we integrate new tools such as scorecards and checklists and mobile health messaging that could foster change on a larger scale?" Kumaresan said there are three factors required to scale up an effort. The first is to show the effectiveness of an initiative. The second is to get the community to understand the value of the initiative. The third is to have a national policy that fosters the effort.

Kumaresan described a project in Ethiopia in which he was involved.

Partners in the Trachoma[10] project included the Carter Center and Pfizer. Water, sanitation, and hygiene were important elements of the project and getting people to build latrines was a high priority. The Carter Center target was the building of 10,000 latrines in one particular community. In 1 year there were 92,000 latrines built because the members of the community saw their value. The women of the community had decided that there needed to be one toilet per household. They saw that children did not have trachoma disease or diarrhea. When President Carter visited the community and asked what they needed, the response was: "Our children are now healthy. Will you please build us a school so our children can go to school?" It is interesting to note that the Ethiopian government now has a policy of one latrine per household.

Len Epstein, a Roundtable member, asked how health literacy can more effectively integrate culturally and linguistically appropriate health and health care perspectives. Baur responded that literacy is a culturally specific activity. When one talks about literacy, one must speak in terms of a particular context. In the U.S. context, there is the issue of limited English proficiency and the need to provide interpretation and translation. But there is a move to go from this traditional approach to a broader notion of understanding. It is not just interpretation and translation; it is ensuring that people have a better understanding of what the encounter is about.

One participant who identified herself as coming from Indonesia and working with the Indonesian delegation to the UN General Assembly shared information about what is going on in Indonesia. The country is, she said, building an integrated health intervention program at seven pilot areas to reorient the primary care system. The reorientation aims for community empowerment and health literacy. Many sectors work together—private, government, and nongovernmental organizations, including Nokia. Indonesia has a population of 240 million people. About 80 percent of those people have mobile phones. Nokia built an application (app) that will be given to women. Questions will be asked and, based on the responses, the app will direct the user to the appropriate information.

Diane Levin-Zamir said that public–private partnerships in Israel are required to be open to any private-sector company that would like to be a partner. Those who express an interest are evaluated based on specific criteria that include health promotion. In this way the public sector is able to address the ethical questions that would arise if it were choosing one

---

[10]"Trachoma is the result of infection of the eye with *Chlamydia trachomatis*. Infection spreads from person to person, and is frequently passed from child to child and from child to mother, especially where there are shortages of water, numerous flies, and crowded living conditions" (http://www.who.int/topics/trachoma/en [accessed November 29, 2012]).

company or one private investor. Levin-Zamir asked Cabe to what extent the private-sector partners for CRI are required to have a health promotion or health literacy agenda within their companies.

Cabe responded that she was uncertain how well a system that required allowing any and all private companies to participate would work in the United States given the very competitive nature of business. There are many companies that probably would worry too much about revealing their secrets. There are also antitrust issues that might be a challenge. Also, Cabe said, the cultural fit of organizations is very important to the success of a program. Her organization partners only with organizations that have a strong belief in promoting health and wellness, organizations like Clorox, the Red Cross, and others involved in disaster relief. Ratzan added that transparency is also key to successful partnering.

Isham said this discussion highlights a key issue when attempting to establish partnerships: the need to maintain a balance between respecting a company's right to privacy and the need for cooperation. That balance must be negotiated in each partnership arrangement, he said.

Sabrina Kurtz-Rossi, a principal in a woman-owned small business specializing in health education, literacy, and evaluation, said she is interested in supporting professional and organizational development in the field of health literacy. Many people have come to identify themselves as health literacy professionals even though they come from many different professions and different kinds of organizations. How can new technologies be used to share information and tools and to build collaboration among these individuals? How can best practices and basic competencies be shared? There seems to be a need for a mechanism that would allow this, she said.

Baur said that when the CDC launched its health literacy website (CDC.gov/healthliteracy) it included links to known international activities, but the traffic for this information was nonexistent. No one was using the information. People were using U.S. state-based data. So the international links were moved to a second-level page.

In terms of information sharing, Baur said, that is one thing the website was intended to do; however, not many people have responded to the postings. The blog is supposed to facilitate sharing, but it will not work if those reading the blog do not post comments. There is also a health literacy mailbox but the kind of feedback received is generally about a problem with an online system. There is a huge opportunity, Baur said, but it has not been taken advantage of.

Ruth Parker, a Roundtable member, said that the IOM Roundtable on Health Literacy commissioned a paper on international health literacy activities which Andrew Pleasant prepared based on a survey he conducted. There is now this compilation of what is happening internationally in policy, programs, and research on health literacy. The next version of the report will focus on the United States. In addition to what Baur mentioned, then, these papers are another tool for better understanding what is going on in health literacy.

Ratzan said that the *Journal of Health Communication* also provides information about health literacy efforts. Also, the U.S. Agency for International Development is holding a summit in December 2012 on social and behavior-change communication.[11] The extent to which health literacy is highlighted will depend on the strength of the evidence.

REFERENCES

BBC (British Broadcasting Corporation). 2012. *More mobiles than humans in 2012, says Cisco.* http://www.bbc.co.uk/news/technology-17047406 (accessed March 13, 2013).

Cabe, J., and S. Thompson. 2012. *From policy to implementation.* Presentation at the Institute of Medicine workshop on Health Literacy: Improving Health, Health Systems, and Health Policy Around the World, New York, September 24.

CDC (Centers for Disease Control and Prevention). 2012. *Become a Text4Baby partner.* http://www.cdc.gov/women/text4baby (accessed November 26, 2012).

ECOSOC (United Nations Economic and Social Council). 2009. *Implementing the internationally agreed goals and commitments in regard to global public health.* Ministerial Declaration—2009 High-Level Segment. Geneva, Switzerland: ECOSOC.

Editorial. 2012. *Lancet* 380(9840):447.

Emanuel, E. 2012. *In medicine, falling for fake innovation.* http://opinionator.blogs.nytimes.com/2012/05/27/in-medicine-falling-for-fake-innovation (accessed February 28, 2013).

European Communities. 2008. *High-level pharmaceutical forum 2005-2008.* Brussels: European Communities.

HHS (U.S. Department of Health and Human Services). 2010. *HHS releases National Plan to Improve Health Literacy.* http://www.hhs.gov/ash/news/20100527.html (accessed March 8, 2013).

Johnson & Johnson. 2012. *Digital health scorecard.* http://www.digitalhealthscorecard.com (accessed November 15, 2012).

Kumaresan, J. 2012. *WHO's health literacy work.* Presentation at the Institute of Medicine Workshop on Health Literacy: Improving Health, Health Systems, and Health Policy Around the World, New York, September 24.

Parker, R. 2009. *Measuring health literacy: What? So what? Now what?* Presentation at the Institute of Medicine Workshop on Measures of Health Literacy, Washington, DC, February 26.

---

[11] "In December 2012, USAID will hold an Evidence Summit on the theme of Social and Behavior Change. The purpose of this Summit, which will bring together US Government, multilateral and nongovernmental partners, is to distill the most compelling evidence about the impact of social and behavioral change strategies, and to communicate that data for improved health and development decision-making" (http://sph.bu.edu/careerservices/viewjob.aspx?id=2977 [accessed December 3, 2012]).

Pronovost, P., D. Needham, S. Berenholtz, D. Sinopoli, H. Chu, S. Cosgrove, B. Sexton, R. Hyzy, R. Welsh, G. Roth, J. Bander, J. Kepros, and G. Goeschel. 2006. An intervention to decrease catheter-related bloodstream infections in the ICU. *New England Journal of Medicine* 355(26):2725-2732.

Ratzan, S. C. 2000. *Quality communication: The path to ideal health. Joseph Leiter Lecture.* National Library of Medicine/Medical Library Association. NLM Lister Hill Center Auditorium, Bethesda, MD, May 17, 2012.

Ratzan, S. C. 2012. *Policies and programs promoting health literacy globally.* Presentation at the Institute of Medicine Workshop on Health Literacy: Improving Health, Health Systems, and Health Policy Around the World, New York, September 24.

Ratzan, S. C., and R. M. Parker. 2000. Introduction. In *National Library of Medicine current bibliographies in medicine: Health literacy,* edited by C. Selden, M. Zorn, S. Ratzan, and R. Parker. NLM Pub. No. CBM 2000-1. Bethesda, MD: National Institutes of Health.

Rees, M. J. 2000. *Just six numbers: The deep forces that shape the universe.* New York: Basic Books.

Treatman, D., M. Bhavsar, V. Kumar, and N. Lesh. 2012. Mobile phones for community health workers of Bihar empower adolescent girls. *WHO South-East Asia Journal of Public Health* 1(2):224-226.

UN General Assembly. 2011a. Non-communicable diseases deemed development challenge of "epidemic proportions" in political declaration adopted during landmark General Assembly summit. GA/11183. September 19, 2011. http://www.un.org/News/Press/docs/2011/ga11138.doc.htm (accessed November 15, 2012).

UN General Assembly. 2011b. *Political declaration of the high-level meeting of the General Assembly on the prevention and control of non-communicable diseases.* http://www.un.org/ga/search/view_doc.asp?symbol=A/66/L.1 (accessed March 8, 2013).

WHO (World Health Organization). 2006. *Constitution of the World Health Organization.* Geneva, Switzerland: World Health Organization.

WHO. 2011. *Global status report on noncommunicable diseases 2010.* Geneva, Switzerland: World Health Organization.

4

Health Literacy Policy and Programs

HEALTH LITERACY IN CANADA

Sandra Vamos, Ed.D., Ed.S., M.S.
Senior Advisor on Health Education and Health Literacy for
the Centre for Chronic Disease Prevention and Control
Public Health Agency of Canada

Vamos said that the Public Health Agency of Canada (PHAC) is the main public health agency in that country and could be seen as equivalent to the U.S. Centers for Disease Control and Prevention. For the past 2 years, the PHAC has been linking health literacy work with agency, branch, and center public health objectives. Approximately 60 percent of adult Canadians have low levels of health literacy, with certain populations experiencing much lower levels. These vulnerable populations include older adults (approximately 88 percent of seniors have low levels); the aboriginal populations; and recent immigrants and those with lower levels of education, socioeconomic status, and low English and French proficiency. To improve health literacy, Vamos said, one must improve the knowledge and skills of the populations who receive health information programs and services as well as those who provide such programs and services.

Health literacy efforts in Canada have been anchored in health promotion efforts and have not been driven by the medical system. Recognition is growing that health literacy plays an important role in public health initiatives, Vamos said. As an emerging field, there are many pockets of innovative health literacy programs, initiatives, and activities across Canada and stronger research on health literacy has been evolving. However, there are no governmental policies that are specific to health literacy at any level of government in Canada and there is little private-sector engagement, Vamos said.

The Canadian path to health literacy began in the 1980s with the Ontario Public Health Association project on literacy and health. This led to interest by the Canadian Public Health Association and a national conference on literacy and health. A second national conference was held in 2004, during which delegates called for the establishment of an expert panel on health literacy. The panel began its work in 2006 and issued its report, *A Vision for a Health Literate Canada: Report of the Expert Panel on Health Literacy,* in 2008. Data used in drafting the report came from a health literacy scale used in the International Adult Literacy and Skills Survey (IALS) of 23,000 Canadians. The report recommended a pan-Canadian strategy for health literacy and called for policies, programs, and research to increase low levels of health literacy and reduce disparities in health. In 2010 the Canadian Medical Association passed two resolutions to promote health literacy. The first resolution urged governments to develop a national strategy to promote the health literacy of Canadians; the second one addressed raising health literacy awareness of physicians in clinical practice.

Vamos went on to say that in 2012 the Public Health Association of British Columbia issued a discussion paper, *An Intersectoral Approach for Improving Health Literacy for Canadians,* which is a framework for action. It is guided by the following vision: "A health literate Canada in which all people in Canada can access, understand, evaluate and use health information and services that can guide them and others in making informed decisions to enhance their health and well-being" (Mitic and Rootman, 2012). The mission of the intersectoral approach is "to develop, implement and evaluate an approach that will support, coordinate and build health literacy capacity in Canada." Figure 4-1 presents a conceptual model of the intersectoral approach. The three fundamental components are identified on the left and deemed essential for the development of a comprehensive approach or strategy for improving health literacy. A list of objectives has also been developed for each component, and associated sample activities (relevant and effective actions for each) have been suggested, which can be found in the approach document. The five collaborative partners or sectors involved are displayed across the top. Within each sector, individuals, groups, and organizations are invited to develop recommendations related to each objective for what can be done to move health literacy forward throughout Canada.

There are a number of health literacy projects in which the PHAC has

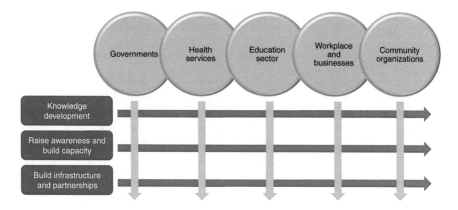

FIGURE 4-1 An intersectoral approach to health literacy.
SOURCE: Vamos, 2012.

been quite active, including the health literacy scan project,[1] the health literacy examples in the field project,[2] and Learning for Health[3]—the health literacy embedded learning demonstration project. There are also online health literacy modules for public health professionals. A PHAC module is anticipated to be launched in French and English in the spring of 2013, Vamos said. The Canadian Medical Association, the Canadian Nurses Association, and others worked together to develop a module that was launched in both official languages in 2012.

Vamos said the objectives of the health literacy scan, which was conducted by the University of British Columbia, were to address the following questions:

1. What examples exist of noteworthy health literacy activities at a federal or national level in Canada and a set of comparable countries?
2. What have been the successes, areas of innovation, and challenges of those activities?

[1] See http://blogs.ubc.ca/frankish/selected-projects/health-literacy-scan-project (accessed December 10, 2012).

[2] This project showcases examples of health literacy activities across Canada (http://www.ihahealthliteracy.org/files/DDF00000/Vamos-Canadian%20Health%20Literacy%20Examples%20in%20the%20Field%20Project%20-%20Final%20Apr%2027%202012.pdf [accessed December 10, 2012]).

[3] "The goal of Learning for Health is to design, pilot test and evaluate embedded learning approaches to improve health literacy outcomes across a range of populations and settings" (http://hpclearinghouse.net/blogs/hlel/pages/home.aspx [accessed December 10, 2012]).

3. What are the emerging opportunities and responsibilities for divisions, agencies, and organizations to address the area of health literacy?

The scan involved looking at federal government initiatives and perspectives of federal employees engaged in health literacy work, an examination of what is happening in Canadian health literacy outside of the government, and a scan of what is happening outside of Canada. Key findings from the scan can be seen in Figure 4-2.

The Canadian health literacy examples from the field project gathers a range of peer-nominated health literacy projects using the Canadian definition of health literacy, Vamos said. This definition is "Health literacy is the ability to access, understand, evaluate, and communicate information as a way to promote, maintain, and improve health in a variety of settings across the life course" (Rootman and Gordon-El-Bihbety, 2008). Three- to five-page vignettes were prepared on the identified projects and will be placed online to share with others. There are 33 projects across Canadian provinces, territories, and regions. They address different settings (e.g., schools, libraries, and workplaces), have different foci (e.g., oral health and mental health), and address different populations (e.g., aboriginals, children and youth, families).

Capacity building/awareness raising
- Training/educating the public/patients
- Educating health professionals
- Working with vulnerable groups
- Producing tailored, targeted programs, reports, and other materials
- Utilizing social media sites for communication

Knowledge development
- Health literacy definition and concept development
- Measurement of health literacy levels
- Identification of best practices by research/demonstration projects

Infrastructure building and partnerships
- Organizing cross-agency and cross-sectoral collaboration
- Developing supports to inform policies, regulations, and standards for health literacy work
- Requests for additional resources and positions for health literacy work

FIGURE 4-2 Key findings: types of health literacy initiatives in Canada.
SOURCE: Frankish et al., 2011.

Learning for Health, the health literacy embedded learning demonstration project, has three demonstration sites and works with three different vulnerable groups (urban seniors, rural families, and urban immigrants and refugees). The goal of this 18-month project was to build capacity. A key finding of the project was that organizations and their staff need time and learning resources to build capacity of staff across all levels to become health literate.

Vamos concluded her presentation with the following examples of potential work that could be done in Canada: (1) develop supports and materials to inform policies and legislation; (2) increase availability and accessibility of resources that could lead to further action within a supportive environment; and (3) create clearer incentives and rewards for engaging in health literacy work.

HEALTH LITERACY AS PART OF A NATIONAL APPROACH TO SAFETY AND QUALITY OF LIFE

Nicola Dunbar, Ph.D.
Program Manager
Australian Commission on Safety and Quality in Health Care

Dunbar said that the Australian Commission on Safety and Quality in Health Care, established in 2006, is a national, government-funded body that aids and coordinates safety and quality nationally for both the public and the private sector, and for acute and primary care. It is a small organization (about 40 staff) that works through consultation, collaboration, dialogue, and discussion. The key functions of the commission are to

- set national standards;
- develop accreditation schemes;
- develop data and indicators;
- monitor, report, and publish; and
- provide knowledge and leadership for safety and quality.

The Australian Safety and Quality Framework for Health Care was developed by the commission in 2010 and endorsed by the health ministers. The vision for safe and high-quality care has three components: it is consumer-centered, driven by information, and organized for safety. The framework provides actions that health care systems should take and, as can be seen in Figure 4-3, several of the actions in the consumer-centered component relate to health literacy: making sure people have information they can understand, are involved in their own health care, receive

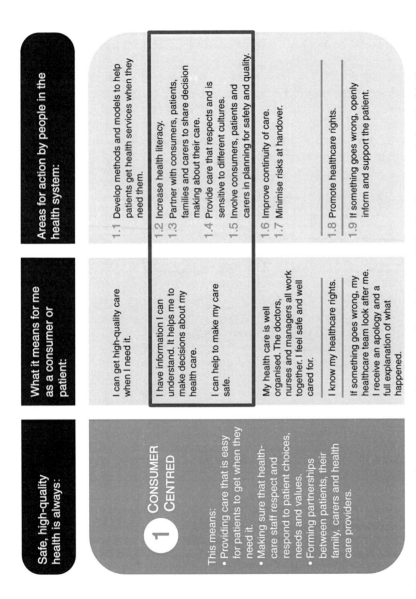

FIGURE 4-3 Consumer-centered component of the Australian Safety and Quality Framework for Health Care.
SOURCE: Australian Commission on Safety and Quality in Health Care, 2010.

services that are sensitive to their culture, and are involved in planning for safety and quality.

The Australian Safety and Quality Goals for Health Care support the framework and contribute to achievement of its vision. The goals address the areas of importance that are amenable to national action and on which efforts should be focused during the next 5 years. Actions are those that can be taken by government, providers, health services, hospitals, patients and caregivers, and the commission. The three high-level goals for safety and quality are

1. **Safety of care:** People receive their health care without experiencing preventable harm. There are a number of priority areas for this goal, including medication safety and health care–associated infection.
2. **Appropriateness of care:** People receive appropriate, evidence-based care. The two priority areas are stroke and acute coronary syndrome.
3. **Partnering with consumers:** There are effective partnerships between patients, consumers, and health care providers and organizations at all levels of health care provision, including planning and evaluation.

For each of the goal priority areas, the framework identifies a number of outcomes desired during the next 5 years. Table 4-1 provides an example of health literate outcomes for effective partnerships. In the area of partnering with consumers, identified outcomes include

1. Consumers are empowered to manage their own condition, if clinically appropriate and desired. The focus is on chronic disease self-management.
2. Consumers and health care providers understand each other when communicating about care and treatment.
3. Health care organizations are health literate organizations. This area picks up on work that has been done at the Institute of Medicine on the attributes of a health literate organization. Outcomes in this area can be seen in Table 4-1.
4. Consumers are involved in a meaningful way in the governance of health care organizations.

The final part of the Australian Safety and Quality Framework for Health Care that makes reference to health literacy is the National Safety and Quality Health Service Standards (NSQHSS). Accreditation and accreditation reform has been a core part of the commission's work since

TABLE 4-1 Examples of Health Literate Organization Outcomes

Goal 3	That there are effective partnerships between consumers and healthcare providers and organisations at all levels of healthcare provision, planning and evaluation.
Outcome 3.0.3	**Healthcare organisations are health literate organisations.**
What would success look like after 5 years?	Healthcare organisations are designed in a way that makes it easier for consumers to navigate, understand, and use their information and services.
How will we know that success has been achieved?	By monitoring changes in consumer experiences of health literacy barriers through patient experience surveys.

What actions are needed to reach these outcomes?

Possible actions by consumers	Consider being involved in the development and review of consumer information and resources. Consider being involved in the planning, design, and delivery of policies, strategies, and projects to reduce barriers to health literacy within their healthcare organisation. Provide feedback to their healthcare organisation on the accessibility of the organisation's physical environment or information.
Possible actions by healthcare providers	Provide feedback to the healthcare organisation on their experience of barriers to health literacy within the healthcare organisation. Participate in improvement projects aimed at reducing barriers to health literacy within the healthcare organisations' physical environment and information. Use health literacy strategies to improve healthcare safety and quality and encourage colleagues to do the same.

TABLE 4-1 Continued

Possible actions by organisations that provide healthcare services or support services at a local level	Develop and implement health literacy policies and processes that aim to reduce complexity of information materials, the physical environment and local care pathways (NSQHSS 1.18). Establish consumer engagement strategies within the organisation (NSQHSS 2.1 and 2.2). Undertake an audit of the organisation's materials and environment to identify and eliminate barriers to health literacy (NSQHSS 1.18). Partner with consumers using a variety of techniques when designing information and services (NSQHSS 2.4). Use health literacy design principles when designing information and services (NSQHSS 1.18). Develop targeted health information materials and resources for local population groups with identified health literacy barriers and involve consumers in this process. Embed health literacy considerations into all planning, implementation, evaluation and safety and quality improvement processes.
Possible actions by government organisations, regulators and bodies that advise or set health policy	Establish health literacy and consumer engagement strategies within the organisation. Embed health literacy principles into all policies. Explore options for including implementation of strategies to address health literacy as a core requirement of healthcare service design and delivery. Support the design and delivery of policies, pathways and processes that reduce the complexity involved in navigating the health system including across sectors and settings.
Possible actions by education and training organisations	Include health literacy strategies in undergraduate, postgraduate and ongoing professional development education and training for healthcare providers. Produce healthcare providers who understand the health literacy barriers for their patients and have the skills to employ strategies to address those barriers.

continued

TABLE 4-1 Continued

Possible actions by research and information organisations	Investigate the most effective environmental health literacy strategies relevant to the Australian healthcare system.
	Develop and disseminate clear summaries of health literacy research for consumers.
	Establish policies and implement processes to involve consumers in research and research translation.
	Non-government organisations support the provision of peer support, information and education materials to strengthen consumer understanding of their health care and the health system.
Possible actions by the Australian Commission on Safety and Quality in Health Care	Support the development of a national network aimed at sharing information on health literacy initiatives including environmental and organisation based health literacy strategies.
	Support the development of tools and resources identifying health literacy strategies and processes which can be implemented at a healthcare organisation level.
	Support the development and dissemination of measurement and audit tools and resources identifying health literacy barriers.

NOTE: NSQHSS = National Safety and Quality Health Service Standards.
SOURCE: Australian Commission on Safety and Quality in Health Care, 2012.

its inception in 2006. The central components of the commission's work in this area include developing safety and quality standards and coordinating accreditation nationally. While accreditation has existed for a long time in Australia, until the commission became involved there was no consistent set of mandatory safety and quality standards for all hospitals and data procedure services. The commission's approach is to move away from an accreditation process that is seen as checking a list of processes to one where the standards provide the basis for continuous quality improvement. The commission standards are mandatory and will be used for assessment beginning in January 2013.[4]

There are two overarching standards that address governance for safety and quality, and partnering with consumers, Dunbar said. The other eight standards cover what one might expect from a patient safety perspective: health care–associated infection, medication safety, clinical handover or handoff, patient identification, use of blood or blood prod-

---

[4]As of January 1, 2012, the standards became mandatory for all public and private hospitals as well as data procedure services.

ucts, pressure ulcers, falls, and deteriorating patients. Health literacy is not explicitly included in the standards; however, throughout the standards are issues that relate to health literacy. Some, but not all of these, are the following:

- 1.18 Implementing processes to enable partnership with patients in decisions about their care, including informed consent to treatment
- 2.4 Consulting consumers on patient information distributed by the organization
- 2.5 Partnering with consumers and/or caregivers to design the way care is delivered to better meet patient needs and preferences
- 4.15 Providing current medicines information to patients in a format that meets their needs whenever new medicines are prescribed or dispensed

Between December 2011 and March 2012, the commission collected information about activities in health literacy in Australia. This was not a systematic or comprehensive process, Dunbar said. There were 66 submissions with more than 200 separate initiatives reported. There are many different approaches to improve health literacy or reduce barriers being taken by many different organizations. Yet, these activities are fragmented, Dunbar said, with few opportunities for learning and sharing information.

The types or strategies taken can be seen in Figure 4-4. There were few policy approaches to health literacy, although one of the state governments in Australia does have a health literacy policy. Most of the initiatives focused on health information for specific target groups, such as fact sheets for people with disabilties or radio campaigns for different ethnic groups. A number of projects looked at skills improvement. An example in this category was a project working with people who had a chronic illness to develop their self-management capabilities. Some projects focused on workforce training and capacity building. The research and knowledge sharing initiatives included projects such as measuring health literacy, evaluating decision support tools, and measuring effectiveness of information resources.

Dunbar concluded her presentation by describing next steps. These include determining how to more specifically build health literacy into the standards, and focusing on health literacy as a core component of safe and high-quality care, Dunbar said. She concluded that the main approach is likely to be focused on supporting health services to make it easier for people with low health literacy to use and understand health information and health services.

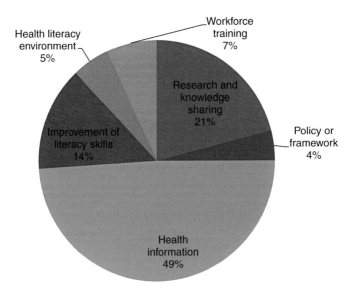

FIGURE 4-4 Types of health literacy strategies and approaches.
SOURCE: Dunbar, 2012.

HEALTH LITERACY IN ITALY'S EMILIA ROMAGNA REGION

Federica Gazzotti, Ph.D.
Director of Communication Staff
Reggio Emilia Health Trust

Gazotti said that the Emilia Romagna region is in the north of Italy. It is the region that produces Parma ham, Parmesan cheese, and Ferrari cars. It is also, as is the rest of Italy, facing a severe economic crisis, she said, and the government is implementing a spending review to reduce public expenditures.

In Italy, the regions and the national government guarantee all citizens universal and equal access to health care. The Regional Health Service with which Gazzotti is associated includes 11 local health trusts, 4 university hospital trusts, and 3 research hospitals. It employs 62,527 people, of whom 3,176 are general practice physicians and 602 are contracting pediatricians, she said. In terms of demography, there are 4,432,439 residents in this region, of whom 13 percent are recent immigrants, mainly from Albania, China, India, Morocco, and Romania. People over 65 years of age make up 22.3 percent of the population.

Gazzotti said that data from the 2008 Adult Literacy and Life Skills Survey showed that the adult population of Italy is ranked second from the bottom among the countries surveyed in terms of health literacy skills. The average literacy skill level in Italy is below the one required to fully access, understand, and use written medical material or to have health-related conversations with doctors and nurses. She hypothesized that one of the reasons for this may be that, in Italy, half of the adult population leaves school with only a middle-school diploma.

In 2008, the Reggio Emilia Local Health Trust's General Director-ate instituted a working group on health literacy techniques. Then, in 2011, the idea of a regional group focused on health literacy and defin-ing needed activities was proposed to the Regional Health Service. The 11-member regional group is composed of the communication directors of the local health trusts and hospitals and the training manager and com-munication manager of the regional health system, Gazzotti said.

There is a mismatch between the skills of the public and the demands of the health system, Gazzotti said. Therefore, the main objective of this group is to improve the oral and written communication skills of health professionals. Dr. Rima Rudd worked with Gazotti to develop and hold a regional training session composed of two separate weeklong workshops that focused on the communication skills for hospital oncology units. The workshops were held in November 2011 and February 2012. There were 74 participants in these courses. Each Health Trust sent one doctor, one nurse, one communication person, and one person from the front office to the workshop. There were lectures and discussions, exercises and group work, field exercises, and reports.

For the clinicians, special attention was paid to the imbalance between the expectations of the system and the skills of the patients, Gazzotti said. Action options, such as teach-back and shame-free environments, were explored. For the communication attendees, critical issues addressed included community relations, communication exchanges, institutional barriers, and analyses of critical texts. Emphasis was placed on language used, and techniques for creating, reviewing, and assessing information materials was explored.

Between the two workshops, homework was assigned, Gazzotti said. The clinicians conducted self-assessments and experimented with the teach-back and question-asking methods. The communication par-ticipants assessed critical materials and searched for barriers in the envi-ronment. These assessments indicated several areas of need, including the need for tools for assessment and measurement tools, training for all levels of staff, skill building for materials development, and policy change. Participants in the workshops thought that staff training should be mandatory for people who work in hospitals. They also emphasized the importance of commitment at the regional level, Gazzotti said.

Following the two workshops, the decision was made to implement two parallel paths of effort in oncologic care (breast, prostate, and colorectal cancer) in each Regional Health Trust. One path focuses on the professional–patient relationship, with training courses to improve relational skills. In this path, clinician participants in the regional course are trained to teach their colleagues in each Local Health Trust. There will be repeated courses because the aim is to train all the health professionals working in the three oncological sectors, Gazzatti said.

The second path focuses on using partnerships with patients and relatives to assess existing materials. Information will be reviewed, first at the local level and then a second time at the regional level in order to create a regional template that can be customized by the region. The emphasis is on the identification of key information and development of explanations in clear and simple language.

Gazzotti said that the goal, by the end of 2012, is for each Local Health Trust to have held a 2-day training course for clinicians working in the oncological field using the peer training method described above. A second goal is to complete the materials assessment by the end of 2012.

Gazzotti concluded by saying that the Regional Health Department is working to become a health literate organization. Every year, the Regional Health Department develops goals that Health Trusts must achieve. This year those goals include the development of health literacy attributes for Health Trust directors, Gazzotti said.

HEALTH LITERACY IN IRELAND

Jennifer Lynch, M.A.
Projects Coordinator
National Adult Literacy Agency

Ireland has a population of 4.5 million, Lynch said, and the country is currently experiencing a baby boom, with the highest birthrate in the European Union. Ireland also has an aging population and a diverse population of immigrants (12 percent of the total population) from many countries, including Poland, Lithuania, Sri Lanka, and the Philippines.

The National Adult Literacy Agency (NALA) is a nonprofit, volunteer organization established 30 years ago, Lynch said. Membership is open to all adults. NALA focuses on five main areas in literacy: policy, research, training, mainstreaming, and promotion and awareness.

While the Department of Education provides some core funding, the organization is independent from the government, which means it can engage in lobbying work. Additional funding for specific projects comes from FAS (the Irish employment authority), the Department of Social and Family Affairs, and the Health Service Executive, which is responsible for providing health care and social services to the population.

As with many others, funding for NALA activities is very tight, Lynch said. Seventy percent of the education and health budgets in Ireland go to paying for staff, she said. That leaves only 30 percent of the budget for discretionary spending on such programs as those sponsored by NALA.

Literacy involves listening and speaking, reading, writing, numeracy, and using everyday technology to communicate and handle information, Lynch said. The definition of health literacy that NALA uses is, "Health literacy emerges when the expectations, preferences, and skills of individuals seeking health information and services meet the expectations, preferences, and skills of those providing information and services." It includes more than the technical skills of communication (reading, writing, and math), Lynch said. It also has personal, social, and economic dimensions. Figure 4-5 provides an illustration of how an individual uses literacy skills throughout life.

In Ireland, Lynch said, there are 55,000 adults attending local vocational education activities, Lynch said. The Vocational Education Committee (VEC) is the main body responsible for providing adult literacy services nationwide. Professionally trained tutors with support from volunteers provide the training. Individuals usually start out in one-on-one sessions and then move into group sessions when ready. A member of the public who wishes to improve his or her literacy skills contacts the local VEC, which then conducts an assessment and provides the teaching. Lynch said that accreditation for people with relatively weak literacy skills is available following training and that this is an important development.

In 1997, the Organisation for Economic Co-operation and Development (OECD) conducted an International Adult Literacy Survey (IALS) and published a report in 2000 (IALS, 2000). The survey tested the skills necessary to understand everyday material such as a bus timetable and the text on a packet of aspirin. For the aspirin packet, respondents were asked to read the packet and then answer questions such as, "How many days can you safely take these tablets?" Twenty-three percent of the Irish population could not answer that question correctly, Lynch said. These results provided data to support the concerns of health care providers who were calling NALA and saying that they did not think their clients were understanding medication instructions. New data from the Programme for the International Assessment of Adult Competencies (PIAAC) are forthcoming in 2013.

NALA contacted the Department of Health and Children to work with them to come up with a strategy to address health literacy issues. The strategy was developed and put forth in the report *The National Health Promotion Strategy* (Department of Health and Children, 2000). This report

52

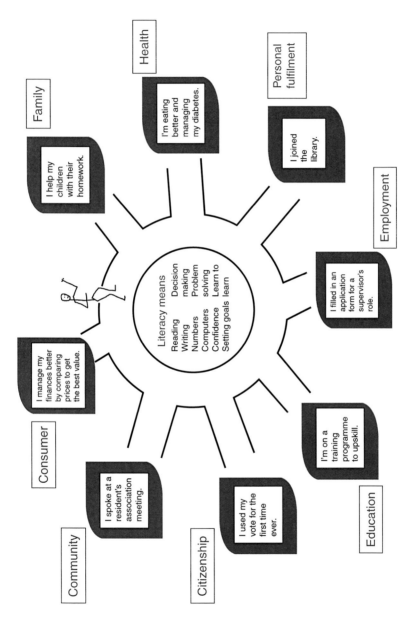

FIGURE 4-5 Literacy and numeracy: essential lifelong learning throughout life events.
SOURCE: Lynch, 2012.

is, Lynch said, the most important health literacy publication in Ireland because it was the first paper that acknowledged health literacy and talked about literacy being a barrier to health promotion. The strategy was launched in 2002, and since that time, NALA has developed health literacy initiatives that have been funded by the Health Promotion Unit of the Department of Health and Children.

One strategy focuses on plain English. More than 300 communicators have been trained in using plain English. The plain English strategy is frequently used for national strategies. One example is a national breast screening program where staff are literacy-friendly and the material has been developed using health literacy principles.

Another strategy is to produce health literate teaching materials, such as *The Health Pack: Resource Pack for Literacy Tutors and Healthcare Staff* (NALA, 2004). These materials are prepared by health promotion staff working with literacy staff. NALA has also produced the *Literacy Audit for Healthcare Settings* (Lynch, 2009), a health literacy tool for use in clinical settings. The publication focuses on translating health literacy into practical steps, Lynch said.

Objectives of the Irish health literacy program are to develop understanding of health literacy issues among key health stakeholders, share best practices across the health care sector, highlight and support good practice, and develop government debate and policy in the area.

In 2007, NALA was approached by Merck Sharp & Dohme to develop a collaboration promoting health literacy in Ireland. The collaboration has developed a health literacy website (www.healthliteracy.ie) and has instituted Crystal Clear Awards[5] for health practitioners who make their material and practices literacy-friendly.

NALA received funding from the national lottery so that it could take part in the European Health Literacy Survey. Results of that survey show that 40 percent of the Irish public has weak literacy skills, with only 21 percent having excellent skills. Merck Sharp & Dohme supported a number of road shows to publicize the findings of the survey and engage in plain English training, Lynch said. In 2008, Merck Sharp & Dohme also sponsored a survey on health literacy awareness among 1,000 general practitioners. The results (see Figure 4-6), Lynch said, were fairly depressing.

Lynch said that future efforts in health literacy in Ireland need to focus on five areas. First, Irish research to provide Irish solutions is needed. One area of focus for research is the literacy demands of Irish health care settings. Second, health literacy needs to be integrated into all national

---

[5]"The Crystal Clear MSD Health Literacy Awards are designed to recognise and reward excellence in health literacy in the healthcare sector" (http://www.healthliteracy.ie/crystal-awards/why-enter [accessed December 12, 2012]).

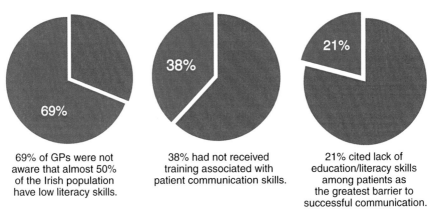

69% of GPs were not aware that almost 50% of the Irish population have low literacy skills.

38% had not received training associated with patient communication skills.

21% cited lack of education/literacy skills among patients as the greatest barrier to successful communication.

FIGURE 4-6 Health literacy awareness among general practitioners in Ireland.
NOTE: GPs = general practitioners.
SOURCE: Lynch, 2012.

health campaigns and screening projects. Third, health literacy needs to be integrated into training at the undergraduate level for range of practitioners. Fourth, incorporating health literacy into health care accreditation is desirable. Finally, she said, there needs to be a national awareness campaign about the problem of low health literacy.

It will be important, Lynch said, to incorporate health literacy into future Department of Health and Children strategies. The department will launch a public health strategy and it is hoped that health literacy will be mentioned in that because it is, in effect, a refreshed health promotion policy. Other opportunities include strategies in the areas of development of primary care structures and of professional competency for general practitioners, she said.

DISCUSSION

Benard Dreyer, a Roundtable member, said that much of the workshop discussion had focused on practice and moving ideas into action. Where, he asked, should the first steps be taken? Should they be in health care organizations? Should they be in the public health arena? Should they focus on some broad area of disease or prevention? Where do we start in trying to move the needle toward health literate health care?

Dunbar responded that the Australian Commission on Safety and Quality in Health Care has also been wondering where to begin because issues of health literacy seem to be such a huge problem. Although it is recognized that health literacy is an important aspect of high-quality care, where can one begin to do something? For a long time, the problem was looked at as a public health and health promotion issue, she said. But once health literacy was seen as an issue on which health services can take action, the organization has begun to move forward, Dunbar said. Raising the profile of health literacy nationally is important and is a strategy that was successful in other areas of commission work, she said.

Gazzotti said that the regional health service she works with had to decide between beginning its efforts in a chronic disease such as diabetes or focusing on cancer. Cancer was chosen because it is a well-defined area. The aim is to extend training to other sectors and also to public health.

Lynch said that it is important to find out who is ready for health literacy because timing is important. A new government took office in Ireland 2 years ago. They are busy producing their own policy papers and health strategies. When new national or health strategies are developed, it is easier to incorporate health literacy from the beginning than to try to add it later. Start reading policy papers and action papers, start examining new health initiatives, she said.

Vamos said she thinks an intersectoral approach is a step in the right direction. While there are pockets of health literacy across Canada, the nexus of activity is in British Columbia, largely because there is a health literacy network there which is, in reality, a network of networks and includes a mental health network, a library network, and a seniors' network. This intersectoral work provides momentum and infrastructure, she said. For example, the mental health network has a health literacy director, funding, and a provincial mandate and strategy for mental health literacy work.

George Isham described some of the ideas he gleaned from the presentations. One point is the importance of defining health literacy in a way that is appropriate to the individual country and the local population and culture. There are also economic constraints to moving forward. Three presenters talked about the attributes of health literacy. There was also an Institute of Medicine discussion paper that described the attributes of a health literate organization. Sharing these ideas is a good way to move forward. Also important, he said, was the idea that expertise should be shared among those involved in health literacy.

Baur said that in the past few years she has presented the U.S. National Action Plan for Health Literacy in three different international contexts with resulting interesting conversations about cultural specificity. She wondered whether it was possible for each country to identify something about health literacy that is specific to its culture.

Roundtable member Susan Pisano said that all four presenters on the panel mentioned immigrant populations. One of the challenges in the United States is diversity and making sure attention is paid to the cultural differences among the population. How is that done in the countries represented on this panel?, she asked.

Gazzotti said that the region she is from in Italy has developed a sophisticated system of mediators in every hospital and in primary care. These mediators speak in ways that the immigrant can understand. They use everyday language to explain things and translate material into everyday language. But that does not happen for the Italian population. The Italians do not receive information in everyday language, nor is the material in everyday language because it is assumed they understand what they are given.

Wilma Alvarado-Little, a Roundtable member, said that a big issue in the United States is the limited resources available for translating and disseminating information to many very diverse populations. Are there particular strategies the can be used to address this issue?

Lynch said that in Ireland there was a translation fund that health writers could use to pay for the translation of national information leaflets. That fund, however, has dissipated in the last few years. As a result, organizations of different minority populations are working to help their colleagues translate material into other languages.

Thomas Sang from Merck Sharp & Dohme said that the U.S. health care market seems to be shifting from a fee-for-service environment to a much more holistic payment policy with many delivery and payment reforms. Some of the newer payment policies are looking at value-based purchasing and quality measurement of the way in which care is delivered. Sang said that until recently he was involved in developing quality measures at the federal level. They were thinking about how to develop measures for assessing patient engagement and shared decision making. He asked whether any of the panelists are using measures to evaluate provider engagement of patients and what type of clinical quality measures are being used.

Gazzotti, Vamos, and Lynch said that is not happening in their countries. Dunbar said the discussion was beginning in Australia. There is a new pricing model for public hospital services—the efficient price. Initially this was conceived of as including measures of safety and quality and the patient experience. However, such measures were not included in the initial draft of the efficient price. There are some agreed-upon national indicators around safety and quality, Dunbar said, and work is beginning for the area of patient experience.

Building on the previous question, Isham asked whether the panelists anticipate health literacy meaurement as part of accreditation. Lynch said that Ireland's accreditation system is quite new but provides a good opportunity to develop a credible way of measuring communication. Dunbar said that each item in the standards in Australia will be marked as met with merit, met, or not met. They do not examine the detail of what communication might look like, but starting a conversation on this is something the commission would like to do.

Andrew Pleasant, a Roundtable member, asked how efforts such as this Roundtable discussion could be kept going internationally. How can best practices be shared yet still allow for the localization of those practices to fit the specific culture in which they will be used?

Kristine Sørensen from Maastricht University said that nine countries and many other partners are working on the European Health Literacy Survey. One issue confronted is how to translate the word *literacy* since this has different meanigs for different countries. In many of the European languages, *literacy* is changed into *health competencies*. In response to Pleasant's question, she said, this meeting is hopefully just the first step in a global dialogue. Sørensen said that she and a colleague from the United Kingdom launched a small survey to find out what individuals thought might be an international platform for health literacy. She said she would be happy to distribute it to the audience members in order to obtain their input.

Diane Levin-Zamir said the International Union of Health Education and Promotion has a global working group composed of people who want to work together on different aspects of health literacy. This might be a mechanism for communication and sharing more globally.

REFERENCES

Australian Commission on Safety and Quality in Health Care. 2010. *Australian Safety and Quality Framework for Health Care*. http://www.safetyandquality.gov.au/wp-content/uploads/2012/04/Australian-SandQ-Framework1.pdf (accessed December 11, 2012).

Australian Commission on Safety and Quality in Health Care. 2012. *Partnering with consumers: Action guide.*

Department of Health and Children. 2000. *National Health Promotion Strategy*. http://www.injuryobservatory.net/documents/National_Health_Promotion_Strategy_2000_2005.pdf (accessed December 13, 2012).

Dunbar, N. 2012. *Health literacy as part of a national approach to safety and quality*. Presentation at the Institute of Medicine Workshop on Health Literacy: Improving Health, Health Systems, and Health Policy Around the World, New York, September 24.

Frankish, J., D. Gray, C. Soon, and D. Milligan. 2011. *Health literacy scan project report*. Ottawa, ON: Centre for Chronic Disease Prevention and Control, Public Health Agency of Canada.

IALS (International Adult Literacy Survey). 2000. *Literacy in the information age: The final report of the International Adult Literacy Survey*. Paris, France: Organisation for Economic Co-operation and Development.

Lynch, J. 2009. *Literacy audit for healthcare settings*. NALA: Dublin, Ireland. http://www.healthpromotion.ie/hp-files/docs/HSE_NALA_Health_Audit.pdf (accessed December 13, 2012).

Lynch, J. 2012. *Health literacy in Ireland.* Presentation at the Institute of Medicine Workshop on Health Literacy: Improving Health, Health Systems, and Health Policy Around the World, New York, September 24.

Mitic, W., and I. Rootman, editors. 2012. *An intersectoral approach for improving health literacy for Canadians.* Victoria, BC, Canada: Public Health Association of British Columbia.

NALA (National Adult Literacy Agency). 2004. *The Health Pack: Resource pack for literacy tutors and healthcare staff.* Dublin, Ireland: NALA. http://www.nala.ie/resources/health-pack (accessed December 13, 2012).

Rootman, I., and D. Gordon-El-Bihbety. 2008. *A vision for a health literate Canada: Report of the Expert Panel on Health Literacy.* Ottawa, ON, Canada: Canadian Public Health Association.

Vamos, S. 2012. *Health literacy in Canada.* Presentation at the Institute of Medicine Workshop on Health Literacy: Improving Health, Health Systems, and Health Policy Around the World, New York, September 24.

5

Innovations in Health Literacy

HEALTH LITERACY IN ISRAEL:
POLICY, ACTION, RESEARCH, AND BEYOND

Diane Levin-Zamir, Ph.D., M.P.H., MCHES
National Director, Department of Health Education and Promotion
Clalit Health Services
Lecturer, School of Public Health, University of Haifa, Israel

Levin-Zamir began with introductory data about Israel, a country with significant cultural diversity. About 20 percent of the people who live in Israel are Arab-speaking. Another 20 percent are native Russian speakers. Many of the remaining 60 percent have immigrated from other countries. A growing number of residents are Hebrew-speaking from birth. The diversity of cultures presents a tremendous challenge for health services, health literacy, and health promotion, Levin-Zamir said.

Life expectancy in Israel is 82 years, Levin-Zamir said. There is universal health care coverage for all citizens of Israel, which includes primary, secondary, and tertiary care. In terms of risk factors, 20.9 percent of people smoke, more than 60 percent are overweight or obese, and only 20 percent to 30 percent engage in regular physical exercise. Arab women and religious men and women are the least physically active, Levin-Zamir said. The average number of physician visits is about six to eight per capita. Rates of chronic diseases are growing and there is concern about increases in out-of-pocket expenses, which may contribute to disparities in health.

Israel has a literacy rate of 97 percent; it ranks 17th among 192 countries for digital communication; and 68 percent of households regularly use the Internet. Two definitions of health literacy have been used in Israel. The first is one developed by Nutbeam (1998), which defines health literacy as "the cognitive and social skills which determine the motivation and ability of individuals to gain access to, understand and use information in ways which promote and maintain good health." The second, developed by Ratzan and Parker (2000), defines health literacy as "the degree to which individuals have the capacity to obtain, process, and understand basic health information and services needed to make appropriate health decisions."

There is not yet a national overall initiative for health literacy in Israel; however, there are several policy landmarks that are encouraging, Levin-Zamir said. The 2020 development goals and objectives include developmental goals on health literacy. The goals include improving awareness of health literacy on a national level, as well as specifically among elected representatives of the public and journalists through local and media interventions. In addition, the national strategic plan for reducing health disparities includes health literacy. A major challenge is the yet-unfunded mandate of the Israeli director general on cultural and linguistic accessibility in the health system. The mandate specifies cultural mediators, information and signage in four to five languages, simultaneous translation of services, capacity training for health professions, culturally appropriate health promotion in communities, and empowerment and involvement of the community. Finally, the Clalit hospital system has voluntarily adopted the Joint Commission's international accreditation that includes elements promoting health literacy.

Clalit Health Services is the second-largest nongovernmental health organization in the world, Levin-Zamir said. Figure 5-1 provides data on the system. Health literacy action takes place in many settings, including community/primary care, the hospital, and online. In the community, for example, a program called "Refuah Shlema" (initiated in the late 1990s), aims to promote health and health literacy among new immigrants from Ethiopia. The program is a partnership of Clalit and the Ministry of Health. The program locates, trains, and employs cross-cultural liaisons, mediators, and primary health care providers. An integral part of the team is a cultural liaison serving the Ethiopian population. There are telephone translators, a community diabetes program, and training and coaching health staff on cultural competence skills. The program has been sustained for more than 14 years and is the longest community program for cultural mediation implemented in Israel, Levin-Zamir said.

An evaluation was conducted after the first 5 years of the program.

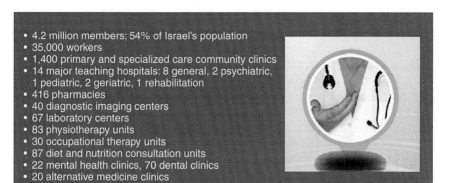

- 4.2 million members; 54% of Israel's population
- 35,000 workers
- 1,400 primary and specialized care community clinics
- 14 major teaching hospitals: 8 general, 2 psychiatric, 1 pediatric, 2 geriatric, 1 rehabilitation
- 416 pharmacies
- 40 diagnostic imaging centers
- 67 laboratory centers
- 83 physiotherapy units
- 30 occupational therapy units
- 87 diet and nutrition consultation units
- 22 mental health clinics, 70 dental clinics
- 20 alternative medicine clinics

FIGURE 5-1 Clalit Health Services.
SOURCE: Levin-Zamir, 2012.

Levin-Zamir said that results showed that the program, with no significant increase in expenditure on services, was effective at improving

- physician-patient relations,
- availability and accessibility of medical services, and
- the ability to navigate the health system.

Another area for action in the community is diabetes and chronic illness. A systematic review by Renders and colleagues (2001) found that "no specific intervention, if used alone, led to major improvements in management of chronic diseases." Complex problems require complex solutions, Levin-Zamir said. Clinical quality indicators for the community have been developed for management of diabetes, congestive heart failure, hyperlipidemia, hypertension, and rehospitalizations. Improvement in these indicators reflect community action in patient empowerment.

A number of health literacy tools have been developed, Levin-Zamir said. More than 3,000 physicians and nurses engage in in-service training each year. Culturally appropriate lifestyle and self-management workshops have been held for the people in the community, with tailored programs for special populations. The program has expanded every year since its inception in 1996. In terms of outcomes, HbA1C[1] measures have greatly improved for those who participated compared to those who did not participate, Levin-Zamir said.

---

[1]HbA1C is a lab test that shows the average level of blood sugar (glucose) over the previous 3 months. The test indicates how well diabetes is controlled in an individual.

There are also actions aimed at health literacy in hospitals. Israel recently joined the World Health Organization Network of Health Promoting Hospitals, Levin-Zamir said. Teaching hospitals, community pediatric clinics, and gynecological clinics have adopted the "Ask Me 3" initiative that encourages each patient to ask three questions. What is my health problem or condition? What am I to do about it? Why is it important? This has been translated into Hebrew, Arabic, and Russian. The teach-back method is also being implemented.

One additional initiative is a program for health literacy online. Health information in Hebrew, Arabic, Russian, French, and Portuguese has been posted online. A user can obtain his or her examination results and an interpretation of what those results mean. Appointments can be made in all languages. There are approximately 2.5 million entries each month, about 80 percent of which are unique entries. To engage children there is an online game about nutrition; this app was the most popular app in all of Israel during the previous month, Levin-Zamir said.

GlaxoSmithKline and Pfizer have provided grants for health literacy and capacity building. The grants were used to build a computer-based program called "You Can Make a Difference" with the aim of improving communication skills using the models of motivational interviewing and brief interventions (the five As), applied in different topics in healthy lifestyles, including smoking cessation, nutrition, early detection of breast and colon cancer, and physical activity. More than 1,100 physicians and nurses have participated in the training based on group learning during weekly staff meetings in primary care clinics, Levin-Zamir said.

Israel is building its research base on health literacy, Levin-Zamir said. The first piece of research conducted was on developing and validating a Media Health Literacy (MHL) scale tested among adolescents. Results showed there is an association between MHL and other important aspects of health and empowerment, including family/peer co-viewing, sources of health information, selected health behaviors, health empowerment, and social and personal demographic characteristics.

Israel is also mounting the National Survey on Health Literacy, which is similar to the European Health Literacy Survey. The survey was developed based on focus groups with key informants. This is an in-person survey of a representative sample of 600 people in home interviews. It will be available in four languages: Hebrew, Arabic, Russian, and Amharic.

Levin-Zamir said that in Israel there are tremendous challenges in bridging the health literacy gaps. New and preliminary policy initiatives for health literacy are part of a systems approach to change, with complex action being taken in the community, health service, and media settings. This provides the potential for building a strong evidence base.

Research is in its early stages with promising studies and projects under way, Levin-Zamir said.

Levin concluded with some observations about the future. She recommended that countries should adopt a "health literacy in all policies" approach, collaborate in research, build on the experience of partners and colleagues, and create international initiatives for professional training and capacity building.

THE EUROPEAN HEALTH LITERACY SURVEY

Kristine Sørensen, Ph.D.
Project Coordinator, European Health Literacy Project
Maastricht University

Prior to the European Health Literacy Project little data about health literacy were available at national and cross-national levels, Sørensen said. There was also little funding. Owing to the efforts of a persistent handful of people led by Ilona Kickbusch and Helmut Brand, funding was obtained from the European Commission for a project that began in 2009, Sørensen said. The project was led by the European Health Literacy Consortium, which is a consortium of nine institutes and universities from eight countries: Austria, Bulgaria, Germany, Greece, Ireland, the Netherlands, Poland, and Spain.

There were three aims of the project: to set up national advisory boards on health literacy in the eight countries, to establish a European health literacy network, and to measure health literacy in Europe. Measuring health literacy required developing a questionnaire that could be used in the eight countries. The questionnaire is called the European Health Literacy Questionnaire (HLS-EU-Q); it is a conceptually based tool, and it was developed by a multinational cross-disciplinary group of researchers, Sørensen said. The tool is broad in scope and covers health care, disease prevention, and health promotion; it also captures both individual competencies and the complexity of systems.

The tool is both content and context specific and measures the fit or relation of individual competencies, expectations, and experiences versus the situational or contextual demands, expectations, and complexities, Sørensen said. There are three versions of the tool, with the long version, the HLS-EU-Q86, used for the European Health Literacy Survey. There is also a core version (HLS-EU-Q47) and a short version (HLS-EU-Q16). These have been translated into 10 languages, with more language translations in process. They have been used in the European Health Literacy Survey as well as smaller studies of specific target groups.

The process for developing the tool began with defining health literacy. For HLS-EU, "health literacy is linked to literacy and it entails people's knowledge, motivation and competencies to access, understand, appraise, and apply health information in order to form judgment and make decisions in everyday life in terms of health care, disease prevention, and health promotion to maintain and improve quality of life during the life course" (Sørensen et al., 2012).

Conceptual models were reviewed, Sørensen said, and the model agreed upon can be seen in Figure 5-2. At the center are the four steps of processing information: accessing, understanding, appraising, and applying information to make decisions. Moving out from the center circle are the three areas of health: health care, disease prevention, and health promotion. On the left side of the figure are the determinants: personal, situational, and broader societal and environmental determinants. On the right side are the outcomes. At the top is the life-course line indicating change over the lifetime. The model captures individual competencies as well as the public health perspective, Sørensen said.

To develop the questionnaire the group laid out a matrix, an example of which is shown in Table 5-1. There are 12 subdimensions of health literacy, so items were developed to measure each of the 12 subdimensions.

The results were analyzed by the Austrian team in the HLS-EU Consortium led by Jürgen M. Pelikan. The 47 health literacy items in the HLS-EU-Q grounded in the HLS-EU matrix above were converted into a 50-point scale that indicated four levels of health literacy:

- Inadequate level: 0–25 points or 50 percent (1/2)
- Problematic level: >25–33 points or 66 percent (2/3)
- Sufficient level: >33–42 points or 80 percent (5/6)
- Excellent level: >42–50 points or top 20 percent (<5/6)

Those who answered "easy" or "very easy" for up to half of the questionnaire would have inadequate health literacy; those who could answer "very easy" or "easy" up to 66 percent of the questionnaire would have a problematic level; those who answered "easy" or "very easy" for up to 80 percent of the questionnaire would be at the sufficient level; and those who answered "easy" or "very easy" for more than 80 percent of the questionnaire would have excellent health literacy.

The results are presented in Figure 5-3. The health literacy index for the eight countries involved in the survey showed that 47 percent, on average, have either problematic or inadequate levels of health literacy. However, it varies across the different countries. For example, the Netherlands is doing well, but Bulgaria has the most severe levels of limited health literacy.

Sørensen said that the survey results showed that levels of health

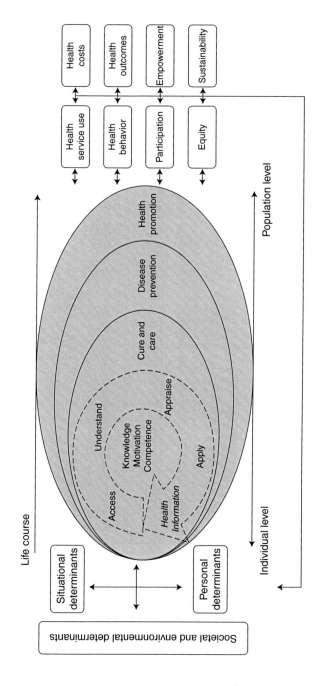

FIGURE 5-2 HLS-EU conceptual model of health literacy.
SOURCE: Sørensen et al., 2012.

TABLE 5-1 Examples from the HLS-EU Questionnaire

On a scale from very easy to very difficult, how easy would you say it is to..."very difficult"—"difficult"—"easy"—"very easy"—(don't know)

Health literacy matrix (examples of items)	Access/obtain	Understand	Appraise	Apply
Health care	Find information about symptoms that concern you?	Understand your doctor's or pharmacist's instruction on how to take prescribed medicine?	Judge how information from your doctor applies to you?	Follow the instructions on medication?
Disease prevention	Find information on vaccinations and health screenings that you should have?	Understand why you should need health screenings?	Judge when you should go to a doctor for a health check-up?	Decide if you should have a flu vaccination?
Health promotion	Find information on healthy activities such as exercise, healthy food, and nutrition?	Understand information on food packaging?	Judge how where you live affects your health and well-being?	Make decisions to improve your own health?

SOURCE: Sørensen, 2012.

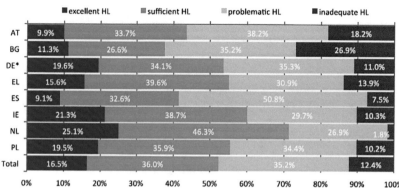

AT [N=979]|BG [N=925]|DE (NRW) [N=1045]|EL[N=998]|ES[N=974]|IE[N=959]|NL[N=993]|PL[N=921]|TOTAL[N=7795]
*only NRW

FIGURE 5-3 Levels of health literacy for the eight countries participating in the European Health Literacy Survey.
NOTE: AT = Austria; BG = Bulgaria; DE = Germany; EL = Greece; ES = Spain; HL = Health Literacy; IE = Ireland; N = number of respondents; NL = Netherlands; NRW = North Rhine-Westphalia (state in Germany); PL = Poland.
SOURCE: HLS-EU Consortium, 2012.

literacy were associated with age, socioeconomic status, and perceived health. In seven of the eight countries (Netherlands is the exception), increasing age is associated with decreasing health literacy. In all countries, there is a strong social gradient, with those with very low socioeconomic status having limited health literacy. The survey results also show that those who rate their health as bad or very bad have limited health literacy, Sørensen said.

Research is now being conducted using national data to look at differences among the consortium countries. The hypothesis, Sørensen said, is that a country's health system and society shapes levels of health literacy. The future research will look at where people find information; who the gatekeepers are; and what the national beliefs, religions, and societal effects of the educational system are.

Health literacy is a challenge in Europe; it varies across countries and is content and context specific, thereby demanding local solutions, Sørensen said. The European Health Literacy Consortium provides a platform for action. The consortium is now being approached for advice by other organizations, such as the World Health Organization (WHO) and the Council of Europe, and by European parliamentarians.

Next steps include working with additional countries to implement the European Health Literacy Survey, Sørensen said. Including health literacy in the curriculum of educational institutions is another approach being taken and is working with politicians to put health literacy on national agendas. Austria, for example, has made health literacy part of its national health targets.

But when 47 percent of adults have poor health literacy, that is too high, Sørensen said. She concluded that more must be done, and she looks forward to the continuing global dialogue begun at this conference.

HEALTH LITERACY COMMUNICATION(S)

Franklin Apfel, M.D.
Managing Director, World Health Communication Associates Ltd.

It is commonly agreed that there is no universal consensus of what is and what is not a health literacy project or policy, nor a universally equitable means to translate the concept of health literacy, Apfel said. Furthermore, there is no global organization for health literacy and the population of interest is undefined. While many see this as a deficit, from a communication perspective, Apfel said, the lack of consensus about these things has helped enable the field to progress in a unique way.

The process of progression has been more viral than controlled. This has catalyzed a dynamic, growing, changing, and expanding discourse, Apfel said. Initially concerned about the health impacts of low literacy on medical system compliance issues (i.e., medication adherence), the health literacy lens has now been applied in a wide variety of settings (e.g., schools and workplaces) to many broader public health and societal concerns, including inequalities, advocacy, empowerment, community engagement, resilience, and risk reduction. Multiple definitions, approaches to, and champions of health literacy have emerged. This seemingly "chaotic" process has helped position health literacy as a whole-of-society concern and a platform for intersectoral communication and cooperation, Apfel said.

A useful slogan for efforts to further define the field of health literacy is "Don't hem me in," an American expression that means be open, not restrictive, Apfel said. Also of critical importance for health literacy–related communications is measurement. The Institute of Medicine's (IOM's) pioneering health literacy research efforts and the more recent European Health Literacy Survey have provided critically important evidence of the extensivity, health impacts, and costs of weak health literacy, Apfel said. These data give scientific authority to the area and have been used to support advocacy aimed at raising professional and political awareness of and attention to health literacy. Yet, the potential communication and advocacy impact of measurement has not been fully realized, Apfel said, because available metrics have not been democratized. Research to date has been too dominated by providers measuring the skills and abilities of individuals (users) and has not adequately empowered people with tools they themselves can use.

Ratzan in an earlier presentation showed a graphic developed by Parker that illustrates how health literacy is a product of the interaction between the skills and abilities of individuals and the demands and complexities of the system within which information is sought and/or obtained (Figure 3-3). There has been some work on measuring the supply side with the use of checklists and health system assessments. What is needed, Apfel said, are tools people can use to hold systems accountable, tools to make sure that institutions, communities, and government authorities invest in creating and supporting more systems that are health-literacy-friendly. Such an approach builds on the old adage that "what gets measured gets done."

One such tool being explored by some patient associations and Healthy City groups, Apfel noted, is a simple, outcome-focused scorecard. It builds on the WHO's list of best buys for noncommunicable diseases (NCDs), which identifies interventions that have been shown to be effective in terms of cost, saving lives, and reducing suffering. Citizens could use this list as a scorecard (see Figure 5-4) to rate institutions or communities on how well they are doing in enacting these "best buys" related to tobacco control policy, alcohol, salt, *trans* fat, and exercise. The institutions or communities would get a score: for example, five stars for excellence in all areas, four stars for needing to improve in one. Such a scoring approach would raise awareness of the value of certain policies and could serve as a strong incentive for targeted action, Apfel said.

Individual scorecards are also useful, as Dr. Ratzan pointed out earlier, Apfel said. Scorecards such as the Digital Health Scorecard (http://www. digitalhealthscorecard.com) can help individuals strengthen their health literacy by examining their own key risks, understanding where they need to act, and identifying where resources are available. The Digital Health Scorecard generates a single number score from 0 to 100 for seven common risk factors. The single number makes it easier for people to keep track of their health risks and establishes simple goal ranges. Including a range of medical and health indicators and behaviors helps people create a mental model of how lifestyle choices and NCDs are connected, Apfel said. Having a scorecard that reflects risk and preventability can motivate action, with sequential ratings serving as incentives for improvement. Importantly, Apfel said, the individual scores can be collected so that systems can be informed (and measured) by the aggregated outcome mea-

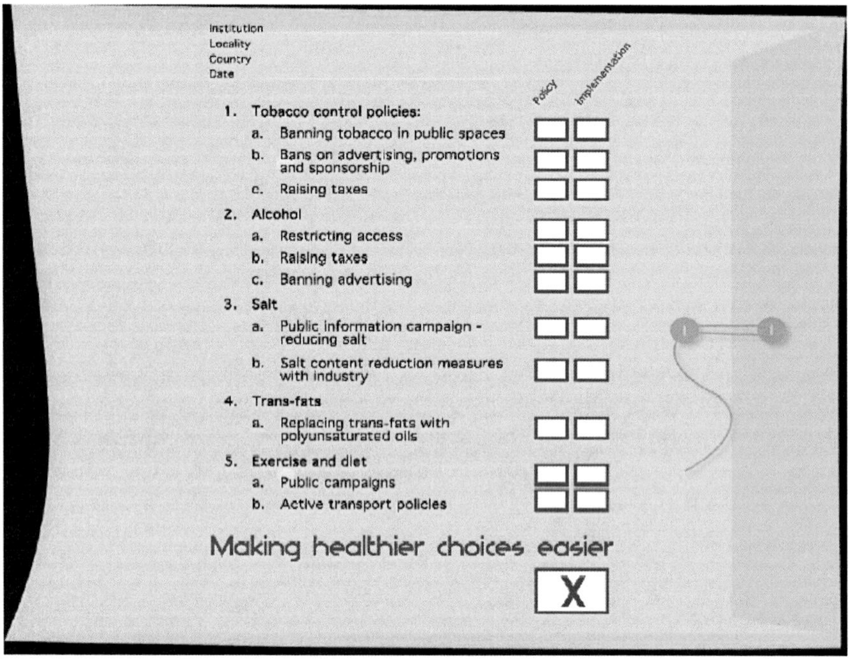

FIGURE 5-4 Making healthier choices.
SOURCE: Apfel, 2012.

sures of their users. Areas needing attention can be identified and appropriate evidence-based interventions and investments made, Apfel said.

Another important area for health literacy communication is the need to counter misinformation in information marketplaces—the public and private places where people obtain health information (e.g., billboards, media, blogs, leaflets, advertising). There are many examples of disinformation, or, as some say, "health glitteracy," where risk and hazards, for example, are glamorized and promoted. These groups include the tobacco and arms industry as well as many drinks and fast-food chains, Apfel said. Strengthening health literacy not only means providing reliable, understandable, and accessible information but also requires actively countering the disinformation. This can be done through a combination of regulation, education, and social marketing initiatives. Although a full discussion of these approaches is beyond the scope of this workshop, one key factor in any strategy aimed at countering hazard promotions relates to "framing," shaping the contexts within which people perceive and understand issues, Apfel said. Those providing disinformation, Apfel noted, know that if one gets people asking the wrong questions, the answers do not matter—for example, framing tobacco as a rights issue: that is, "the right to smoke." As long as people see tobacco as a rights issue, Apfel said, those saying one should not smoke (like public health authorities) will be seen as representing the nanny state or health "fascists." To raise health literacy about tobacco control, the WHO and other public health agencies have worked to reframe perceptions of tobacco and raise awareness that it kills half of its users when used as directed.Immunization is another topic about which there is much misinformation and confusion. Opponents of immunization actively frame the issue around vaccine safety concerns. Agencies like the Centers for Disease Control and Prevention and the European Centre for Disease Prevention and Control have been working on reframing vaccine debates around the issue of protection from the significant diseases that vaccines provide for individuals and populations, Apfel said.

Those working to enhance health literacy can benefit from learning from the rapidly growing expertise and experience of public health communication science, especially in the area of social marketing and audience segmentation techniques, Apfel said. These approaches build communication strategies based on first understanding "customers" and insights into people's health literacy and how it is influenced by their everyday lives, hopes, fears, values, beliefs, and behaviors. With this knowledge, messages can be shaped and programs tailored to specific groups' needs and demands. Information can be packaged and delivered in ways that more effectively motivate, inform, and empower individuals to make healthier choices. There are many health literacy campaigns that have used this approach to raise awareness about important health issues. Examples include campaigns related to seat belt wearing in Hispanic populations[2] and education initiatives for mothers through Head Start programs on what to do when one's child is sick.[3]

Apfel said that the final area he wanted to discuss is the communications revolution. Those interested in improving health literacy need to engage on a continuing basis with new media technologies, tools, and platforms because that is where vast numbers of individuals obtain their information, he said. What influences health literacy is changing. In 2010, the International Telecommunications Union[4] reported that two-thirds of the world's population has mobile telephones. There is also media con-

---

[2]See http://www.nhtsa.gov/About+NHTSA/Press+Releases/2001/NHTSA+Launches+Campaign+To+Promote+Seat+Belt+Use+Among+Hispanics (accessed November 16, 2012).

[3]See http://www.ihs.org/documents/literacy/Conference/Debbie%20Boulware%20O%27Neill%20-%20what%20to%20do%20brochure2012.pdf (accessed November 16, 2012).

[4]See http://www.itu.int/newsroom/press_releases/2010/pdf/PR08_ExecSum.pdf (accessed November 16, 2012).

solidation both nationally and globally. Obtaining independent information is more difficult in some respects, Apfel said.

The Internet provides many new platforms. There is the Patients Like Me platform (http://www.patientslikeme.com), where people can communicate with other people who have similar kinds of health conditions and diseases. They can help inform each other and raise each other's health literacy about available options, Apfel said. There are Facebook pages, such as Vaccinate Your Baby (http://www.facebook.com/VaccinateYourBaby). There are various text programs, for example, the Text4baby program (https://text4baby.org). In this program, the mother registers on a website, sending her ZIP code and due date. Using geocoding and the due date, the mother will then receive messages and referrals to local resources. Topics covered are those critical to maternal and infant health, including breastfeeding, mental health, car seat safety, safe sleep, oral health, pregnancy symptoms and warnings, exercise, developmental milestones, and violence. Another approach is the use of "edutainment," that is, using soap-opera formats and storybook formats to communicate health messages.

Mobile devices are also important for providers. Apfel said his son, who went to medical school at the Brighton and Sussex Medical School in the United Kingdom, has not used a textbook since his third year in medicine, when all third-year students received handheld devices. He and his fellow students now access all needed health and medical information through their devices.

Apfel said there is a great need for "universal connectors." Many players and agencies are already taking health literacy–enhancing action in a wide variety of settings, such as schools, workplaces, community-based agencies, political arenas, and in health services and systems. Most do not call these health literacy initiatives. They are often called "education programs," "health promotion initiatives," "interpretation," "translation," and "cultural adaptation services." Others relate to helping people navigate complex systems, linking people with needed resources, or connecting them with others like themselves. Many of these health literacy agents do not even know what health literacy is. Those who have had the privilege of engaging with, defining, and identifying the many ways health literacy is a determinant of health have important roles to play as connectors, Apfel said. As health systems work to embrace new governance models (which emphasize whole-of-society and whole-of-government approaches), health literacy–related communications provide both a common meeting ground and a way of measuring the success of our individual and collaborative initiatives, Apfel said.

INNOVATIONS FROM A CORPORATE PERSPECTIVE

Innovations—Wellness and Prevention: A Corporate Perspective

Fikry W. Isaac, M.D., M.P.H., FACOEM
Vice President, Global Health Services
Chief Medical Officer, Wellness & Prevention, Inc.
Johnson & Johnson

Isaac described his responsibilities as managing the health and wellness programs for 120,000 Johnson & Johnson employees and their families worldwide, 60 percent of whom are outside the United States. These employees work in 250 operating companies in 75 countries. What brings them together, Isaac said, is the credo, the value system within Johnson & Johnson that was developed and established about 65 years ago by General Johnson. That credo is, "We are responsible to our employees, the men and women who work with us throughout the world." Johnson & Johnson has a responsibility to provide resources that foster healthier lives, not only to its workers but also to communities and the environment. As Bill Weldon, the former chief executive of the company, said, "Good health is also good business."

The company's global health strategy has five components: (1) foster a culture of health; (2) integrate service delivery with innovative solutions that focus on prevention, behavior modification, and linkage to benefit design; (3) use appropriate incentives; (4) include family and the community; and (5) commit in the long term. Promoting and sustaining a culture of health within an organization requires finding approaches that incorporate these five components in such a way that they become part of the fabric of the organization rather than an add-on, Isaac said. Taking a holistic view of the individual and the organization is also key; an organization should offer programs that simultaneously address the mental, physical, nutritional, and spiritual aspects rather than taking one area or one condition at a time. The five-part strategy also uses incentives to get people interested in improving health, but, Isaac said, the way to sustain behavioral changes is to motivate people to make changes in their lifestyle, which has been a key focus in the company's prevention and wellness programs for the past 30 years.

Also of major importance is to commit for the long term, Isaac said. Employee health goals for 2015 include

1. Ninety percent of employees have access to "culture of health" programs.
2. Eighty percent of employees have completed a health risk profile and know their key health indicators.

3.   Eighty percent of measured population health risk will be characterized as low health risk.

The "culture of health" program includes programs and policies related to becoming tobacco free, HIV/AIDs management, how to prevent cancer in the workplace, and how to address healthy eating in the workplace, as well as wellness programs and access to employee assistance counselors. The second and third goals above relate to the individual's ability to understand and know his or her health risks, and to take action to reduce those risks. Achieving the third goal will demonstrate the impact the program is having on the health of its employees, Isaac said. Progress is tracked with mandated annual reviews. Local teams report progress against goals annually through the online Global Health Assessment Tool. The results for each location feed into a Culture of Health Scorecard, which is reviewed by senior management to raise awareness around progress locally and to facilitate action planning.

The strategy requires offering access for employees to centrally provided resources and tools that make it easier for them to implement programs to improve health. However, one can not address only individual workers' health, Isaac said; one needs to reach out to the homes and communities where workers live. Programs offered to spouses and families include a health profile, an e-health website, tobacco cessation programs, a family activity challenge, and Weight Watchers®, among others. Meeting people where they are is part of the philosophy in offering programs. This is accomplished through offering multiple approaches to health programs, from person-to-person efforts within the clinic, to fitness or wellness centers and energy break rooms, to e-health messages when the environment allows for such an approach.

Johnson & Johnson also has a population health risk assessment process that tracks 11 indicators: obesity, high cholesterol levels, high glucose, high blood pressure, tobacco use, physical inactivity, high stress levels, high alcohol use, unhealthy eating, no use of seat belts, and depression. The risk assessment profile is offered in 19 countries and 18 languages and has been modified as needed to be culturally appropriate. The U.S. program has been in place for more than 30 years, and data show that the low-risk group (those with no more than 2 of the 11 health risks) has risen from 78 percent of the population in 2006 to about 88 percent in 2011.

One approach piloted in the United Kingdom and France was placement in the workplace of kiosks that provide an effective and fast, front-line method of screening large populations for the key health metrics of weight, body mass index, body fat, blood pressure, and heart rate. Results have been positive, and there is consideration of placing them elsewhere. Other approaches include a digital health coach with a plan for modifying or changing an undesirable health-related behavior that is available 24 hours per day. This approach includes the following:

1. A detailed assessment to understand a person's unique motivation, confidence, and change barriers
2. A supportive plan for treatment that
   a. Establishes an emotional connection,
   b. Follows proven clinical guidelines,
   c. Incorporates proven behavioral science models,
   d. Is uniquely tailored to each individual,
   e. Is longitudinal, and
   f. Offers tools, tips, and resources
3. Quantifiable outcomes measures

The final innovation area that Isaac discussed was energy management. The Energy for Performance in Life program is designed to achieve optimal performance for the organization and arm employees with personal energy management skills. The practice of energy management can produce employee engagement, resiliency, and the potential for greater employee innovation, creativity, and optimal performance. This program currently reaches 16,000 employees who attend either a half-day, 1-day, or 2-day training session that teaches them how to expand their energy beyond their current status.

Isaac said that in terms of overall impact of the health promotion program on health outcomes and cost in the United States, "company employees benefited from meaningful reductions in rates of obesity, high blood pressure, high cholesterol, tobacco use, physical inactivity, and poor nutrition. Average annual savings were $565 in 2009 dollars, producing a return on investment equal to a range of $1.88 to $3.92 saved for every dollar spent on the program" (Henke et al., 2011).

Isaac concluded his presentation by saying he wished to impart six key messages. First, success springs from a culture of health, which is built into the fabric of business, communities, and health systems. Second, phased approaches and pilots are critical to successful implementation. Third, there must be both short- and long-term goals and measurement of outcomes. Fourth, a focus on health risk factors can yield strong results. Fifth, increased productivity and engagement can generate significant cost savings and improved performance. Finally, investment in prevention and health innovation can yield significant economic and social returns.

Innovations in Health Literacy at Merck & Co., Inc.

Michael Rosenblatt, M.D.
Executive Vice President and Chief Medical Officer
Merck & Co., Inc.

Rosenblatt spoke about what could be industry's unique role in the health literacy movement and described the journey Merck is taking. One step along Merck's journey was broadening its perspective—coming to the understanding that its products are not just the "chemical or the mixture that is in the bottle," but include all of the information surrounding its medicines and vaccines. The "chemical" would be of no use to a physician unless the physician understood what was in it, what it was good for, and what would be the problems or risks in using it, Rosenblatt said. The same is true for patients, especially at critical moments such as when receiving a new diagnosis.

Rosenblatt said company founder George Merck framed up its broad responsibilities to patients very well back in 1950, when he said:

> We cannot step aside and say that we have achieved our goal by inventing a new drug. . . . We cannot rest until a way has been found with our help to bring our finest achievement to everyone.

Stories heard every day show that there is much opportunity to help create better understanding for patients. Rosenblatt said that as an endocrinologist he has placed many patients on thyroid hormones and told them they must take it every day of their lives because it is substituting for a hormone that normally circulates in the body. But numerous times patients stop taking the medicine when they assumed it might interfere with a newly prescribed antibiotic, for example. Similarly, he noted, patients placed on cholesterol medications sometimes abandon them as soon as their cholesterol reaches appropriate levels.

The challenge is to communicate effectively, in a language that patients can understand, especially at critical times, such as when they are assimilating a new diagnosis. There is a large emotional overlay and, even if the language used is quite right, the patients may not be in a position to accept or understand that language, Rosenblatt said. One must consider people's state of mind when designing patient information.

The significant challenges faced in health care today place more responsibility on us all to do better. When patients do not participate in their care, do not follow important lifestyle changes, and do not show up for appointments, bad things can happen. And of course medicines do not work if people do not take them correctly.

Years ago, Rosenblatt said, the pharmaceutical industry considered their contributions to be mainly "chemical" in nature—discovering new medicines and vaccines and getting them approved. But there has been a shift—a true evolution—to a focus on the whole patient, and the whole ecosystem surrounding the patient.

That is where efforts to improve health literacy come in. Research-focused companies like Merck are in a unique position to contribute, as they shepherd discoveries from the lab to the marketplace. It is a journey that involves multiple touchpoints with the patient and with others affecting the patient experience—providers, advocates, payers, and policy makers. Each touchpoint is an opportunity for education and greater understanding.

Unfortunately, many patients have a fundamental distrust of medicine, Rosenblatt said. They might be concerned because the medicine is a chemical, or because it was made by a for-profit company. One of the things the industry can do to build trust is spread the message about medications to help people better understand where a medicine comes from and that the industry does not work in a vacuum. Rather, there is extensive research and clinical trials behind medicines and rigorous evaluations by health authorities such as the U.S. Food and Drug Administration. If people understand all this better, they might have fewer inner struggles, and more confidence in their medicines. And, said Rosenblatt, trust levels would go up considerably if patients also had an understanding not only of why they need to take a medicine for a particular disease but also about the risks of their medical condition alone.

Rosenblatt highlighted where Merck is on its journey to embed health literacy into its work across many aspects of its business. He said that while creating understanding about diseases and its medicines in patient prescribing information and medication guides is not new, the company has been helping advance health literacy through more formal initiatives in three main areas: advancing the understanding of health literacy as a discipline, including research and its communication; developing and applying health literacy principles in disease education and related materials; and developing tools and services for patients, health care providers, and the broader environment, such as online resources and speaker programs.

Rosenblatt added that health literacy principles enable all to help patients better understand and weigh their choices—not only the risk–benefit of medicines but also the risk–risk ratio—as well as the possible risk of letting the disease take its natural course versus the possible risks of treatment. There is the risk of the disease, the natural history of the disease, and the events associated with that disease. Then there is the risk of side effects of the medicine. If the balance among these factors is not in favor of the medicine, then the patient should not be taking the medicine, Rosenblatt said. But for many people, the concept of *benefit* means something else; it means that something wonderful is going to happen when they take the medicine. That is not always the case, he said. It is usually that the patient will not get some sequelae of the disease.

He said the industry can work to apply health literacy principles and standards to efforts ranging from clinical trial recruitment to the packaging of medicines. By increasing the development of expertise in this relatively new area of health literacy, there is the chance to improve patients' understanding at even more points along their health journeys.

There are many avenues to take in addressing issues of health literacy. In the end, there is probably no "one-size-fits-all" approach. There will be a menu of opportunities, a menu of ways to communicate with different patients, Rosenblatt said. Certain things will work for some but not for others. And it is important to realize that there is no average patient.

Rosenblatt said that the workshop under way has the potential to be a turning point in the field. It can have great impact for patients and can elevate things to the point that health care policy has health literacy as a priority. Merck shares the goals of elevating patient health through patient literacy, he said, and his colleagues at Merck are fully committed to this field.

DISCUSSION

The floor was opened for discussion. One participant addressed his question to Sørensen, saying that the European survey data show there is a social distribution of health literacy in the population: that is, those who are wealthy and better educated have higher levels of health literacy compared to those who are more disadvantaged. Also, he said, the data show that level of health literacy is related to perceived health. The participant asked if an analysis will be conducted of whether or not health literacy acts as some kind of mediator that might help those who come from more socially disadvantaged backgrounds—that it might protect them somewhat in relation to their health. If it were identified that those having higher health literacy, even when poor, experienced a protective effect on their health, that would be a profound finding on a population basis, he said.

Sørensen said this was something that is beginning to be looked at. The data do show a strong social gradient, and there are additional burdens related to age, low education, or social deprivation. Pelikan also responded to the question and said the analysis is examining the distribution of health literacy across the population and looking at determinants of health literacy. Health literacy is not a dichotomous concept, he said; rather, it is a more-or-less concept, and the data from the survey show very interesting social gradients. The data also show that health literacy has consequences for some health behaviors, especially for physical activity, which has a positive correlation. There are also correlations with body mass index. But the evidence concerning alcohol use and smoking is very different in different countries. Another finding is that health literacy is second only to age as an important predictor for health. There is also an interesting relationship between health literacy and use of health care services, that is, people with higher health literacy have less use of health care services than people with low health literacy. That, Pelikan said, is a very interesting finding and has implications for costs.

Elena Rios, president of the National Hispanic Medical Association in the United States, addressed her question to Apfel. In the United States, she said, there has been a rise in ethnic media, not just Hispanic but also Asian and African American media, including television, newspapers, and magazines. How, she asked, can one measure the impact of ethnic media as well as how it interconnects with mainstream media at the national level? Apfel responded that this is a tough question. One component relates to how populations are segmented; another relates to how to develop audience-centered communication strategies that address the needs of the users. At the core is finding out where those you want to reach are getting their information, he said.

Apfel said that a recent study on immunization programs had, as a major focus, the Roma populations because there is concern that these populations are either not immunized or underimmunized. In many instances, they were labeled as hard-to-reach populations. Information obtained from talking with people from these populations, conducting focus groups, and examining people's perceptions and behaviors around vaccination, resulted in an understanding that the Roma populations are poorly reached because of the current system for providing immunizations and information about immunizations.

Apfel said that his organization conducts media audits that examine who the spokespeople are. Those are the individuals one wants to involve in planning whatever effort is under way because the influence of the local media is very important, he said. Local spokespeople also need to be involved in the implementation and evaluation of the program. People from the community one is trying to reach are critical to the effort, he said.

Sabrina Kurtz-Rossi asked Sørensen if she could explain a bit more about the survey and how to access it since it is something that might benefit from the involvement of a wider group of participants. Sørensen said that there is the potential to work much more closely with a broader group. At this stage, the project is sharing results and discussing tools to use to measure policy frameworks and activity plans, and how to develop curriculums. The question is one of how to involve a broader group. She said she talked with Professor Jeanne Rollins from South Bank University in London to see if it might be possible to establish a federation of health literacy networks. Questions to consider, she said, include how formal such a federation should be; what kind of networks should be involved, or should it be an organization that individuals could join; should it focus on policy, practice, research, or all three; should membership be free, should membership cost something, or is there another way to fund the effort; and what should be the goals of the organization. Apfel said that he hoped a certain kind of credential would not be needed to become involved in health literacy, and that a network seems like a great way to expand and develop a global consciousness.

Isham pointed out that the IOM Roundtable on Health Literacy does not have any requirement for credentials for members, sponsors, or participants in its meetings. Furthermore, the Roundtable appreciates the opportunity to draw upon the expertise of the field, and the strength of the dialogue comes from the mix of backgrounds and people joining together in the conversation.

Jennifer Cabe addressed her remarks to Isaac and Rosenblatt. She said that Isaac talked about Johnson & Johnson engaging with employees to try to improve health outcomes, and that Rosenblatt talked about employees' interest in health literacy and how that is influencing Merck's thinking. She asked how employees influence internal policy. Isaac said that part of the engagement and participation strategy has to do with the entry point, which is the health risk assessment process that includes an online survey and response to a number of questions about modifiable risk factors and behaviors. The initial way employees were engaged was by offering a $500 discount on their health or medical contribution. Over the past 17 years' use of this process, participation rates went from 26 percent in 1993–1994 to a current participation rate of 80–85 percent and a rate of 90 percent satisfaction with the process. The company also has health targets, as discussed earlier. Promotional materials are placed everywhere—from the cafeterias to bulletin boards to restrooms. Representatives from the employee population are asked what they like and what they do not like about various programs. For example, employees who smoke were involved in putting a tobacco-free policy in place. An annual survey is conducted to determine employee attitudes about whether Johnson & Johnson cares about employee health and well-being. Results of that survey vary from company to company and reflect company leadership. These results help identify where additional effort is needed.

Sørensen said that the European Health Literacy Project, in a joint venture on health literacy with Corporate Social Responsibility Europe, conducted a scan to determine to what degree various companies are involved in health literacy. The results showed that Johnson & Johnson, Merck, and Nestlé were in the forefront. They have moved health literacy from the fitness room to the boardroom, she said. What messages do these companies have to take to the other companies that do not have a health-related product, she asked.

Once resources are available, a participant said, employees take more and more advantage of them, and the early indicators are that they are having an impact. Corporations need to understand the link between good health as well as the impact of caring and engagement on people's happiness and productivity in the workplace. In the United States, most of the message is centered around health care. When discussions are held with senior management, health care cost is emphasized. However, when one travels outside the United States, what is discussed is engagement, using health programs as a method for recruitment and retention, especially in emerging markets.

Rima Rudd congratulated Sørensen and Pelikan for the efforts and findings of the European survey. Can these findings be replicated? Can the same insights and the same findings emerge from different methods and different perspectives? Answering her own question, Rudd said that the answer is an enthusiastic yes because different measures of the health literacy of populations in the United States, Canada, Australia, New Zealand, and the Netherlands came to the same conclusions. Literacy may not be a mediating factor, but it could well be a social determinant of health, she said. That question has not yet been answered. Is a respondent in the survey saying he or she does not have access to needed information because of his or her own lack of skills or because the information is so poorly constructed that it is not accessible? The answer to that question has profound implications for action, Rudd said. Perhaps one needs to focus on the demand side of the equation—improving information, the accessibility of information, and on communication.

Sørensen responded that it is important not to focus on blaming the individual. But the shocking thing is that only 47 percent of individuals are doing well in terms of health literacy. Change must occur, but where that change should start has yet to be determined, she said. It is important to use the results of the comparative study to look at what are the best practices in different systems. Who can we learn from? What is the best approach for different situations?

Isham asked what the impact has been on the countries that participated in the survey in terms of engagement of those in policy and leadership positions. Sørensen said that a network at the European level is being created that will share practices and policies. Activity has varied from country to county, however. Within each participating country there is a national advisory board. Those boards are very different from country to country. In Ireland, for example, they have created the health literacy award, which serves as an example for other countries. In the

Netherlands, there is also an active group of researchers that is developing a health literacy alliance that already has 60 organizations engaged. For Bulgaria and Poland, however, there has been no established activity. In Austria, the results were quickly taken up, and health targets are being established.

Joan Kelly said that it might be useful to look at the Worldwide Wellness Alliance at the World Economic Forum. This alliance brought together 60 multinational companies to begin to share data and information on what works in worksite wellness programs.

REFERENCES

Apfel, F. 2012. *Health literacy communications.* Presentation at the Institute of Medicine Workshop on Health Literacy: Improving Health, Health Systems, and Health Policy Around the World, New York, September 24.

Henke, R. M., R. Z. Goetzel, J. McHugh, and F. Isaac. 2011. Recent experience in health promotion at Johnson & Johnson: Lower health spending, strong return on investment. *Health Affairs* 30(3):490-499.

HLS-EU Consortium. 2012. Comparative report of health literacy in eight EU member states. *The European Health Literacy Survey (HLS-EU).* Available at www.health-literacy.eu (accessed March 26, 2013).

International Telecommunication Union. 2010. *Measuring the information society.* Geneva, Switzerland: International Telecommunication Union.

Levin-Zamir, D. 2012. *Health literacy in Israel: Policy, action, research and beyond.* Presentation at the Institute of Medicine Workshop on Health Literacy: Improving Health, Health Systems, and Health Policy Around the World, New York, September 24.

Nutbeam, D. 1998. Health promotion glossary. *Health Promotion International* 13(4):349-364.

Ratzan, S. C., and R. M. Parker. 2000. Introduction. In *National Library of Medicine current bibliographies in medicine: Health literacy,* edited by C. Selden, M. Zorn, S. C. Ratzan, and R. M. Parker. NLM Pub. No. CBM 2000-1. Bethesda, MD: National Institutes of Health.

Renders, C. M., G. D. Valk, S. J. Griffin, E. H. Wagner, J. T. Van Eijk, and W. J. Assendelft. 2001. Interventions to improve the management of diabetes in primary care, outpatient, and community settings: a systematic review. *Diabetes Care* 24:1821-1833.

Sørensen, K. 2012. *The European Health Literacy Survey.* Presentation at the Institute of Medicine Workshop on Health Literacy: Improving Health, Health Systems, and Health Policy Around the World, New York, September 24.

Sørensen, K., S. Van den Broucke, J. Fullam, G. Doyle, J. Pelikan, Z. Slonska, H. Brand, and Consortium Health Literacy Project European. 2012. Health literacy and public health: A systematic review and integration of definitions and models. *BMC Public Health* 12(1):80.

6

Concluding Panel

WHERE DO WE GO FROM HERE?

Ilona Kickbusch, Ph.D.
Director, Global Health Programme,
Graduate Institute of International and Development Studies

Kickbusch said that when she was at Yale University years ago and met with such people as Ratzan and Parker, she thought about how to further the dialogue between a more European perspective on health literacy and the way health literacy is discussed in the United States. Upon returning to Europe, one of her goals was to strengthen health literacy in Europe and be able to have data to determine whether the levels of health literacy in Europe were better, worse, or the same as they were in the United States. Joining with other health literacy professionals, the European Health Literacy Survey was initiated.

In thinking about how to move forward, it is important to keep in mind why many dedicated people pushed for health literacy in general and the European Health Literacy Survey in particular, she said. It was because what was needed was an outcome measure at the population health level that would indicate the composite impact of health promotion measures. It was important to move away from just having a program-by-program success or failure rate. What was needed was to be able to show at the aggregate population level how health literate a population is and, from that, deduce how well a society has been doing in terms of investment in skills and capacity of its population to deal with health issues.

The key point, Kickbusch said, is that future activities depend on a composite figure that can be used when talking with politicians and other decision makers about whether they are fulfilling their responsibilities as a state, as an employer, or as a society. That now exists in Europe. And the figure for Europe is just as ominous as the figure for the United States, she said. Forty-seven percent of the population does not have enough health literacy. When one has such data, one starts to obtain attention. Not long ago the Austrian media attended a press conference where data were presented that show Austria has a low level of health literacy compared to other European countries. That was news. That was a political issue. It is not acceptable for a European welfare state to have such low levels of health literacy, particularly if they are low in comparison to others, Kickbusch said.

Should health literacy be measured only at the individual level or at the community level, or should it be measured at the population level? A population-level measure can be a politically critical figure, Kickbusch said. But this also means there must be a better definition of health literacy. It is important to be clear when communicating with decision makers what the dimensions of health literacy are. What is it that needs to be addressed? Kickbusch said there are four things to get across:

1. There is a need to equip people with the possibility of making healthy choices in an environment that is basically detrimental to their health. It is also important to show how this is influenced or not through health literacy.
2. There is a need to indicate how people get the skills they need and whether they have the skills to self-manage their health behaviors, to live with chronic disease, and to support their families. How can individuals be part of a coproduction of health?
3. Can people be taught the skills to navigate increasingly complex health care systems that are not only complex but also nontransparent and undemocratic? How?
4. Can people be taught the skills needed to communicate with health professionals?

Looking at these four dimensions, then, health literacy is about measuring how well equipped people are to function in these four dimensions, Kickbusch said. Is society equipping people and supporting citizens in the pursuit of health? It is unacceptable in a modern democracy, she said, that 47 percent of a population does not have the necessary skills and society does not make available the environment for them to adequately use the health care system and access health. This is not only about the health care system but also includes looking at every single supermarket, at labeling, and at the range of determinants of health, including the social, political, and commercial determinants that prevent people from accessing their citizen and patient rights, Kickbusch said. Health literacy is a debate about human rights, patient rights, and citizen rights, she stated.

In terms of where to go from there, first, the debate about health literacy needs to be integrated into the key global health debates, including the noncommunicable disease challenge, the millennium development goals, and the inequality debate. Health literacy is inextricably linked to the debate on inequality, she said. Second, the link between adult literacy and health literacy needs to be strengthened, she said. If some kind of alliance is to be built, the Organisation for Economic Co-operation and Development (OECD) must strengthen the health literacy dimensions of the surveys they conduct.

Third, Kickbusch said, an initiative should be begun with the World Economic Forum, possibly also with the World Health Organization (WHO) and the International Telecommunication Union, on mobile health and health literacy in developing countries. This could include cross-national roundtables involving the African countries and the association of emerging national economies (BRICS). Health literacy advocates should, she said, start developing policy briefs with economic arguments about the cost of low health literacy, about the unacceptability of 47 percent of the population having low health literacy, about the contributions of health literacy to achieving healthy life-years, and about health literacy's contributions to the quality agenda and to a patient-centered health care system.

The health literacy of key decision makers also needs to be addressed, Kickbusch said. What is the health literacy of parliamentarians, mayors, business leaders, and journalists? Work must also be done with patients and citizens about how they exchange health information with each other.

Kickbusch quoted from *The Art of Choosing* by Sheena Iyeangar of Columbia University: "We wish to see our lives as offering us choices and the potential for control, even in the most dismal of circumstances." This quote echoes what Amartya Sen wrote in *Development as Freedom*, which is that one needs to have both. There needs to be choice plus control. That is empowerment. What modern societies often offer, Kickbusch said, is choice without control, without knowledge, without skills. And that, she concluded, is irresponsible.

A PUBLIC HEALTH PERSPECTIVE FOR HEALTH LITERACY

Jürgen M. Pelikan, D.Phil.
Professor Emeritus, Vienna University
Key Researcher and Director,
WHO-CC for Health Promotion in Hospitals and Health Care
Vienna, Austria

Pelikan said that health literacy of both people and systems is a relevant social determinant of health that can be defined, measured, compared, and influenced. This holds true even though there are concerns about some of the definitions and, when measuring, there are a number of instruments that differ in scope, content, and psychometric qualities. Health literacy can also be measured in different ways for general populations. Health literacy can be measured for specific vulnerable groups, especially patients. And it can be measured for health relevant or health care systems, organizations, services, and products. With measurement, results can be compared. They can be compared cross-sectionally and longitudinally, which enables determination of the effects of policies and health promotion interventions. This possibility of diagnosis and evaluation of measures taken is very important for practice and for politics, Pelikan said.

There are two kinds of strategies to undertake toward achieving health literacy: improving the competencies of people and decreasing the demands of systems, organizations, services, and products. The latter is much less well explored at this time.

Pelikan said there is only fragmented knowledge, especially for general populations, about the distribution of health literacy and its associations with social causes, conditions, and determinants of lower health literacy. There is also growing knowledge about the association of health literacy with vulnerable population groups and with health relevant consequences (e.g., health behavior, health status, use of services, and costs).

Results of the European Health Literacy Survey, which used an identical and comprehensive instrument in eight countries, showed four major results, Pelikan said. First, health literacy is not only complex but, because it is complex, it is quite diverse within and across countries. Therefore, one must measure in every country because there are differences, not only for averages or distributions or standard deviations but concerning associations with determinants and consequences of health literacy as well. In some countries, low health literacy is related to age; in others, there is no relationship to age. There are also remarkable differences in bivariate and multivariate associations (and explained variance) of health literacy with social determinants or covariates. This is not just a consequence of HLS-EU survey's complex measure; the same kinds of variance hold true for the newest vital sign health literacy test or standard measures of self-assessed health.

Pelikan said that from a public health perspective there are four main deficits or challenges for health literacy research, practice, and policy. The first challenge relates to Ilona Kickbusch's discussion—comparable, comprehensive, and economic population measures for continuous monitoring of a population's health literacy need to be developed. Second, health literacy is about both personal competences and situational demands. Currently, there is still an imbalance in focus. More investment is needed in organizational change and development, he said, and in measures of health literate organizations. There is a need for systematic and sustainable integration of health literacy in health care services, in their goals, mission statements, outcome definitions, structures and processes, quality management, and everyday diagnosis and intervention. Finally, regular comparative and longitudinal population studies of health literacy need to be conducted, Pelikan said.

Where do we go from here? Pelikan asked. From a public health perspective, health literacy could be established as a new type of index for societies. Or a population health literacy index (combining a person's skills and the health literacy friendliness of key systems and settings) could be developed as a measure of health development. This cannot be done by scattered research and practice efforts. A much more integrated approach is needed, he said, and there are some good models of such efforts. There is the OECD International Adult Literacy Survey, the Adult Literacy and Life Skills Survey, the Program for International Student Assessment, and the Programme for International Assessment of Adult Competencies. Another example is the WHO's Health Behavior in School-Aged Children study, which began with 5 countries in 1983 and by 2009 included 40 countries. Characteristics that made these international projects successful include being open; they can start with a few countries and then can grow. There also needs to be obligatory core measures, but every nation should have the option of also adding specific topics and themes for themselves, Pelikan said. In the long run, what is really needed, Pelikan said, is to include health literacy in official health statistics and health reporting on a regular basis.

What are the next steps to take to reach these goals? Having continuous population measurement is a necessary but difficult goal as it puts a great deal of stress on accepted measurement systems. Pelikan said agendas must be set, alliances need to be built, and resources must be allocated by relevant stakeholders to tackle four priority areas:

1. Develop of an accorded, comprehensive, economical health literacy population measuring instrument.

2. Develop measures for the health literacy demand of different systems.
3. Conduct comparative population and system studies using these instruments.
4. Systematically integrate health literacy into health care services.

Pelikan also recommended the creation of international working groups with clear goals, time frames, and resources to start and prepare some open international projects. Such projects need strong leadership, he said, and therefore should include the OECD and the WHO. In terms of orienting health services to health literacy, the Institute of Medicine (IOM) has provided excellent leadership already. Others from Europe should become involved now and begin an American-European initiative to move broadly and quickly in this direction. Pelikan concluded his presentation by inviting all present to help attain the important goal of improving population health by investing in health literacy.

THE EVOLVING CONCEPT OF HEALTH LITERACY

Don Nutbeam, Ph.D., FFPH
Vice-Chancellor, University of Southampton

Nutbeam said that in 1991 he and a group of colleagues at the University of Sydney were commissioned by the Australian government to review and revise Australia's national health goals and targets. Over an 18-month period, the group worked on what they perceived to be a visionary and radical set of proposals for health goals and targets that included not only conventional goals related to mortality and morbidity and healthy lifestyles but also proposals for two new major areas: the creation and promotion of healthy environments and health literacy. Health literacy at that time was defined as the ability to gain access, understand, and use information in ways that promote and maintain good health.

There were three national goals for health literacy published in *Goals and Targets for Australia's Health* (Nutbeam et al., 1993). The first goal was to achieve the goals of the Australian Language and Literacy Policy because it was clear that improving health literacy in the population was fundamentally dependent upon levels of literacy. The second goal was to enhance knowledge and improve health literacy to enable people to make informed choices about their health. The third goal was to enhance knowledge and improve health literacy to enable people to take an active role in bringing about changes in the environments that shape their health.

Unfortunately, an election was held shortly after publication and the health minister who supported this work did not survive the election, and neither did the recommendations for a radical change to the nation's health goals and targets. What actually happened was a narrowing of the national goals and targets to focus only on preventable mortality and morbidity. Health literacy basically disappeared without a trace in terms of public discourse in Australia for about a decade when it then began to reemerge in the early 2000s.

This brief history provides some context for what is happening today. It is great to see that health literacy has finally "taken off," as shown in the commissioned paper by Pleasant (see Appendix A), Nutbeam said. There is a far better appreciation of the nature of the relationship between literacy and health. Nutbeam said that the presentations made throughout the day demonstrate there is a much more sophisticated understanding of the importance of informed choice, of patient engagement, of community engagement, and of the role that literacy and health literacy can play in empowering people to do things that will improve their health.

On the other hand, he said, there is some cause for worry. Health literacy has become rather fashionable and is being represented as a panacea for all ills and ambitions in the health system. Nutbeam expressed concern that this is exacerbating conceptual confusion and could actually result in holding back scientific advancement and the translation of health literacy into policy and practice.

Nutbeam identified three important tasks necessary for improving health literacy. First, there is a need to sort out conceptual confusion and competing paradigms. Although there is the alternative view expressed earlier that all concepts should be welcomed, there are real risks associated with such an approach, he said. Second, it is important to put into practice what is already known to be useful and effective; not only should new knowledge be generated but existing knowledge must be communicated and shared as well. Finally, as Pelikan said earlier today, a more systematic and collaborative approach is needed to address the challenge of measurement.

There are a number of areas of conceptual confusion, Nutbeam said. First, health literacy is not an action, it is an outcome or status measurement. People do not "do" health literacy, they educate and communicate. Second, there is continuing confusion about the relationship between language and literacy. Individuals may be highly literate in the language they speak at home but not fluent in the language used in their community or current country of residence. Translation and interpretation services would address this issue, which is not an issue of health literacy, Nutbeam said.

The third conceptual confusion relates to the fundamental relationship between literacy and health. On a population basis, there is a direct relationship between literacy and health status. Some people have low literacy levels and, at a population level, this both directly and indirectly affects health status. Literacy is a social determinant of health. Programs to promote improved access to education and improved education would address this, Nutbeam said.

The fourth area of confusion is that there is a difference between health-related literacy and health literacy, Nutbeam said. Health-related literacy reflects the impact that low general literacy (and numeracy) may have on an individual's ability to engage with health information and the health care system. People who enter a health system with low general literacy will often have problems with the system and problems responding to what the system might demand of them. The difficulties are due to a deficit of general literacy rather than a specific deficit in health literacy.

Health literacy is a distinctive domain of literacy that is content and context specific and can be assessed in absolute and relative terms, Nutbeam said. It can be built and improved through educational intervention across the life span. There are many different kinds of literacies—financial, science, media, information technology—and health literacy is one kind of literacy that is contextualized by age and stage of life.

Nutbeam said our collective research efforts have demonstrated several things about health literacy. There is good evidence derived from research in clinical settings that has linked poor health-related literacy with a range of clinical outcomes. Research has also shown that the rapid assessment of health literacy is feasible in normal clinical settings. There have also been intervention trials in clinical settings that show both the potential effectiveness and the cost savings that can come from interventions that take into account differences in health-related literacy. Outside of the clinical setting, Nutbeam said, there is promising but as yet largely undeveloped intervention research in schools, adult education, and online learning.

It is important to continue to broaden and test different types of interventions beyond health care settings and disease groups into schools, adult learning, and community development. There is also great potential for e-health and mobile health initiatives. There is also a need for development of measures that incorporate a wider set of skills and capacities represented by health literacy, he said, such as the inclusion of measures of context-specific self-efficacy or the confidence and capacity to act.

In clinical policy and practice, there is a need to continue to promote understanding among clinicians of the effect poor literacy has on clincial outcomes, Nutbeam said. Furthermore, there is a need for different forms of education and communication methods than are commonly used in clinical practice, such as the use of the teach-back method. Also, effective communication can be supported by service management and organizations that are "literacy sensitive," such as minimizing filling out forms.

In terms of public health policy and practice, because health literacy is fundamentally dependent on population literacy levels, a link needs to be made between these two social goals, Nutbeam said. School health also has an important role to play in building a foundation for future health literacy. There is a need to exploit the great potential in existing educational interventions in health care, such as prenatal education and patient education for chronic disease management. Nutbeam concluded by saying that adult education and skills-development programs can provide ideal partnerships for adult health literacy development.

DISCUSSION

Benard Dreyer, Roundtable member, said the presentations demonstrate that issues of health literacy are international. There may be diffrerent associations in different countries, but overall, the issues are the same. This means, he said, there is an opportunity to collaborate to address the problems. One specific and important problem to work on is to decrease the health literacy load the health system places on people. Such an issue might form the focus of a follow-up meeting to this one, he said.

Dreyer also said the points made by the closing panel—the issues of justice and of health inequality Kickbusch described, the need for measures identified by Pelikan, and the comments on research needs discussed by Nutbeam—were powerful. In addition to these, Dreyer said, there is a need for research on medication labeling. There is a huge problem with medication errors and the use of medication.

Patrick McGarry, Roundtable member, commended Nutbeam for highlighting school health education and comprehensive health education. A meaningful solution to ameliorate problems in health literacy, McGarry said, is to provide comprehensive school health education.

Lisa Khan-Kapadia, a health literacy program manager with Community Healthcare Network, commented that the need for research on what companies are doing internally to integrate health literacy into their organizations is very important. She said that her job is to change the culture of the network of federally qualified health centers to become health literacy organizations. Her organization has defined health literacy for their purposes, has moved forward with infrastructure initiatives (e.g., a health literacy task force that reviews information), and involved both clinical and nonclinical staff. The difficulty in moving forward is that there are no funding streams that support the kind of research needed on organizational change. Such funding is key to moving beyond a focus on patients or a diagnosis, she said.

Will Ross, Roundtable member, directed his comment to Kickbusch, saying that he agreed that health literacy should be viewed as a human right and it should be codified into policies at the highest level. The relationship between health literacy and human rights needs to be explored as part of the discussion on conceptual issues for health literacy, he said. Rights-based public health might be a realm in which such exploration could occur, he said.

Ratzan said that Pelikan made specific comments about advancing health literacy by working through the OECD. An Economics of Prevention meeting is held every year, and that could be a forum in which data such as the European Health Literacy Survey results (e.g., 47 percent low levels of health literacy) could be presented. Furthermore, it would be good to develop a policy brief on the state of and impact of health literacy, he said. Second, World Economic Forum documents contain the term *health literacy* but there is a need for more—again, policy briefs and, perhaps, an index of health literacy are needed, he said.

But what is also needed, Ratzan continued, is advocacy backed up by evidence. The ambassadors to the OECD, including the business sector, need to learn about the importance of improving health literacy. The United Nations Innovation Working Group is another place to provide information about health literacy and its impact on health. This working group has mobile health and e-health working groups that anyone can participate in. These are important potential avenues to explore, Ratzan said. Finally, the next time there is such an international meeting as the current workshop, there should be representatives from additional continents and countries. Continuing the momentum in both the academic and private sector, and with the work of the IOM Roundtable on Health Literacy, great progress can be made, Ratzan concluded.

Nutbeam said he agrees that it is important to engage in the political process. The critical thing, he said, is that if one does not have a sound scientific base, there is only so far one can go. It is important both to advocate and to advance and strengthen the science, but if there are lots and lots of things going on, it is harder to advance the science; a balance is needed, Nutbeam said.

Kickbusch agreed that a balance is needed, but she pointed out that one needs to advocate in order to obtain funding to develop the scientific base. Health literacy is important to public health. There are enough exemplars and evidence to document that health literacy is a critical issue. What is needed is funding of research that will strengthen the evidence base. The European Health Literacy Survey is a case in point. It took 3 years of advocacy to obtain the funding to implement the survey. Today, these data are very important.

Rima Rudd, Roundtable member, asked, "Are we done? Are we finished? Do we really need funding for health literacy? Or do we need funding to take health literacy insights and reinfuse health communication with those insights and bring health literacy into health education programs or health promotion programs? Is more health literacy work really needed?" She also asked whether the materials and information offered to the public were accessible. Providing her own answer, Rudd said that with more than 3,000 studies, the answer is no. Information is poorly designed whether it is on a website or in print.

Pelikan responded that he did not think research into health literacy was finished because the concept of health literacy is not only complex but also dynamic. Because things change, additional research is needed. One must measure the effects of health interventions; if a change is implemented, one must measure that change, he said. Furthermore, many areas monitor what is occurring, and there is a need for monitoring concerning health literacy because health literacy is a very important outcome of how society is working, Pelikan said. Just as there is monitoring of an organization's quality of health care, one needs to monitor to determine whether one can improve the health literacy of a hospital organization. All of these things require data, and from both an epidemiological perspective and a quality perspective, there needs to be continued measurement of health literacy, Pelikan concluded.

Nutbeam responded that as he said in his presentation there are three things needed. One is to continue to explore the concept of health literacy and what it is. Second, one must put into practice what is already known. As Rudd pointed out, a lot is known but more knowledge and evidence is needed. Finally, improved measurement used in creative ways is needed, he said.

Kickbusch added that despite the fact that a great deal is known, it is not translated into what gets done, often because there are not enough resources to bring a program to scale. And the lack of resources can be traced to lack of political support, she said. Many in the health literacy field are grappling with trying to determine what kinds of arguments and what kinds of data are needed in order to be able to obtain funding. It would be great, she said, to find a measure that would help in political measurements, such as a measure that showed "low health literacy costs x amount of dollars." Kickbusch said that in discussions with European insurance companies those companies have expressed concern about health literate people because they fear such individuals will use the health system more. Do health literate people use the health system more? Do they use it better? Data are needed to answer these questions and concerns, she said.

Kickbusch said she believes that with all the knowledge about health education, communication, and health promotion it is a tragedy that better advances in population health have not been made in developed societies in the world. The measurement of health literacy as an outcome is, she said, a tool to further improve population health.

Nutbeam said he believes there have been advances in population health, but these have not been accompanied by advances in equity in health. There is something in health literacy that might be useful, both in the discourse it prompts about the way the health care system works and in the approach that it promotes in terms of empowering individuals. And this, in turn, might make a difference in advancing population health and improving equity, he said. Kickbusch agreed.

Cindy Brach, Roundtable member, said that although *health literacy* may not be a verb it is evolving to be more of an adjective, such as becoming a *health literate organization*, engaging in *health literate* health promotion, and promoting *health literate* patient safety. The discussion is about doing things differently.

Also, Brach said, what has been largely absent from the workshop discussion is exploration of incentives and alignment. Hospital readmissions in the United States can serve as an example. Seven years ago the U.S. Agency for Healthcare Research and Quality (AHRQ) sponsored a study to examine a new way of performing hospital discharges, a health literate way. A randomized controlled trial was conducted, and it was found that this health literate approach reduced hospital readmissions by 30 percent. But was there a groundswell wanting to know how to do this? No. Not until there was a change in reimbursement by the Centers for Medicare & Medicaid Services regarding readmissions did many show interest. Now there is a huge increase in interest. What is needed, Brach said, is a focus on tools to help organizations implement health literate strategies.

Finally, Brach said she is nervous about population-based measurement and national or international surveys of health literacy for two reasons. The first reason concerns the sensitivity of the measure. The other reason concerns what is the measure of success. On the one hand, one talks about the capabilities and abilities of individuals. On the other hand, one talks about the demands and complexities of the health system. It may not be necessary to address individual abilities if the demands of the system have been reduced so individuals are better able to navigate, access, and understand information. "What kind of tools can be used to measure these system demands?" Brach asked. What tools can be used to measure the attributes of a health literate organization, to monitor progress?

In response to Brach, George Isham, chair of the Roundtable, said that as a member of the Measurement Application Partnership[1] he is advising

---

[1]The Measurement Application Partnership (MAP) is an effort of the National Quality Forum. "MAP is a public-private partnership that reviews performance measures for potential

the U.S. Department of Health and Human Services on the use of quality measures for incentives in their various programs. Health literacy is
being discussed for inclusion. Second, the recent IOM report *Best Care at
Lower Cost* includes several references to health literacy. Health literacy
needs to be embedded into the main line of policy development, into the
use of information technology, and into the delivery of high-quality care,
Isham said. There are many opportunities, and it is important to broaden
understanding of the impact of health literacy beyond the core of health
literacy researchers and experts. Working across silos, within each country, is a tremendous opportunity for policy makers, he said.

Kickbusch agreed that there are many opportunities to link existing
programs. For example, one might revisit the definition of what defines
a health-promoting school and add a dimension of health literacy. One
could also move forward with Pelikan's idea of comparing schools to see
whether those that fulfilled the health-promoting schools criteria have
more health literate students, teachers, or directors, she said. One could
build a composite program with the support of existing networks, be they
health-promoting hospitals, the schools, the cities, or other groups.

Pelikan said there is an interest from the Health Behavior in School-
Aged Children Consortium in incorporating a measure of health literacy
into their measurement instrument. In terms of sensitivity of the measure,
Pelikan said, measuring always is a risk. But that risk must be taken in
order to advance learning. Saying one should not measure because it
might be misinterpreted is not a good strategy, he said. Also, the measures of individual skills and abilities are relative measures, not absolute
ones. They are measures of how difficult it is in a certain system and how
much competence one needs in that system to do something. More work
is definitely needed to make systems more user-friendly.

One participant said she would like to hear more from developing
countries. The United States has a lot to learn and there are many partners for learning more about cultural competency. What does research
in that area show? There is also, she said, much to be learned from the
fields of adult literacy and education, such as theories about adult learning. The participant said she felt very strongly that health literacy is part
of the critical issue of literacy and adult-learning theory, which is about
empowerment. Health literacy is not only a systems issue, she said, but
also a patient-rights issue.

---

use in federal public reporting and performance-based payment programs, while working to align measures being used in public- and private-sector programs. MAP is the first
group of its kind to provide upstream, pre-rulemaking input to the federal government on
the selection of measures" (http://www.qualityforum.org/Setting_Priorities/Partnership/
Measure_Applications_Partnership.aspx [accessed March 6, 2013]).

Andrew Pleasant, Roundtable member, said he agreed with Nutbeam about the need for a conceptual framework. The reason why this is important is because the field of health literacy would not fare well in a systematic review without such a framework. It takes solid evidence to influence policy, Pleasant said. That solid evidence base does not yet exist, mainly because the methodology has been inconsistently applied and there is no agreement on the fundamentals. The other problem is that most of the studies have been conducted from a deficit model, Pleasant said. It is known what happens when health literacy is not present. But what happens when health literacy is present; how do people actually use health literacy? Finally, now is the time to create an international organization of health literacy, Pleasant said.

Lisa Bernstein from the What to Expect Foundation, said that she has been working in developing nations that either are building or do not have health care systems. Of concern is the potential for exporting the current dysfunctional health care system in these countries as doctors and others trained in the United States or a European country return to their home countries and work to build the same systems over again. Bernstein said she hopes the international health literacy efforts will grow and include developing nations so that such dysfunction will not continue.

Sofia Leticia Morales of the Pan American Health Organization said she believes health literacy is an outcome. It is also a political goal in a modern democracy. And it is a challenge. What is needed is an understanding of how to work with the politicians, the parliaments, and the other ministers to achieve the outcome of health literacy.

Isham concluded the workshop by announcing that a summary of the presentations will be prepared and published, and that it will include the full paper on international health literacy programs, policies, and strategies as an appendix.

REFERENCE

Nutbeam, D., M. Wise, A. Bauman, E. Harris, and S. Leeder. 1993. *Goals and targets for Australia's health in the year 2000 and beyond.* Canberra: Australian Government Publishing Service.

Appendix A

Health Literacy Around the World: Part 1 Health Literacy Efforts Outside of the United States[1]

by

Andrew Pleasant, Ph.D.
Director of Health Literacy and Research
Canyon Ranch Institute
Tucson, Arizona

Commissioned by
Institute of Medicine
Roundtable on Health Literacy

---

[1]The author is responsible for the content of this article, which does not necessarily represent the views of the Institute of Medicine.

CONTENTS

ACKNOWLEDGMENTS

First and foremost, I want to offer my sincere gratitude to every participant who took the time to respond to the request for information. When investigating what is essentially an unknown phenomenon such as the subject of this discussion paper, it becomes increasingly difficult to design an efficient data collection tool. The data collection tool employed in this exercise inherently had no choice but to place the bulk of the burden on respondents to respond in English. I dearly wish that reliance on the English language and the burden created by an open-ended inquiry could have been reduced. However, the resources available, the context of health literacy as a field of research and practice, and my own personal skills required an open-ended inquiry in English. Truly, and necessarily, this was not a health literate process of collecting information. I had to rely on the motivation and health literacy skills, in English, of the respondents. Thus, I cannot thank the participants enough. This effort would also not have been possible without the inspiration and support from the staff and members of the Institute of Medicine Roundtable on Health Literacy. In particular, I would like to recognize the tireless role that Lyla Hernandez plays in keeping the Roundtable on Health Literacy moving forward.

While many of the many hours I had the pleasure to invest in this project occurred in the evening and weekends, many hours also necessarily overlapped with my primary employment at Canyon Ranch Institute (CRI), which is a 501(c)3 nonprofit public charity located in Tucson, Arizona, in the United States. Without the active support of my colleagues at CRI, this discussion paper would have never materialized. Thus, I want and need to extend my heartfelt thanks to my colleagues Dr. Richard Carmona, Athena DeLay, Jan McIntire, Russell Newberg, Chuck Palm, Maura Pereira-Leon, and must offer a special thank-you and acknowledgment to CRI Executive Director and Board Member Jennifer Cabe. Nothing that anyone at CRI accomplishes—including this project—would occur without her inspiring leadership.

Additionally, I want to acknowledge a few specific individuals who supported this process in a variety of ways, including reviewing reports on specific countries, encouraging colleagues to participate, helping to gather specific data, or just being necessary in other ways. These individuals are Andre de Quadros, Nicola Dunbar, and the entire staff at the Australian Commission on Safety and Quality in Health Care, Mahiri Mwita, R.V. Rikard, Irv Rootman, Gillian Rowlands, Mallika Sarabhia, and Kristine Sørensen. If you do not know of those individuals already, please take my advice and get to know their work.

First efforts such as this will necessarily be burdened with errors.

Any faults are my own. Hopefully, I will be able to correct any errors and improve the process and reporting in the future.

Respectfully,
Andrew Pleasant, Ph.D.
Health Literacy and Research Director, Canyon Ranch Institute
Member, Institute of Medicine Roundtable on Health Literacy

INTRODUCTION

In the history of health and medicine, health literacy is a dramatically new idea and area of activity.

That newness of the concept of health literacy creates the motivation and the possibility for an effort to better understand the health literacy efforts ongoing around the world. That newness is also what makes such an effort challenging, if not impossible, to truly and systematically complete. The source of that challenge lies in multiple realities. For example, there is no international organization of health literacy practitioners, researchers, or academics. There is no existing database of individuals and organizations that actively work with health literacy. Further, there is not universal agreement of the definition of health literacy and, partly as a result, translation of the concept across languages is fraught with difficulty.

The results of an effort to learn about health literacy activities ongoing around the world are reported in this discussion paper, and a companion paper to follow that will focus on health literacy efforts in the United States. The idea for this discussion paper emerged during the planning for an Institute of Medicine Roundtable on Health Literacy workshop on health literacy in international contexts titled "Improving Health, Health Systems, and Health Policy Around the World." More details about the workshop are available at http://www.iom.edu/Activities/PublicHealth/HealthLiteracy/2012-SEP-24.aspx.

This paper is prepared to stimulate workshop discussion and help to

- Initiate a dialogue among existing organizations from all sectors.
- Document the use of health literacy in international contexts (policy, practice, and research).
- Examine health literacy interventions, measurement, practice, and research.

HEALTH LITERACY: A BRIEF SYNOPSIS OF THE FIELD

The first use of the phrase "health literacy" in the peer-reviewed academic literature occurred in 1974 (Simonds, 1974). That use had, by the author's own report, nothing at all to do with the current understanding of the concept and was more an accident of English than an intentional representation of a singular concept. Health literacy began appearing in the academic peer-reviewed literature in earnest in the early 1990s and has experienced nearly exponential growth since that beginning (Pleasant, 2011).

From a total of 569 peer-reviewed publications identified in 2011 through a search of multiple scholarly databases,[2] the first author of more than 200 of the articles is from a nation other than the United States (Table A-1). Several nations were represented by a single peer-reviewed publication during 2011. These are the Czech Republic, Denmark, Italy, Jamaica, Portugal, Qatar, the Republic of Korea, Romania, Saudi Arabia, Serbia, Slovakia, South Korea, Sri Lanka, Turkey, and the West Indies. This indicates a growing internationalization of the field of health literacy—a field that has been dominated in at least quantitative aspects by the United States but truly does have very international roots, for example, in the work of Brazilian scholar Paulo Freire.

Mapping the number of peer-reviewed articles in 2011 by country (Figure A-1) clearly indicates that health literacy has spread around the world and is definitively not a U.S.-only phenomenon.

The field of health literacy has grown in many ways beyond the academic peer-reviewed literature. For example, there are an increasing number of conferences with an explicit focus on health literacy. Equally, conferences with a more general focus on public health, for example, seem to also be featuring a growing number of presentations that address health literacy. Anecdotally, at least, these also seem to be attracting larger and larger audiences as more individuals are becoming aware of the importance of health literacy.

What we have learned about health literacy has steadily increased over the years as well. For example, numerous research efforts over the years have demonstrated that patients with low health literacy experience less understanding, poorer use of health services, and are less healthy. Specific outcomes associated with low health literacy include, but are not limited to, poor adherence to medical regimes, poor understanding of the complex nature of their own health, a lack of knowledge about medical care and conditions, poorer comprehension of medical information, low understanding and use of preventive services, poorer overall health status, and earlier death (IOM, 2009, 2011a,b).

The growth in the field of health literacy has, in fact, been so rapid that the field of health literacy is becoming at risk for losing track of its own successes and failures. This and the forthcoming report are an attempt to inform the field about its growth and diffusion around the

---

[2]With the assistance of R. V. Rikard, Doctoral Candidate at North Carolina State University, the review searched for articles with "health literacy" in either the title, abstract, or keywords published from 1950 to 2011. The databases searched include Pubmed, ISI Web of Science, Academic Search Premier, the Cumulative Index to Nursing and Allied Health Literature (CINAHL), Ingenta, and Science Direct. Duplicate citations were removed and/or collapsed into a single citation. In addition, Google Scholar was used to obtain any missing citation information such as the country of the lead author and/or publication year.

TABLE A-1   Peer-Reviewed Publications on
Health Literacy by Nation of First Author (2011)

Country	Frequency
United States	360
Australia	48
United Kingdom	37
Canada	25
Netherlands	14
Germany	12
Japan	7
Spain	6
South Africa	4
Sweden	4
Brazil	3
China	3
Iran	3
Israel	3
Netherlands	3
New Zealand	3
Nigeria	3
Taiwan	3
Argentina	2
Belgium	2
India	2
Malaysia	2
Norway	2
Singapore	2
Switzerland	2
Thailand	2

world as well as about how health literacy is appearing in policy, research, education, and on-the-ground projects.

METHODOLOGY

Gathering information about any social phenomenon on a global basis is a significant undertaking that is often rife for failure and nearly always guaranteed to draw criticism. Critiques of this effort and discussion paper are certainly possible and warranted, and the main areas the approach used in this initial effort to collect information about health literacy activities on such a large scale is certainly open to future improvements.

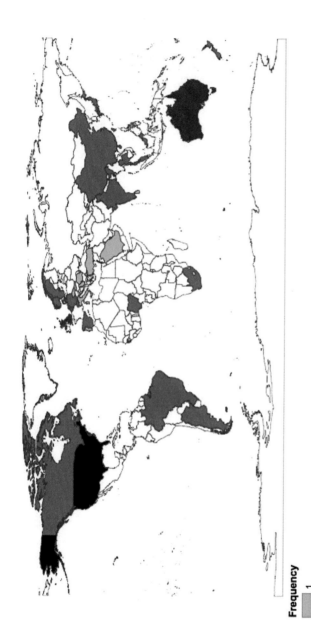

FIGURE A-1 Frequency of health literacy publications by country (2011).

The central challenge to this project was to try to gather information, catalogue, and analyze all of the health literacy activities currently ongoing around the world. That is an ambitious goal and one that has still not been accomplished. Thus, this effort is essentially a baseline against which future efforts can be compared to learn of changes and improvements in methodology and of the status of health literacy work around the world. This first attempt to reach the goals of identifying, cataloguing, and analyzing efforts in health literacy around the world relied upon three distinct methodologies. Overall, data collection for this effort occurred between June 7, 2012, and September 6, 2012.

First, this effort employed a non-probability purposive sampling strategy of snowballing. Snowball sampling is often the best method to reach a population that is unknown or inaccessible to the researchers. Both conditions were true in this case. In snowball sampling, the sampling process begins with individuals who are known to be members of the population of interest (Faugier and Sargenat, 1997). Those individuals are then contacted, asked to provide information, and asked to identify other members of the population of interest they may know. The hope is that the sample literally grows like a snowball rolling down a hill and accumulating more snow with each revolution. In this project, the snowball sampling process was initiated by sending e-mail invitations directly to individuals who worked in health literacy or worked in a position such that they should be aware of health literacy work in their country or organization. These individuals were requested to participate in the online survey *and* to forward the e-mail invitation to others they knew of who work in health literacy. This process started with an initial e-mail, with at least one reminder at a later date, sent to 574 individuals around the world believed to be associated with health literacy, health promotion, or health communication efforts. This initial effort garnered 169 responses from 32 countries.

Second, the same snowball method was used but with a distinctly different delivery mechanism. Versus sending the invitation to participate and to forward the invitation to participate to known individuals, electronic listservs and discussion groups were the means of delivery in the second method employed in this project. In this instance, the invitation to participate and to forward the invitation to others was delivered to 13 topically related e-mail discussion lists or organizational membership lists. This effort garnered 195 responses from 27 countries.

Additionally, a small group of fewer than 10 individuals responded directly via e-mail versus using the online survey platform and are not reflected in the above tallies. Furthermore, not all e-mail addresses included in the initial invitation rounds were valid. Response rates cannot be determined in this methodology, as there is no way to truly know how many people received the initial invitation.

The third method employed was a direct online search for health literacy projects and policies. The main search phrase used in this method was "health literacy" and a country name in combination. For countries that do not primarily use English, the term health literacy was translated via freely available online translators. This method was focused primarily on nations where the expected response rate was very low. In addition to identifying online resources that became a part of the evidence reported on here, this method also identified new individuals who were included in the sampling strategy for the first methodology described above.

Finally, a small number of nations were selected for a final "fact-checking" stage with an in-country expert. Nations selected for this stage were those that received the most responses. Fact checkers in the selected nation were recognized experts in health literacy working within that nation. This was essentially a validity and reliability check on the basic methodology. Very few errors in fact were discovered in this process and the volunteer fact checkers reported that they actually learned something new about health literacy within their own nation that they were unaware of prior to reviewing the information collected through this process.

While a goal of this project was to catalogue all the health literacy activities ongoing around the world, that goal is clearly unreachable. The many realities that transform that ideal into an impossibility include

- There is not a universal consensus of what is and is not a health literacy project or policy. This is due to underlying variations in theoretical approaches; definitions; desired outcomes; and to political, social, and cultural contexts in which participants in this project work.
- There is not a global organization for health literacy researchers, practitioners, and policymakers. Therefore, there is no known structure through which to contact practitioners, researchers, academics, and policymakers working with health literacy.
- As the actual population of interest is undefined, probability sampling techniques are not possible to employ.
- This project did not have the resources to conduct the inquiry in multiple languages. However, using English only is clearly a very limiting factor. Hopefully, future efforts will have the resources to expand to multiple languages.
- Further, there is no universally equitable means to translate the concept of "health literacy" into multiple languages. The conceptual understandings of health literacy reported from around the world have far exceeded the literal understanding of both "health"

and "literacy." As a result, accurate translation between languages is increasingly problematic.

- Given timelines and costs, this project was solely conducted online using e-mail as the means of recruiting participants and the Internet as the sole means of gathering responses and information. Clearly, that makes it impossible for many around the world to participate. Further, many potential recipients have indicated that the timeline this project was conducted within made it difficult for them to participate.

- Verifying the accuracy of all responses is impossible. Therefore, analysis must proceed in good faith. However, the responses do make it very clear that there are multiple conflicts in how people understand, define, and operationalize health literacy. This project recruited fact-checkers in some, but not all nations. The hope is that recruiting fact-checkers in nations from which multiple people participated in this country provided the best means to validate the methodology. To date, this seems to have been a fruitful approach.

- Many participants seemed to be unclear as to whether the efforts they described were policies, practices, or projects. At times, participants used these three words (policy, practice, project) interchangeably. Therefore, the editing process is another source of potential error as participants may have intended to indicate something that did not survive the editing and analysis process.

- Many participants either explicitly stated or clearly assumed that the organizer of this project possessed prior knowledge about their work or about other health literacy work ongoing in their country. While that may or may not be true, what is clear is that several responses were deliberately less than complete because of that assumption. For example, one participate wrote, "I know of all the standard policies in the U.S. that I'm sure you are already familiar with. I'm not sure if you are trying to determine what is going on, or if you're more interested in how many people know about what is going on. So I'm assuming you are just trying to learn what is happening. Therefore, if I believe you already know the answers for the U.S., I'm not going to spend much time on the question." Several similar responses were received from participants in several nations. That perception (of prior knowledge on the part of the researcher) may have unfortunately negatively influenced this discussion paper as well.

Readers of this and the forthcoming discussion paper focusing on the health literacy activities in the United States may too quickly assume that health literacy research, practice, and policy are more advanced in the United States than elsewhere around the world. A necessary and warranted caution to be offered to those coming to that conclusion is that the findings of this project, given the above caveats, should in no way be taken to prove that health literacy is more advanced in one country versus another.

The information in this discussion paper and the companion paper on U.S. efforts is not based on a perfect sample of respondents, nor is it fully representative of the health literacy work ongoing around the world. Nonetheless, the effort reported on in these two companion papers does seem to represent the largest documentation of health literacy efforts around the world to date and will hopefully serve as a functional baseline for future efforts to help better understand how health literacy is advancing around the world.

BOX A-1
How Did You First Learn About Health Literacy?

As a part of this effort, some participants were asked how they first learned about health literacy. These stories will be interspersed throughout the two reports. They will be anonymous to the extent possible according to the nature of the story and are shared with permission.

RESULTS

Information from each country follows and is organized by sections on governmental policy, health literacy initiatives (governmental and nongovernmental), education efforts focusing on health professionals, and how health literacy is defined in each nation or effort.

Australia

GOVERNMENTAL POLICY

Australia is one of the few nations around the world to have completed a national assessment of health literacy to provide evidence upon which to base future policy and practice. A complete summary of the methodology and findings can be found at http://www.abs.gov.au/AUSSTATS/abs@.nsf/Latestproducts/4233.0Main%20Features22006?

opendocument&tabname=Summary&prodno=4233.0&issue=2006&num
=&view=.

The assessment of health literacy in Australia is a component of the Adult Literacy and Life Skill Survey (ALLS)[3] that was last completed in 2006 and reported by the Australian Bureau of Statistics. The methodology consisted of 191 items in four conceptual domains of prose, document, numeracy, and problem solving. These items were also classified according to relevance to health promotion, health protection, disease prevention, health care maintenance, and systems navigation. The assessment indicated that health literacy for Australians generally increases between the ages of 15 to 19 until 40 years of age and then begins to decline for older adults. There were not regional variations of note except for the Australian Capital Territory, where health literacy was generally higher than the rest of the nation (Australian Bureau of Statistics, 2006).

Respondents varied in their qualitative assessments of health literacy policies in Australia. Some reported a forward-moving robust process of policy development while others characterized that same effort as lacking except for the acknowledgment that there is a problem. For instance, participants reported that currently there is not a national health literacy policy in Australia and that there has not been a systematic comprehensive review of government policies that include health literacy in Australia.

One participant offered an observation that Australia's health policies are moving in the direction of a more "joined up" health system with less silos between health providers. The hope is that this will change the experience of consumers with the health system. Also, this participant adds, the government is sending a very strong message that people need to be self-responsible for their health through funding health promotion and health literacy programs and through a tax for those who don't invest in private health insurance.

Notably, participants reported that there is a national safety and quality policy that explicitly includes health literacy in its framework (http://www.safetyandquality.gov.au/our-work/national-perspectives/australian-safety-and-quality-framework-for-health-care). This policy sets

---

[3]According to the Australian Bureau of Statistics, "the ALLS is an international survey that has been completed by participating countries in successive waves. In 2003, the first wave of countries that participated in the Adult Literacy and Life Skills Survey were Bermuda, Canada, Italy, Mexico, Norway, Switzerland and the United States. Second wave countries to take part were Australia, New Zealand, the Netherlands, Hungary and South Korea. The health literacy domain was only derived for some countries, as it was provided as an additional service (requiring additional funding). It also was not derived on the same basis for all countries. To date, Canada is the only country with a health literacy domain comparable to Australia's; however, due to the unavailability of Canada's health literacy microdata, no detailed health literacy comparisons have been made between the two countries."

out to describe safe and high-quality care and the actions needed to achieve those goals for Australia. The goals specified by the policy are that safe, high-quality health care is always consumer-centered, driven by information, and organized for safety (http://www.safetyandquality. gov.au/wp-content/uploads/2012/01/32296-Australian-SandQ-Framework1.pdf). The consumer-centered goal discussion within this policy specifies health literacy as an action area. A participant in this project reported that the goal is to ensure that there are effective partnerships between consumers, health care providers, and organizations at all levels of health care provision, planning, and evaluation. One of the outcomes identified within this goal is for health care organizations to become health literate organizations. The Australian Health Ministers, participants noted, recently endorsed these goals.

Participants in this project reported that starting in January 2013, that all hospitals in Australia will be assessed against a set of 10 standards, the National Safety and Quality Health Service Standards (http://www. safetyandquality.gov.au/our-work/accreditation/nsqhss). Participants also reported that while health literacy is not explicitly included, health literacy concepts are embedded throughout the standards. For example, the standards include action items regarding

- Having mechanisms in place to align information provided with the patient's capacity to understand;
- The need to get feedback from consumers on patient information publications developed by the hospital, and take action to incorporate this feedback into final documents;
- Developing a medication management plan in partnership with patients and carers[4];
- Providing information to patients about medication treatment options, benefits, and associated risks; and
- Developing fall prevention plans in partnership with patients and caregivers.

Health literacy and related concepts are also reported to be included in a range of other Australian national health policies that focus on the educational and societal aspects of health literacy, including issues such as raising awareness, prevention, self-management, and shared decision

---

[4]The term "carers" in Australia and the United Kingdom is roughly equivalent to "caregivers" in the United States, usually referring to someone who is responsible for the care of someone who has poor mental health, is physically disabled or whose health is impaired by sickness or old age. The terms are most often used to refer to unpaid relatives or friends versus health care professionals.

making. Two examples of such policies that were highlighted by survey participants are:

- National Male Health Policy (http://www.health.gov.au/internet/main/publishing.nsf/content/0547F4712F6AB5D3CA257457001D4ECF/$File/MainDocument.pdf)
- National Mental Health Plan (http://www.health.gov.au/internet/main/publishing.nsf/Content/360EB322114EC906CA2576700014A817/$File/pla2.pdf—note this link is to Priority area 2: Prevention and early intervention)

At the state level in Australia, two Australian states are reported to have developed policies that include health literacy as a key priority area. The Department of Health and Human Services in Tasmania developed a Communication and Health Literacy Action Plan (http://www.dhhs.tas.gov.au/pophealth/health_literacy). This plan outlines the actions that will be taken between 2011 and 2013 to improve communication across health and human services, and to help improve health literacy in Tasmania. The four areas to be focused on are (1) raising awareness of the importance of effective communication and health literacy; (2) helping people access, understand, and use services and information; (3) helping staff, volunteers, and those who use health services to be more health literate; and (4) improving health literacy across Tasmania. The report is available at http://www.dhhs.tas.gov.au/__data/assets/pdf_file/0009/75870/poh_Action_Plan_communication_and_health_literacy_20120313.pdf.

Victoria is the second Australian state reported to have developed health literacy policies. For example, participants reported that the Victorian Health Priorities Framework 2012–2022 developed by the Victorian Department of Health establishes a framework for the planning and development of priorities for health services across the Victorian health care system by the year 2022, and then articulates the particular planning and development priorities. The framework identifies that improving health literacy is a fundamental precursor to improving health outcomes of the population and that better health literacy improves access to a range of programs to help maintain good health. See http://www.health.vic.gov.au/healthplan2022.

In that report, health literacy underpins the seven priority areas for reform. Those reform priorities are to develop a system that is responsive to people's needs; improving every Victorian's health status and health experiences; expanding service, workforce, and system capacity; increasing the system's financial sustainability and productivity; implementing continuous improvements and innovation; increasing accountability and transparency; and using e-health and communication technology.

BOX A-2
How Did You First Learn About Health Literacy?

"I became interested in health literacy in 2007 when I read a UNAIDS report and was alarmed with HIV/AIDS statistics in Africa. In December 2007, I made a presentation at a youth conference highlighting the impact of HIV/AIDS on the youth."

Participant from Malawi

One participant reported that regulations set by the Australian government also are reported to require private health insurers to present information regarding coverage in a standardized format so that consumers choosing between them can compare "apples and apples."[5] Participants also reported that Australia has just moved to a national registration for health providers, a unique health identifier for consumers, and have launched a person-controlled electronic health record that hopes to facilitate consistent communication between different providers dealing with the one patient.

A participant reported that most population specific (e.g., children, adults, older people) and disease specific (e.g., mental health, diabetes) policies in Australia do have a community education and health literacy–related component. Others reported that policies at national and state/territory levels do address needs of people from culturally and linguistically diverse backgrounds such as Aboriginal and Torres Strait Islander Australians.

Other relevant policies indicated by participants in, or aware of, health literacy efforts in Australia include

- National Primary Health Care Reform: This effort explicitly addresses health literacy, cultural appropriate and timely care, increased focus on prevention, including support of health life-

---

[5]According to a 2009 report from the Commonwealth Fund, "Australia has a mixed public and private health care system. The core feature is public, taxation-funded health insurance under Medicare, which provides universal access to subsidized medical services and pharmaceuticals, and free hospital treatment as a public patient. Medicare is complemented by a private health system in which private health insurance assists with access to hospital treatment as a private patient and with access to dental services and allied health services. There is a strong reliance on out-of-pocket payments." See http://www.commonwealth fund.org/~/media/Files/Publications/Fund%20Report/2010/Jun/1417_Squires_Intl_Profiles_622.pdf.

styles, better management of health information, including use of e-health and flexibility to best respond to local community needs, and workforce development. See http://www.yourhealth.gov.au/ internet/yourhealth/publishing.nsf/Content/nphc-draftreport supp-toc#.UDk4jBwoSKI and http://www.yourhealth.gov.au/ internet/yourhealth/publishing.nsf/Content/nphc-draftreport supp-toc~nphc-draftreportsupp-ch4~nphc-draftreportsupp-ch4-elem2#.UAOAWxwWWvw.

• Australia is a signatory to the United Nations Convention on Rights of People with Disability 2006. Article 2 described the breadth of communication modes, Article 9 addresses issues of accessibility, and Article 21 of the Convention addresses related to freedom of expression and opinion and access to information. Further discussion can be found in Basterfield (2009) "Raising awareness of the importance of functional literacy skills." *Australian Communication Quarterly* Vol. 11 No. 2.

In the state of Victoria, several other policies are relevant to health literacy. These include

• Victorian Charter of Human Rights and Responsibility Charter of 2007 (http://www.education.vic.gov.au/studentlearning/programs/multicultural/tchhrcharter.htm)
• The Victorian Disability Act of 2006 (http://www.dhs.vic.gov.au/for-individuals/disability/your-rights/disability-act-2006) explicitly addresses issues such as providing information, community inclusion, easy to read information, and information in community languages
• Victorian Equal Opportunity Act of 2010 (http://www.human rightscommission.vic.gov.au/index.php?option=com_k2&view=item&layout=item&id=1123&Itemid=569)
• Other relevant legislation frameworks and government policies can be found linked at http://accesseasyenglish.com.au/easy-english/legislative-framework
• Victorian Government External Communication Access Policy of 2006

In other states and territories, policies relevant to health literacy reported by participants include

• The Western Australia chronic disease self-management strategy http://www.healthnetworks.health.wa.gov.au/abhi/project/self_management.cfm

- The Northern Health Promotion Strategic Framework 2011–2015
  http://health.nt.gov.au/library/scripts/objectifyMedia.aspx?
  file=pdf/66/68.pdf&siteID=1&str_title=NT%20DoH%20Health
  %20Promotion%20Framework.pdf

Key sources of data related to information related to health literacy in Australia are the Australian Bureau of Statistics and the Australian Institute of Health and Welfare.

HEALTH LITERACY INITIATIVES
(GOVERNMENTAL AND NONGOVERNMENTAL)

As a part of its work to encourage patient-centered, high-quality care, the Australian Commission on Safety and Quality in Health Care (http://www.safetyandquality.gov.au) is conducting a comprehensive "stocktake" of health literacy initiatives that is ongoing as of the preparation of this report. The effort, much like what produced this report, sought information on health literacy projects, programs, research, and initiatives at local, state, and national levels within Australia. The goals were to gain a greater understanding of the types of health literacy initiatives being implemented and the potential effectiveness and impact of these initiatives, identify areas of best practices for national promotion, as well as areas requiring further development within the health literacy field, and investigate opportunities for future national activities the Commission could undertake to support improvements to health literacy (http://www.safetyandquality.gov.au/our-work/patient-and-consumer-centered-care/health-literacy).

Working in collaboration with the state government of Victoria, academics Richard Osborne (http://www.deakin.edu.au/health/hsd/staff/index.php?username=rosb) and Rachelle Buchbinder (http://monash.edu/research/profiles/profile.html?sid=440&pid=2691) are reported to have led teams to develop a person-centered measure of health literacy called the Health Literacy Questionnaire. They have assessed 380 patients at four health care provider organizations. The research helped inform the partnership between the government and universities to develop the Victorian Health Literacy Response Framework. The goal of the project is for the partnership to co-create a statewide system to improve equitable service provision through assessment of consumers/patients health literacy who enter community and hospital health care institutions. The project is reported to be funded by the Australian Research Council, Victorian Department of Health, and Deakin University.

The Australian government has also been reported by participants to have formed a partnership with the Pharmacy Guild of Australia to provide access to community pharmaceutical services. This initiative is the Community Pharmacy Health Literacy Research Project. Pharmacy research and development is one of the areas included in this agreement. One of the research projects currently under way focuses on health literacy in the pharmaceutical sector. The aim of this project is to develop, pilot, and refine an educational package for pharmacists and pharmacy assistants around health literacy in order for them to better tailor information to consumers and facilitate improved health outcomes. The methodology involves a comprehensive literature review and identification of existing resources, tools, and relevant best practices of health literacy. That will be followed by the development, evaluation, and refinement of the educational package. To facilitate wide dissemination, a train-the-trainer approach will be used to prepare pharmacists to deliver the training to other pharmacists and pharmacy assistants in the workplace (Duncan et al., 2012). The package will be refined based on outcomes and then made widely available to improve consumer medicines through better quality interactions in the pharmacy setting. See, as an example of this effort, http://www.uq.edu.au/health/healthycomm/docs/IHAMay2012.pdf.

HealthInsite is an online health information service provided by the National Health Call Centre Network, a service funded by the national and state governments in Australia to provide telephone triage, advice, and health information. HealthInsite reports its aim is to improve the health of Australians by providing easy access to quality information about human health. The information provided covers a wide range of topic areas and is reviewed by an assessment panel for quality, authority, currency, accessibility, navigation, format, design, and innovation. See http://www.healthinsite.gov.au.

One participant reported that there is a national health promotion effort targeted at Aboriginal and Torres Strait Islander health needs through Closing the Gap. This effort includes funding and health initiatives aimed at reducing the gap in life expectancy between Indigenous Australians and the general Australian population. See http://www.health.gov.au/internet/main/publishing.nsf/Content/currentissue-P10000005.

Another participant in this process reported on the ongoing efforts of the Health Issues Centre, an independent, not-for-profit organization that began in 1985 to promote equity and consumer perspectives in the Australian health system (http://www.healthissuescentre.org.au). One effort of this organization, Project Participate!, hopes to increase participating organizations' knowledge, skill, and relationship capital by building capacity for sustainable community participation in health. The effort is reported to involve local primary care organizations, community health services, and hospitals, and consumer mentoring, participating staff and consumer leaders will lead and learn from the project by

- Identifying current participation data, activities, policy, standards and stakeholders
- Consulting with stakeholders to analyze current gaps and opportunities
- Developing an action-learning based community participation plan
- Facilitating implementation and monitoring of the plan
- Participating in the delivery of consumer leadership accredited training
- Identifying and disseminating participation resources
- Utilizing participation networks in the health sector
- Collecting and analyzing participation data for internal and external reporting
- Leading the review and improvement of the participation plan (Health Issues Center, 2012)

Several participants reported that the Department of Health, Western Australia, is supporting a Patient First Program that is designed to educate health consumers about the health care process and potential problems that can occur with their health care. The goals are to help people become more active, involved, and informed participants in their health care and reduce medical errors during a patient's care. The Patient First Program aims to increase patients' understanding of their condition(s) to enable better decision making through informed consent, increase patients' awareness of the risks inherent in their health care to minimize the potential for adverse events, and increase patients' health literacy and give them the ability to self-manage their health issues (Department of Health Government of Western Australia, 2012). Participants reported that efforts to reach those goals include the development of booklets and brochures for patients and care givers as part of the program. These materials address issues such as informed consent, managing medications, understanding risks, and making decisions about health care. See http:// www.safetyandquality.health.wa.gov.au/involving_patient/patient_1st. cfm.

Multiple organizations, governmental and nongovernmental, have reportedly created a Health Literacy Network (HLN). This effort, participants report, is convened by the New South Wales (NSW) Clinical Excellence Commission (CEC) (http://www.cec.health.nsw.gov.au/home) and is a collaboration between the CEC, the Australian Commission on Safety and Quality in Health Care, the NSW Health Care Complaints Commission, and the University of Sydney School of Public Health. The HLN is reported to be committed to the improvement of health literacy by encouraging collaboration through this alliance of key stakeholders. To date, participants report that key activities of the HLN include the

- Liaison with health education providers within NSW to encourage inclusion of health literacy–related education in clinical under-graduate or postgraduate curricula;
- Development of a guideline to assist clinicians, public health orga-nizations, and consumer groups to communicate, verbally and in printed form, in a manner that patients can easily understand;
- Development of a repository of health literacy information and resources; and
- Investigation of ways to promote awareness amongst clinicians of the signs and effects of limited health literacy and evidence-based strategies that have been shown to assist lower literacy patients.

The Cue Cards in Community Languages initiative is an effort con-ducted by Eastern health, a health care provider organization in the state of Victoria, that is reported to work to assist health professionals and clients/carers who do not speak the English language well or at all or have problems communicating with each other. Participants reported that in order to develop the cue cards, local government, acute and mental health organizations, residential care facilities, and dental and disability service organizations were asked to provide a list of the most commonly used words they needed to communicate on a daily basis. The organiz-ers then developed a list of words that were used across the spectrum of health care services. Participating organizations also indicated their choices of the languages to be used for translation. Community members with little or no English language chose the images that best represented the 200-plus words listed on the cue cards. The organizers note that the cue cards are not meant to be used in lieu of accredited interpreters, but can be used by clients/carers to communicate simple needs such as hun-ger, thirst, or need to use a telephone and can be used by professionals to indicate simple instructions/concepts. See http://www.easternhealth. org.au/services/cuecards/default.aspx#cuecards.

Goulburn Valley Health, a hospital in Shepparton, Victoria, offers a Hospital Orientation and Health Information Tour for Migrants and Refugees in a pilot program that began in 2010. The effort provides tours of the hospital to small groups of English language students from the local technical college. The objectives of the program are to

- familiarize community members with the hospital layout, car park-ing, and how to find their way around the hospital should they need to in the future, and to
- introduce "key take home messages" provided by health service staff at "stop-off" points in the tour, including pharmacy, pathol-ogy, imaging, and emergency departments.

Participants in this effort reported that evaluations of the pilot program were positive, so the program has been expanded to include

- outpatient clinics, and the Sanctuary (a sacred space within the hospital which is available to people of all faiths) as part of the tour itinerary, and
- tours for multicultural support workers and settlement support service staff so that they can better assist refugee and migrant families to access hospital services.

Participants also reported that the Penola War Memorial Hospital (http://www.sahealth.sa.gov.au/wps/wcm/connect/public+content/sa+health+internet/health+services/hospitals+and+health+services/country/limestone+coast/penola+war+memorial+hospital) of the government of South Australia Health System is conducting a First Impressions Activities project in an effort that has been adapted from Rima Rudd's effort, "The Health Literacy Environment Activity Packet: First Impressions and Walking Interview" (http://www.hsph.harvard.edu/healthliteracy/files/activitypacket.pdf) in order to suit a rural hospital. The First Impressions project is reported to consist of three activities that focus on first impressions: a telephone call to the hospital, a visit to the hospital's website, and a walking interview.

A health literacy project also reported on by participants is the Melton Shire Council, Live Eat Go! Healthy Communities Program (http://www.melton.vic.gov.au/Services/Health_safety_and_wellbeing/Health_promotion/Live_Eat_GO). This initiative aims to reduce the prevalence of overweight and obesity in participating communities by increasing the number of at-risk individuals that engaged in accredited physical activity and healthy eating programs. The program includes a range of initiatives including increasing health literacy and knowledge in groups at risk of pre-diabetes or the onset of type 2 diabetes.

A health literacy project titled "Fear and Shame: Using Theatre to Destigmatise Mental Illness in an Australian Macedonian Community" is reported as ongoing and led by individuals from the South Eastern Sydney Illawarra Area Health Service. This effort used the arts, theater in particular, to address stigma and beliefs surrounding mental health to positive effect. See Blignault, I., S. Smith, L. Woodland, V. Ponzio, D. Ristevski, and S. Kirov. 2010. Fear and shame: Using theatre to destigmatize mental illness in an Australian Macedonian community. *Health Promotion Journal of Australia* 21:120–126.

The Western Australian (WA) Country Health Service Chronic Conditions Self-management program is reported to include building health literacy and training as one of four overarching program goals for 2012–

2015 (http://www.wacountry.health.wa.gov.au/index.php?id=667). This goal includes

- Developing a chronic condition and self-management education and training strategy for WA Country Health staff in collaboration with Learning and Development Units, Metropolitan Health Services, and relevant academic partners.
- Liaise with Allied Health workforce development manager to review the training framework for inclusion of self-management competencies, including those that specifically address health literacy.
- Distribute the DVD titled *Self-Managing Your Long-Term Health Condition* through consumer and health professional networks.
- Distribute the *On the Right Road* diabetes education DVD through the Pilbara Region of WA.
- Develop brochures and other education/promotion resources targeted to consumers and health professionals on topics, including
  o How to better self-manage a long-term condition
  o How to provide better self-management support for consumers living with long-term conditions
  o Long-term conditions such as chronic obstructive pulmonary disease, heart failure, asthma, diabetes, etc.

A participant to the query for information about health literacy activities in Australia reported that "I am challenged by the concept of health literacy as being often written for the 'typical reader.' I work with and for people with limited literacy—the 46% in Australia with non-functional literacy. Health literacy in its traditional description is not useful for this category of people. I write 'Easy English' to assist people with low or limited or non-functional literacy to access health information." This participant reported creating materials related to asthma, domestic abuse, immunization, and other health topics. See the Business section of this report for more information. Examples include

- Privacy release of information: http://www.health.vic.gov.au/pcps/downloads/coordination/translations/consent_easy_english.pdf; http://www.health.vic.gov.au/pcps/downloads/coordination/translations/privacy_easyenglish.pdf
- Rights charter: http://www.health.vic.gov.au/patientcharter/publications/order.htm

A respondent in Australia reported that a group has been working on health literacy interventions regarding oral (dental) health for indigenous adults in rural settings. No other information was supplied.

In general, Australian respondents note that health literacy efforts may be funded by the government, although they are often tendered out to external providers like not-for-profit/nongovernmental organizations such as health promotion charities, community service providers, and universities. The aggregate of responses from other participants clearly indicate that there are many more ongoing and diverse health literacy projects in Australia. Other health literacy–related efforts in Australia according to participants include

- One Life suicide prevention: http://www.mcsp.org.au
- Mental Health First Aid: http://www.mhfa.com.au
- Measure Up (reducing metabolic syndrome risk by targeting obesity): http://www.measureup.gov.au
- Swap it, don't stop it (reducing metabolic syndrome risk by targeting obesity): http://swapit.gov.au
- Mind Matters is a mental health promotion initiative run in schools: http://www.mindmatters.edu.au/default.asp
- Headspace is a program that focuses on mental health literacy and early identification and intervention in mental health and drug/alcohol problems in the 12- to 25-year-old age group: http://www.headspace.org.au
- HealthInfonet provides information about Indigenous health promotion/health literacy programs: http://www.healthinfonet.ecu.edu.au
- The Drug and Alcohol Office in Western Australia and nationally the drug strategies are reported to be very proactive around community awareness and prevention and responsible use: http://www.dao.health.wa.gov.au
- The Department of Health of the Government of Western Australia has produced a toolkit for collecting and using patient stories to improve health: http://www.health.wa.gov.au/hrit/docs/A_toolkit_for_collecting_and_using_patient_stories.pdf
- The Health Consumers' Council Western Australia has created a Patients First Ambassador project: http://www.healthissuescentre.org.au/documents/items/2009/06/280714-upload-00001.pdf
- An overview of ongoing campaigns conducted by the Australian Department of Health and Ageing: http://www.health.gov.au/internet/main/publishing.nsf/Content/relatedwebsites
- An overview of health promotion efforts ongoing in South Australia: http://www.dh.sa.gov.au/pehs/health-promotion.htm

EDUCATIONAL EFFORTS TARGETING HEALTH PROFESSIONALS

Training of health professionals in health literacy is reported to be occurring at several institutions in Australia. A respondent notes that education and training about health literacy is not coordinated in Australia. Examples of efforts conducted in the nation include

- Training/educational classes at the University of Adelaide, University of Melbourne Dental College, Victoria Department of Health.
- The University of South Australia has many different training programs in nursing, allied health, and specialist exercise/nutrition.
- Two-day "Easy English" trainings reportedly draw individuals from all sectors of the health industry, including health practitioners, policy writers, nurses, and support staff.
- A large teaching hospital in Metropolitan Melbourne is currently offering a 2-day course for Community health practitioners.
- The chronic disease coordinator for the Wheatbelt region of the Southern Country Health Service is promoting ways to increase self-management and self-management support using health literacy. Presentations were reported to challenge the audiences of health professionals to adapt their practices when working with and communicating with clients. This work started 2.5 years ago and includes presentations to primary health care teams (physiotherapists, occupational therapists, child health and community nurses, speech pathologists, social workers, health promotion officers, and team managers). The work has also completed a second round of presentations to the primary health care teams. The second presentation focused on how health literacy may be considered even more important than the social determinants of health. The information has also been presented to three District Health Advisory Councils that are comprised of local engaged citizens and a senior hospital representative, Local Health Advisory Groups, and to asthma educators in the Asthma Foundation of Western Australia. Outcomes are reported to include an increasing familiarity with the concept of health literacy and small changes in document adaptations (http://www.acal.edu.au/conference/08/HealthLitKeleher.pdf).
- Monash University offers a short course in health literacy: http://www.med.monash.edu.au/healthsci/shortcrse/health-literacy/health-literacy-index.html.
- The NSW Clinical Excellence Commission and the Australian Commission on Safety and Quality in Health Care offers a Breaking down the Barriers seminar: http://www.safetyandquality.

gov.au/our-work/patient-and-consumer-centred-care/breaking-down-the-barriers-seminar.
- The Royal Women's Hospital in Victoria, Australia, offered a seminar on health literacy: http://www.thewomens.org.au/IntheirShoes.
- La Trobe University is reported to have developed a 5-day course on health literacy.

HOW IS HEALTH LITERACY DEFINED IN AUSTRALIA?

As with many other nations, multiple participants from Australia reported multiple definitions of health literacy. One participant wrote that "there is no national health literacy policy at this stage in Australia, and no agreed definition of health literacy." Another individual observed that, "at the moment it is more of a way of ensuring patients control their own health, particularly those with chronic illness, to reduce costs of a very expensive universal health service."

The Tasmanian government's report on communication and health literacy states that "there is no single agreed way of defining the term 'health literacy.' In this Action Plan, the term means: The knowledge and skills needed to access, understand, and use information related to physical, mental, and social wellbeing" (Department of Health and Human Services Tasmania, 2011). The Australian Bureau of Statistics report on the adult literacy survey conducted in 2006 defines health literacy as "the knowledge and skills required to understand and use information relating to health issues such as drugs and alcohol, disease prevention and treatment, safety and accident prevention, first aid, emergencies, and staying healthy" (Australian Bureau of Statistics, 2006). A participant reported that the Health Literacy Questionnaire developed by Professor Richard Osborne and team defines health literacy as consisting of the following 10 dimensions that were derived from patients, practitioners, managers and policy makers:

1. Quality of health care provider support.
2. Perceived adequacy of health information.
3. Taking responsibility for health.
4. Being health focused.
5. Social support.
6. Critical appraisal.
7. Agency in relationships with providers.
8. Navigating the health care system.
9. Ability to access health information.
10. Reading and writing health information.

Another participant reported that health literacy is defined in Australian practice as the "interaction between the skills of the public and the demands of health systems." Another reported that Australians tend to use the U.S. definition that is based on the World Health Organization (WHO) developed originally through the work of Donald Nutbeam. That is that health literacy is "the degree to which individuals can obtain, process, and understand basic health information and services they need to make appropriate health decisions" (IOM, 2004). This definition was reported as used by the Australian Commission on Safety and Quality of Health Care in its recent "stocktake" of health literacy activities in Australia referenced above.

Another reported definition is that "the ability to understand and apply health-related information is known as health literacy. Health literacy is more than just the ability to read, it includes the ability to understand and interpret health-related information and apply it to a particular situation. Health literacy skills are used every day and are necessary to be able to make decisions about, for example, when to seek treatment, which over the counter medicine might be appropriate, or what to do in a first aid emergency" (Victorian Government, 2011).

On a functional level, the Australian report to support the first national primary health care strategy states: "Health literacy refers to the 'ability of individuals to gain access to, understand and use information in ways which promote and maintain good health. Health literacy is a product of the population's knowledge and skills gained from education and experiences" (Australian Government Department of Health and Ageing, 2009).

Within the context of mental health, a participant reported that mental health literacy is defined as "the knowledge and beliefs about mental disorders which aid their recognition, management, or prevention" (Jorm et al., 1997).

Another participant reported that nongovernmental organizations (NGOs) usually define health literacy in relation to their health focus area, essentially taking a contextual approach to defining health literacy so that the context can become more important than the elements of health literacy (e.g., mental health literacy for an organization that focuses on mental health and social and emotional well-being services/issues).

A participant offering a definition from an Australian NGO perspective wrote that "As per WHO, health literacy has been defined as the cognitive and social skills which determine the motivation and ability of individuals to gain access to, understand and use information in ways which promote and maintain good health. Health literacy means more than being able to read pamphlets and successfully make appointments. By improving people's access to health information and their capacity to use it effectively, health literacy is critical to empowerment."

Austria

GOVERNMENTAL POLICY

In Austria, participants indicated that health literacy is a relatively new entrant into the national policy stage. Participants from Austria reported that health literacy is now one of the 10 health goals of both the national and some official regional policies. These health goals were recently developed via a participatory process and health literacy (Gesundheitskompetenz) is the third of 10 targets identified through that process. For more information on that development, see http://www.gesundheitsziele-oesterreich.at/praesentation/10-rahmen-gesundheitsziele-fuer-oesterreich.

HEALTH LITERACY INITIATIVES
(GOVERNMENTAL AND NONGOVERNMENTAL)

Participants reported that Austria is one of the nations that has participated in the recent European Health Literacy Survey (HLS-EU). The Fonds Gesundes Österreich/Fund for Healthy Austria sponsored this effort. In Austria, the sample for that study was enlarged to 1,800 people in order to allow regional comparisons. Additionally, participants reported that the governmental social security association sponsored a survey using the same instrument for a sample of 500 15-year-olds in Austria.

Participants also reported that Austria is now working to develop measures to begin a process to develop national health targets to guide future activities. Health literacy is one of the proposed targets. The effort is reportedly just beginning and will be conducted in the near future.

Another participant reported that the Women's Health Center (Frauengesundheitszentrum) is offering a self-management program (http://www.fgz.co.at) that addresses health literacy.

EDUCATIONAL EFFORTS TARGETING HEALTH PROFESSIONALS

None reported.

HOW IS HEALTH LITERACY DEFINED IN AUSTRIA?

None reported.

Bangladesh

See the International NGO section of this paper.

Botswana

GOVERNMENTAL POLICY

None reported.

HEALTH LITERACY INITIATIVES
(GOVERNMENTAL AND NONGOVERNMENTAL)

In a report from 2009 on a regional health literacy initiative (http://www.tarsc.org/publications/documents/HLregional%20meeting09.pdf), the Botswana Network of Ethics, Law and HIV and AIDS (BONELA) is reported as introducing a health literacy program beginning in 2007 along with Botswana Federation of Trade Unions (BFTU) with support from Kellogg Foundation. The program is described as being a holistic approach that significantly supports the agenda of health systems strengthening, supporting communities in the abilities to understand, communicate and use information to support action and to create a platform to fully advocate for pertinent grassroots issues at the district and national levels. The program used participatory approaches to hopefully enable full engagement of communities with leadership (the Kogtla), elect leadership, health workers, and other important stakeholders at the local level. The program promoted the "bottom up" approach where communities identify their priority health needs and act upon them. The program was also described as complementing government efforts to revitalize primary health care in Botswana. A total of 30 facilitators in four districts of Botswana were trained in health literacy.

EDUCATIONAL EFFORTS TARGETING HEALTH PROFESSIONALS

None reported.

HOW IS HEALTH LITERACY DEFINED IN BOTSWANA?

None reported.

Brazil

See the International NGO section of this paper.

Cameroon

GOVERNMENTAL POLICY

The government of Cameroon, according to participants, is attempting to increase the number of citizens who enroll in schools of health through the Ministry of Public Health. This effort seems to be limited to schools approved by the government, and thus that falls short of representing all schools focusing on public health. What a respondent refers to as a "cumbersome application process" appears present for hospitals and clinics hoping to participate in governmental efforts, which some feel is reducing access to health coverage for residents. However, NGOs are reported to attempt to fill the gap.

HEALTH LITERACY INITIATIVES (GOVERNMENTAL AND NONGOVERNMENTAL)

None reported.

EDUCATIONAL EFFORTS TARGETING HEALTH PROFESSIONALS

Several programs offer education in multiple areas of professional medical practice, but no efforts aimed at the broader population were reported.

HOW IS HEALTH LITERACY DEFINED IN CAMEROON?

None reported.

Canada

GOVERNMENTAL POLICY

Several participants reported that to their knowledge, there are no governmental policies specifically directed at health literacy at any level of government in Canada. However, participants also noted that the federal government has policies related to communicating with the public using plain/clear language and that it is possible that some provinces and territorial governments do as well.

Participants added that the Public Health Agency of Canada (PHAC) designated health literacy as a priority area of work and has had a position for a Senior Advisor in Health Education and Health Literacy for over the past 2 years. This position, however, is reported to have recently been eliminated due to Canadian federal government deficit reduction action plan (i.e., budget cuts). PHAC was also reported to have commissioned a national think tank to advise on the development of an approach to health literacy within the agency as well as supported the Public Health Association of British Columbia (PHABC) who organized subsequent national think tanks resulting in the development of a national draft approach to health literacy. The report on this effort is available at http://www.phabc.org/userfiles/file/IntersectoralApproachforHealthLiteracy-FINAL.pdf.

Health Canada is the "federal department responsible for helping Canadians maintain and improve their health, while respecting individual choices and circumstances" (Health Canada, 2011). The Department has produced reports that address health literacy at various levels. For example, in 2001 it produced a report compiling multiple documents titled *Certain Circumstances: Issues in Equity and Responsiveness in Access to Health Care in Canada* containing multiple references to the role of health literacy (http://www.hc-sc.gc.ca/hcs-sss/pubs/acces/2001-certain-equit-acces/index-eng.php). More recently, in 2011, the agency produced a report on a workshop, *Health Canada Workshop on Health Product Plain Language Labelling* (http://www.hc-sc.gc.ca/dhp-mps/prodpharma/activit/proj/monograph-rev/workshop_pll_atelier_elc-eng.php).

One participant reported that the current Government of Canada has abolished the formerly mandatory Long-Form Census that provided information about the health and wellbeing of large random samples of Canadians. This participant suggested that the absence of Long-Form Census data has seriously compromised the health literacy situation in Canada due to the lack of valid information upon which to base policy.

Another respondent reported that while there are no health literacy–specific policies, at the provincial level, the Ontario Public Health Standards do require all information and resources to be focused on priority populations and to use equity and the social determinants of health as a way of focusing various social media strategies to reach their target populations and to evaluate what works. One respondent from Ontario also reported that the Accessibility for Ontarians with Disabilities Act includes guidelines and legislation for accessibility (http://www.mcss.gov.on.ca/en/mcss/programs/accessibility/index.aspx). This Act includes elements addressing accessibility of information and communications as well as customer service.

Multiple participants reported on the state of mental health literacy policy in Canada as well. One noted that the significant role of mental health literacy was initially recognized in British Columbia in 2003 when the British Columbia Ministry of Health Services released a mental health and addictions information plan to improve mental health and substance use literacy among all British Columbians. To facilitate implementation of the plan, a coalition of seven nonprofit mental health and addictions agencies was created and called the "British Columbia Partners for Mental Health & Addictions Information."

HEALTH LITERACY INITIATIVES
(GOVERNMENTAL AND NONGOVERNMENTAL)

In general, respondents noted that while many health literacy projects exist in Canada, they are often transient and not embedded in a larger systematic or coordinated approach. One respondent noted that most of the leadership in respect to health literacy has come from nongovernmental program (NGP) and academic sectors rather than government with the exception of the Public Health Agency of Canada and the British Columbia Provincial Health Services Authority and BC Ministry of Health Services. Thus, in turn, efforts are reported from nongovernmental organizations, then national government efforts, and then provincial level governmental efforts in Canada.

Nongovernmental Organizations

In regard to health literacy efforts from the NGO sector, a participant reported that the Canadian Public Health Association (CPHA) has been a leader in relation to literacy and health efforts in Canada, beginning in 1994 with the establishment of the National Literacy and Health Program, that ultimately involved 26 National Professional Organizations and NGOs in health and education. Among other things, this program is reported to have sponsored two National Conferences on Literacy and Health (in 2000 and 2004) and developed various resources on Literacy and Health available online. More recently, CPHA organized and managed the Canadian Expert Panel on Health Literacy (2006–2008), sponsored a national consultation on health literacy, and contributed to the development of a Health Literacy Council. See http://www.cpha.ca/en/search.aspx?cx=004708887294457467309%3A1gs3w1uselq&cof=FORID%3A11&ie=UTF-8&q=Health+Literacy&sa.x=0&sa.y=0.

The Canadian Expert Panel on Health Literacy report recommended that "a comprehensive, coordinated, cooperative and integrated Pan-Canadian Strategy on Health Literacy be developed, funded and implemented to improve the level of health literacy in Canada and the extent to which people receive the support they need to cope with the health literacy demands they encounter" (Rootman and Gordon-El-Bihbety, 2008). Since literacy and health literacy are inextricably linked, the Panel suggested that such a strategy needs to address both by pursuing three fundamental goals:

- To improve literacy and health literacy skills in Canada
- To reduce inequities in opportunities for developing literacy and health literacy skills in Canada
- To enhance the capacities of systems that provide health information and services to do so effectively for people with all levels of literacy and health literacy

Another national organization that is reported by participants to have shown leadership in this area is the now defunct Canadian Council on Learning (CCL). According to participants, the Council provided financial support for the Canadian Expert Panel on Health Literacy and supported a number of research and intervention projects on health literacy, as well as conducted a number of innovative analyses of the Canadian data from the 2003 International Adult Literacy and Skills Survey and published several ground-breaking reports on health literacy. Before the CCL was dissolved in 2011 it also supported efforts to implement the recommendations of the Expert Panel, including the establishment of a National Health Literacy Council. See http://www.ccl-cca.ca/CCL/Reports/Health Literacy.html.

At the provincial level in Canada, participants reported that the Ontario Public Health Association (OPHA) and the Public Health Association of British Columbia (PHABC) have both been active in health literacy efforts. The former is reported to have stimulated interest in "literacy and health" in Canada when it started a project on Literacy and Health in partnership with Frontier College in 1989. That initiative, which lasted until 1993, stimulated the interest of the Canadian Public Health Association and the establishment of the National Literacy and Health Program mentioned above. More recently, the PHABC has shown leadership in this field by coordinating the BC Health Literacy Network that is reported to consist of the mental health network as well as several other networks working on aspects of health literacy such as a Library Network and a Seniors Network. This Association was also reported to be assuming a national role by hosting two national think tanks and a workshop on Health Literacy and making the products of these events, including the discussion paper on the national health literacy approach titled *An Intersectoral Approach to Improving Health Literacy for Canadians* available on their website. See http://www.phabc.org/userfiles/file/ IntersectoralApproachforHealthLiteracy-FINAL.pdf.

Another organization that multiple participants reported has been very active in regard to health literacy both in Quebec and outside of it is the Quebec Centre for Literacy, which has sponsored two Institutes on Health Literacy, one of which produced the *Calgary Charter on Health Literacy: Rationale and Core Principles for the Development of Health Literacy Curricula*. The document was the result of a 3-day institute held in Calgary, Alberta, in October 2008, which brought together participants from Canada, the United States, and the United Kingdom. The *Calgary Charter on Health Literacy* presents a definition of health literacy and core principles to support developing and adapting health literacy curricula and urges anyone involved in developing or evaluating health literacy curricula to incorporate them. Interested individuals may read the charter and become a signatory at http://www.centreforliteracy.qc.ca/Health litinst/Calgary_Charter.htm.

Beyond the effort to produce the *Calgary Charter on Health Literacy*, the Centre for Literacy is a centre of expertise that supports best practices and informed policy development in literacy and essential skills by creating bridges between research, policy and practice. The organization reaches those goals through learning events (including institutes and workshops), action research projects and publications, and also through its library services and website. The Centre has recently completed a scan of French-language resources and tools related to health literacy that is available at http://www.centreforliteracy.qc.ca/sites/default/files/ litensant-mai2012.pdf.

Other provincial literacy organizations reported to have also been active include Decoda in British Columbia and Alberta Literacy, which among other things, has produced a tool and workshop for auditing health literacy. See http://literacyalberta.ca/workshops.

The two university hospitals in Montréal—McGill University Health Center (MUHC) and Centre hospitalier de l'Université de Montréal (CHUM)—are both reported to have developed health literacy efforts. The MUHC has educational tools in French and English on cancer and specializes in medical illustrations through the Molson Medical Informatics (http://www.muhcpatienteducation.ca). The CHUM is reported by participants to have a patient education project that focuses on the coordination of all printed patient information or education material. The organization has implemented a systematic process so that all teams and professionals consistently develop material for their patients using templates and consultants with an external firm (90 Degrés Communications). Respondents noted that this project is funded through a grant from Pfizer Canada.

A participant reported that Accreditation Canada (http://www.accreditation.ca), which accredits hospitals and other organizations, is reported to have general guidelines related to communication and education of patients and families. The organization is a not-for-profit, independent organization accredited by the International Society for Quality in Health Care.

National Governmental Efforts

In regard to efforts of national governmental organizations, the Public Health Agency of Canada's Centre for Chronic Disease Prevention and Control (CCDPC) is reported to have recently supported a number of projects related to health literacy. They include

- Background papers on Research, Analysis, and Knowledge Development, Applying a Health Literacy Framework to Diabetes, and e-health literacy;
- Two National Think Tanks and a Workshop on Health Literacy;
- Development of a Health Literacy Prototype Online Module for Public Health Professionals;
- Development and Evaluation of a Health Literacy Prototype Module for Health Educators K-12;
- Health Literacy Examples from the Field Project;
- Health Literacy Capacity Tool Project;
- Health Literacy Scan Project;
- Regional Health Literacy Synthesis Project;
- Health Literacy Knowledge Translation Project;
- Health Literacy Science Seminars;
- Health literacy content development and publishing for new PHAC Health Literacy website (http://www.phac-aspc.gc.ca/cd-mc/hl-ls/index-eng.php);
- HL2Go Project; and the
- Health Literacy Module and Workshop for Health Practitioners.

In particular, respondents noted that there has been demand among health literacy academics and practitioners for PHAC's Centre for Chronic Disease Prevention and Control to complete and disseminate the Canadian Health Literacy Examples in the Field Project as one means to help advance the health literacy agenda in Canada. This project was reported to be first suggested by health literacy academics and practitioners during the National Health Literacy Think Tank in February 2011, as a way to address a gap in the understanding of the range of possible health-related interventions targeted to priority populations and to contribute to the knowledge base regarding health literacy in Canada. The Canadian Health Literacy Examples in the Field Project gathered and translated 33 examples of health literacy in practices from across the country using a consistent Canadian definition of health literacy. Examples were translated into short, user-friendly "case vignettes" to enhance health literacy awareness (e.g., what is health literacy, what does it look like, and what can it look like in practice in different contexts and in different settings). The project focused on interventions with priority populations (e.g., Aboriginals, families, children/youth, seniors, multicultural groups) and on various settings (e.g., schools, communities, workplaces, hospitals) as well as on a variety of health topic areas (e.g., chronic disease, mental health, obesity) relevant to communities in Canada. The consolidated resource reportedly will be shared online and in print with public health professionals.

Respondents from Canada also reported that an internal PHAC Branch Level Health Literacy Working Group exists, which is an action-orientated group with an interest in creating, implementing, and sustaining an integrated and cohesive health literacy approach among Centres/Directorates within PHAC. Additionally, they noted that the Strategic Initiatives and Innovation Directorate (SIID) within PHAC has provided support for a participatory research project in three provinces on embedding health literacy in existing initiatives as well as a health literacy online curriculum/module in partnership with the Canadian Medical Association, Canadian Nursing Association and others as continuing medical education (available free of charge in both official languages through http://www.mdCME.ca). The Centre for Health Promotion within PHAC was also reported to have started to incorporate health literacy concepts into their information and programming with respect to older adults via the Division of Aging and Seniors. Recent activities in this organization include a poster presentation at the 2011 Canadian Association for Gerontology Conference (The Importance of Health Literacy in an Aging Population) and a report (*Literature Review: Improving Health Literacy among Older Adults in Canada*).

Provincial and Local Government Efforts

In regard to health literacy efforts of provincial governments in Canada, the Ministry of Health Services in British Columbia was reported to have sponsored a Health Literacy Prototype project that involved collaboration between primary care physicians and literacy learners and coordinators in four communities. This effort also produced a *Charter for Health Literacy in Communities* (http://www.impactbc.ca/sites/default/

files/resource/n221_ibc_pasp_health_literacy_prototype_charter_2009. pdf).

Respondents reported that the Direction de la Santé Publique in Montreal (http://www.dsp.santemontreal.qc.ca) is developing guidelines to embed health literacy principles in its structure and activities. This effort is based on the Institute of Medicine's recent report identifying 10 attributes of a health literate organization (http://www.iom.edu/~/media/ Files/Perspectives-Files/2012/Discussion-Papers/BPH_HLit_Attributes. pdf) and on a literature review of guidelines in educational tools that apply to health promotion and disease prevention. The effort is reported to include an algorithm for professionals to use, a set of guidelines for each medium (Web, written, oral, video or multimedia, through primary care clinicians, etc.). The project's aim is to apply universal precautions so that every Montrealer can access, comprehend, and act according to the best available information on health and disease prevention.

At the school system level, a respondent reported that the British Colombia Ministry of Education's Healthy Living Performance Standards allow students, teachers, and parents to assess a student's progress towards accomplished learning by supporting a health literacy approach in a variety of curricular areas. See http://www.bced.gov.bc.ca/perf_ stands/healthy_living/background/health_literacy.htm.

In the province of Ontario, the Ministry of Education is reported to have efforts, including training and components of curricula across the grades that address health literacy, mental health literacy, literacy, and numeracy (http://www.edu.gov.on.ca/eng).

Multiple respondents reported that in regard to mental health literacy, efforts in British Columbia are guided by the Integrated Provincial Strategy to Promote Health Literacy in Mental Health and Addiction that was created in 2007. The goal is to improve public understanding of mental health and substance use issues (including mental health promotion, prevention, early recognition, help seeking, self-management, and recovery), and to reduce the stigma related to mental health and substance use. As a capacity-building initiative, the strategy is reported to focus on coordinating and developing integrated and sustained approaches to information development, dissemination, uptake, and action targeted to the health literacy levels and needs of different population groups within British Columbia. As a result, respondents reported that a variety of mental health literacy initiatives are currently being implemented in the province of British Columbia by BC Mental Health & Addiction Services. Another participant added that the Provincial Health Services Authority in British Columbia has established a position of Director of Health Literacy for the BC Mental Health & Addictions Services (an agency of the Provincial Health Services Authority) and for the past few years the agency has allocated a budget for the support of a mental health literacy network and activities in the province, as noted above. Examples of health literacy initiatives reported include

- The Kelty Mental Health Resource Centre (http://keltymental health.ca) provides free, all-inclusive virtual and in-person support to help all BC children, youth, and their families navigate mental health and substance use resources and services.
- The Provincial Child and Youth Healthy Living Initiative established in 2009 has supported this work through the development of interactive Web resources for the Kelty Mental Health Resource Centre; Healthy Living Toolkits (http://keltymentalhealth.ca/toolkits) designed for families and professionals dealing with mental health and substance use issues; and the development of the Provincial Mental Health Metabolic Program (http://keltymental health.ca/partner/provincial-mental-health-metabolic-program) based at BC Children's Hospital.
- Initiatives aimed at increasing mental health literacy within specific populations and settings include
  o The Disordered Eating and Eating Disorders Mental Health Literacy Initiative, which includes 13 projects that aim to enhance health literacy in the area of eating disorders and disordered eating across the continuum of mental health from promotion to treatment.
  o Cross-Cultural Mental Health Literacy Initiatives, which aim to enhance mental health literacy among culturally diverse families.
  o Mental Health Literacy School-Based Initiatives, which aim to further develop the mental health literacy of educators across British Columbia to support the mental health of children and youth in school environments.
  o A partnership with the Fraser Health Authority resulted in the 2012 provincial expansion and redesign of mindcheck.ca, a youth and young adult–focused interactive website where visitors can check out how they are feeling and get connected to support early and quickly. Support includes education, self-help tools, website links, and assistance in connecting to local professional resources (http://mindcheck.ca).
  o The health literacy portfolio was reported to also include the management of a number of provincial networks, including the BC Mental Health and Substance Use Provincial Health Literacy Network, which aim to support knowledge exchange across the province.

○ Mental health literacy projects are also reported to be high-lighted in the BC government's Healthy Minds, Healthy People, 10-year Plan to Address Mental Health and Substance Use in British Columbia.

The BC Partners for Mental Health & Addictions Information is composed of multiple organizations. These are Anxiety BC, British Columbia Schizophrenia Society, Centre for Addictions Research of BC, Canadian Mental Health Association (BC Division), The F.O.R.C.E. Society for Kids' Mental Health, Family Services of the North Shore (Jessie's Legacy Program), and Mood Disorders Association of British Columbia. The BC Partners health literacy work is reported at http://heretohelp.ca. The BC Partners are reported to have made a number of key contributions which support mental and substance use health literacy in the province. These include

- establishment of the "heretohelp" website and development of indicators to monitor website usage and reach;
- development and dissemination of materials and resources, including fact sheets and interactive toolkits for the "heretohelp" website;
- a range of information dissemination vehicles, projects, and events, including the Visions Journal, Healthy Minds, Healthy Campuses and Beyond the Blues; and
- the provision of evidence-informed resources for a Provincial Health Services Authority Translation Project.

EDUCATIONAL EFFORTS TARGETING HEALTH PROFESSIONALS

A Canadian respondent reported that other than offering training or educational classes for their own staff, the Federal Government in Canada does not "currently" directly offer training or educational classes on health literacy to practitioners or the public.

The PHAC is reported to be currently transitioning an existing Health Literacy Workshop Module for Public Health Professionals into an interactive online module for their National Online Learning Program (Skills Online), which provides continuing education for public health practitioners in Canada. In the meantime, PHAC has reportedly supported training initiatives related to health literacy such as a 2-day, multisite summer school on Health Literacy in 2011 organized by the Public Health Association of British Columbia (http://www.phabc.org/modules/Contentccomp/files/2011%20Public%20Health%20Summer%20School%20Backgrounder.pdf). PHAC also was reported by respondents to have supported the development of an online curriculum now offered through the Canadian Medical Association, Canadian Nursing Association, and others; as well as various workshops, seminars, presentations and conferences related to health literacy.

A training program from Health Canada is available in French online at http://www.alphabetismeensante.ca/lecons.aspx.

In general, respondents note that health literacy workshops and training are frequently organized and provided by local organizations such as hospitals, local health organizations, community-based organizations or nongovernmental organizations often for in-house staff.

HOW IS HEALTH LITERACY DEFINED IN CANADA?

One participant reported that the current Government of Canada defines health literacy as an individual matter even though a few years ago, the Federal Government of Canada, Health Canada, and the PHAC used the social determinants of health as the framework for discussing the health of Canadians. This participant noted that this approach is not as prominent in the current government, which does not seem to have a definition of health literacy in place.

Another participant simply replied that there are many different definitions in place in Canada as there is not an agreed-upon definition. Others offer definitions, such as "the ability to find, comprehend, evaluate and act upon health information in various contexts," and "the ability to access, understand and act on information for health."

The previously mentioned Calgary Charter on Health Literacy defines health literacy as allowing "the public and personnel working in all health-related contexts to find, understand, evaluate, communicate, and use information. Health literacy is the use of a wide range of skills that improve the ability of people to act on information in order to live healthier lives. These skills include reading, writing, listening, speaking, numeracy, and critical analysis, as well as communication and interaction skills" (Coleman et al., 2008). In addition, the Charter fairly uniquely suggests that health literacy applies to both individuals and to health systems, explaining that a system is health literate when it provides equal, easy to use, and shame-free access to and delivery of health care and health information. See http://www.centreforliteracy.qc.ca/Health litinst/Calgary_Charter.htm.

The 2008 Canadian Expert Panel on Health Literacy defined health literacy as, "the ability to access, comprehend, evaluate and communicate information as a way to promote, maintain and improve health in a variety of settings across the life-course" (Rootman and Gordon-El-Bihbety, 2008). Closely, echoing this definition, a report produced by the Public Health Association of British Columbia edited by Wayne Mitic and Irving

Rootman (2012), defines health literacy as, "the degree to which people are able to access, understand, evaluate and communicate information to engage with the demands of different health contexts in order to promote and maintain good health across the life-course." See http://www.phabc. org/userfiles/file/IntersectoralApproachforHealthLiteracy-FINAL.pdf.

Chile

GOVERNMENTAL POLICY

According to the single respondent reporting on Chile, there are no specific health literacy policies in Chile at this time. However, there is a policy that regulates service provision at primary health care centers that does address health promotion and prevention efforts in addition to the provision of medical care. This is based on a family health model.

HEALTH LITERACY INITIATIVES (GOVERNMENTAL AND NONGOVERNMENTAL)

In addition to the health promotion and prevention efforts outlined above at primary health care centers, the participants from Chile notes that there is a program called *Vida Chile* (Chilean Life) that promotes healthy lifestyles in communities and schools. Another program called *Chile Crece Contigo* (Chile Grows With You) focuses on parenting skills from pregnancy to the first year of children's lives.

Reportedly, some schools do create alliances with health centers and work together to improve health literacy of the public. This is reported as mainly focusing on sexual education or healthy lifestyles (nutrition, physical activity, and obesity prevention). These alliances can be part of *Vida Chile* or occur through other funding mechanisms or sometimes as an in-kind effort between participating organizations.

EDUCATIONAL EFFORTS TARGETING HEALTH PROFESSIONALS

None reported.

HOW IS HEALTH LITERACY DEFINED IN CHILE?

None reported.

China

GOVERNMENTAL POLICY

The Chinese government, according to participants, has policies that address health literacy within regulations related to the registration and approval of medical institutions (http://www.gov.cn/banshi/2005-08/01/content_19113.htm) and medical practitioners (http://www.gov.cn/banshi/2005-08/01/content_18970.htm). For example, these regulations require that medical practitioners participate in continuing education and that they spread the knowledge of health care and health to their patients. A respondent also reported that another health literacy relevant policy includes a Nurse Management Act that was issued by the Ministry of Health in 2005 (http://www.gov.cn/banshi/2005-08/02/content_19268.htm). This regulation requires that nurses be committed to preventive health care and to publicize the knowledge to prevent and cure diseases and rehabilitation guidance, provide health education, and are obliged to provide health advice. Also, participants reported that there are regulations related to health literacy regarding the administration of health insurance (http://www.gov.cn/flfg/2006-08/14/content_361968.htm), the administration of drug advertisements (http://www.sda.gov.cn/WS01/CL0053/24527.html), measures for the administration of information reporting on monitoring public health emergencies and epidemics of infectious diseases (http://www.china.com.cn/chinese/PI-c/460481.htm), and measures on the medical and health information services provided through the Internet (http://www.moh.gov.cn/publicfiles/business/htmlfiles/mohzcfgs/pgz/200906/41403.htm).

A respondent also reported that health literacy is addressed within the law of the People's Republic of China on Science and Technology Progress, the law of the People's Republic of China on Popularization of Science and Technology (http://english.gov.cn/laws/2005-10/08/content_75055.htm), and finally within the Outline of the National Scheme for Scientific Literacy for all Chinese citizens released in 2006 (http://www.kxsz.org.cn/portal/findportal.do;jsessionid=D4C22322C5CFFB183 71A6C199EB52B90?failure=true). For instance, the law on popularization of science and technology includes provisions that communication of science and technology efforts that "make it easy for the general public to understand, accept, and participate shall be adopted" (Chinese Government, 2012).

HEALTH LITERACY INITIATIVES (GOVERNMENTAL AND NONGOVERNMENTAL)

Most directly related to health literacy, participants reported there is a National Plan of Health Literacy Promotion Initiatives for Chinese Citizens (2008–2010). This policy was reported to establish a health sector leading, multisector cooperating and social participatory network of "Health Literacy Promotion Initiatives." Goals of the effort are to train at least 80 percent of the professionals in the working network, to establish a Chinese citizens' health literacy surveillance and evaluation system, and to ensure that at least 60 percent of counties all over the country will carry out communication activities related to *Health Literacy 66*.

Health Literacy 66 is a book that compiles 66 health literacy goals for the population of China. The booklet was also used as the basis for an evaluation of the level of health literacy in China that was conducted in 2008. That effort included more than 79,000 individuals and reportedly found that only a little more than 6 percent of the Chinese population could be considered health literate. This effort also included organizing health literacy contests for both rural and urban residents. One report stated that there were 9,196 contests at the county/township level, 207 contests at the prefecture/city level, 46 contests at the provincial level, and 5 national contests.

The Chinese Ministry of Health conducts efforts to highlight and commend efforts related to health literacy according to participants. Examples include conferring the Norman Bethune Medal, honoring advanced collectives and individuals in the health system for their efforts, presenting awards at the 60th anniversary of the Patriotic Public Health Movement, and organizing public participation to select "My Favorite Health Guardian." Through these activities, participants reported that the Ministry of Health gives considerable publicity to advanced collectives and individuals who are working to improve health literacy in China

(http://www.moh.gov.cn/publicfiles/business/htmlfiles/mohbgt/
s3582/201203/54395.htm). For example, the Norman Bethune Medal is
said to be the highest medical honor in China and the honor recognizes
outstanding contributions and humanitarian efforts. Accounts online of
recipients include reference to Wu Dengyun, who is said to have provided
care in a remote area and focused on being culturally and linguistically
appropriate in his interactions with patients.

Other examples of health literacy efforts that participants reported
from China include

- A Chinese national symposium on health education and health
  promotion that was held in Shanghai on May 18–19, 2012. The
  theme of the symposium was "Achieving education and health
  promotion is of great significance for the deepening of the health
  care system reform, the protection of public health, the construction of health culture, and the promotion of harmonious socioeconomic development" (http://www.moh.gov.cn/publicfiles/
  business/htmlfiles/liuq/pldhd/201205/54793.htm).
- The 24th Chinese Patriotic Health Month was held in April 2012
  with a theme of "Everyone takes part in the patriotic health campaign and everyone enjoys a healthy life."
- China's 5th National Healthy Lifestyle Day was held on September 1, 2011. The slogan for the day was "I act, I am healthy, I
  am happy!" and the theme was "Lowering salt intake to prevent
  hypertension."
- China's 14th National Hypertension Day was observed on October
  8, 2011. The theme for the Day was "Be aware of your blood pressure and control your target."
- The efforts of the China Association for Science and Technology
  (http://english.cast.org.cn) that include "to advocate scientific
  spirit, popularize scientific knowledge, and disseminate scientific
  ideas and methods. Defend the dignity of science, popularize the
  advanced technology, and develop the scientific and educational
  activities for the young people, so as to improve the scientific literacy of the whole nation" (CAST, 2011). Activities of this association related to health literacy in China include
  o During the 3rd China Food Safety Forum, about 10 govern-
    mental departments related to food safety are reported by par-
    ticipants to have vowed to implement stricter enforcement to
    assure the quality of food. A publicity week on China Food
    Safety is also beginning around the country. The aim is to make
    people know more about the State's standard of food safety and

the knowledge of additives in food (http://scitech.people.com.cn/n/2012/0626/c131715-18386349.html).

o The special committee on drug dependence toxicology under the Chinese Society of Toxicology recently organized a science promotion activity, according to respondents, that focused on "For a healthy life, keeping away from drug dependence." The activity, with the support of the National Committee on Narcotics Control, the General Drug Prohibition Brigade under the Beijing Municipal Bureau of Public Security, Beijing Hui Long Guan Hospital, Red Cross Society of Peking University Health Science Center, and Tayuan neighborhood committee of Beijing's Haidian District, were attended by more than 1,000 people (http://english.cast.org.cn/n1181872/n1182018/n1182077/13957747.html).

o "Science and Technology Week" has been held annually since 2001 and more than 600 million people have participated in its activities. Various activities were organized in parks, schools or museums across the nation to improve the awareness of science and technology (http://www.cast.org.cn).

o A 2007 International Symposium on HIV/AIDS Prevention and Control.

o An International Symposium on Innovation and Development in Experiment Research of Integrated Traditional Chinese and Western Experimental Medicine demonstrated the achievement of new theories, new technologies in the academic field of the combination of traditional Chinese and Western medicine; explored prospects for organ fibrosis research and the hotspot of Chinese medicine drug development, thus promoting the development of Traditional Chinese Medicine, and making efforts to combining medicine into the mainstream of the world medical system.

• Participants reported that an effort called "Beijing Home of Red Ribbon" aims to use social forces to provide HIV/AIDS patients with comprehensive care, serve their relatives and friends with HIV/AIDS care and prevention knowledge, develop various social activities on HIV/AIDS prevention and control, and promote the public's understanding and concern for HIV/AIDS (http://www.aidschannel.cn/shownews.asp?newsid=1453). The Beijing Home of Red Ribbon program is reported to consist of six separate branches, including medical support, self-help of HIV/AIDS patients, volunteer service, social aid, Internet publicity, and legal aid. Specific efforts of this initiative participants reported on include

o On February 11, 2012, the Beijing Home of Red Ribbon offered

training courses for patients and their families in drug compliance, drug side effects, and nutritional support.
  o Conducted simulated classes for the Project of Health Red Ribbon 2+1 Entering Institutions of Higher Learning ("2" standing for volunteer medical professionals and peer educators from the Beijing Home of Red Ribbon, and "1" for college volunteers).
  o Volunteers held an AIDS awareness campaign in Beijing Ditan Hospital on November 30, 2011.
  o A Lunar New Year party for HIV-infected patients on January 25, 2011 (http://www.aidschannel.cn/index.asp).
• The Chinese Association for Health Education (CAHE) is reported to aim to unite health education work nationwide, promote the undertaking of health education and the construction of socialist material and cultural civilization in China, and increase the knowledge of health and science among Chinese people in order that they develop healthy behaviors and lifestyles (http://www.health-china.com.cn/english/newDetail.asp?id=46). The organization created a delegation of 54 individuals to participate in 17th International Union for Health Promotion and Education World Conference (http://www.health-china.com.cn/english/newDetail.asp?id=83). (See the International NGO section of this paper for more on the IUHPE health literacy efforts.) CAHE also organized the Chinese major hospitals delegation to have a short-term hospital management training in Germany in 1999 (http://www.health-china.com.cn/english/newDetail.asp?id=86). Finally, participants reported that the organization is building cooperation projects with the American Association for Health Education.

EDUCATIONAL EFFORTS TARGETING HEALTH PROFESSIONALS

Courses that include health literacy training for different types of doctors and nurses are reported to be offered in many medical schools, such as Peking University Health Science Center, Chinese Academy of Medical Science, Tsinghua University School of Medicine, and Medical Center of Fudan University, and others. Among these courses are pharmacology, epidemiology, medical immunology, the history of medicine, medical psychology, anthropotomy, health evaluation, basic nursing, community nursing, nursing management, medical nursing, and surgery nursing.

As reported above, aspects of the National Plan of Health Literacy Promotion Initiatives for Chinese Citizens (2008–2010) are focused on the health sector, including creation of a participatory network of "Health Literacy Promotion Initiatives" and efforts to train at least 80 percent of the professionals in the network.

In Hong Kong, based on WHO Trainers' and Trainees' Guides on infection control measures for the health care of acute respiratory diseases (ARDs) in a community setting, a culturally specific train-the-trainer program was reportedly developed for professional health workers and community workers in Hong Kong, with an aim to enhance the health literacy of the Chinese-speaking community in the prevention and control of the spread of ARDs.

HOW IS HEALTH LITERACY DEFINED IN CHINA?

None reported.

Côte d'Ivoire

GOVERNMENTAL POLICY

A participant indicates that in Côte d'Ivoire there is not yet governmental policy related to health literacy. There are reports that policy formulation related to health literacy is under way in the Western African Health Organisation. That organization, consisting of 15 member states, including Benin, Burkina Faso, Cabo Verde, Côte d'Ivoire, Gambia, Ghana, Guinea, Guinea-Bissau, Liberia, Mali, Niger, Nigeria, Senegal, Sierra Leone, and Togo puts forth the promotion of dissemination of best practices as a central concern. That program identifies that "lack of knowledge of behavioural best practices, of the effective approaches to disease prevention and management strategies limits health coverage and compromises the quality of care" (WAHO, 2009).

HEALTH LITERACY INITIATIVES
(GOVERNMENTAL AND NONGOVERNMENTAL)

No specific projects were reported.

EDUCATIONAL EFFORTS TARGETING HEALTH PROFESSIONALS

A participant from Côte d'Ivoire reported that the Biblotheque UFR Sciences Medicales Université de Cocody provides training in health information literacy in the medical school. A participant reported that policies of Association of African Universities License-Master-Doctorate system are involving information literacy policies for the next school year and that training of librarians at the university will begin as well. Additionally, the Western African Health Documentation and Information

Network was reported to offer trainings to enhance the competencies of librarians.

HOW IS HEALTH LITERACY DEFINED IN COTE D'IVOIRE?

None reported.

Denmark

GOVERNMENTAL POLICY

None reported.

HEALTH LITERACY INITIATIVES
(GOVERNMENTAL AND NONGOVERNMENTAL)

The Danish Ministry of Children and Education is reported to conduct a national assessment to map human resources in 10 key competency areas. These are health, literacy, learning, self-management, creativity and innovation, culture, environment, social relationships, communication, and democracy—factors that affect growth and welfare (Rushforth et al., 2006).

A participant reported that health literacy activities in Denmark are conducted by the Danish Committee for Health Education. This organization reports it was founded in 1964 and is a nonprofit nongovernmental organization with close working relations with public authorities like the Ministry of Health, the National Board of Health, and private organizations in the health field. The membership organizations are primarily professional associations in the health field and the associations of county councils and local authorities. Sponsored by mainly public health authorities, the Committee develops and produces health promotion material on many themes and to many target groups. Themes include pregnancy prevention, child and maternity health, sexually transmitted diseases, breastfeeding, child raising, and alcohol problems (http://www.sundhedsoplysning.dk).

EDUCATIONAL EFFORTS TARGETING HEALTH PROFESSIONALS

None reported.

HOW IS HEALTH LITERACY DEFINED IN DEMARK?

One government report seems to define health literacy (sundheds-kompetence) as including the ability to maintain both good physical health and good mental health. Health literacy is thus defined as the ability to meet the complex demands and challenges encountered in work and in civilian life, including the ability to exhibit behaviors that help to maintain or improve a healthy state of health. This construct is reported to have been measured in Denmark as consisting of three domains: Action level (skills of a person to promote and maintain and good health); Reflexive level (ideas and knowledge about interactions with the surrounding environment relevant to health); and Opinions level (physical and psychosocial experiences that a person ascribes as relevant to health).

Finland

GOVERNMENTAL POLICY

A participant reported that new recommendations and guidelines for Finnish health care professionals make promoting health literacy a central goal in health counseling.

HEALTH LITERACY INITIATIVES
(GOVERNMENTAL AND NONGOVERNMENTAL)

A participant from Finland also reported that discussions about health literacy have been increasing in Finland. During the last decade, health promotion practitioners have reportedly underlined the importance of supporting health literacy in order to improve population health and cost-effectiveness of health promotion programs.

Despite that policy development for health care professionals reported above, however, a participant reported that few empirical health literacy studies have been conducted. Commonly used health literacy measurement tools have not yet been translated in Finnish. However, some ongoing studies apply the concept of health literacy in order to explore health literacy in different age groups and circumstances.

A participant reported that the most common context where health literacy is encountered in Finland is in health education in schools. Further, another participant indicated that health education has been an obligatory subject in Finnish schools since 2002, and is based on a national curriculum.

A participant also reported that health literacy among adults and seniors has received less attention. The project "Health Information Practice and Its Impact" is examining the impact of information by looking at three thematic areas of knowledge production, information content and transfer, and the use of information. That project is funded by Academy of Finland and it is conducted by University of Oulu and Åbo Akademi. One subproject aims to find out how senior citizens understand information provided by health professionals during counselling, and what kind of information strategies do they use if they lack understanding (http://www.oulu.fi/hutk/info/tutkimus/HeIP/english.html).

Participants also note a growing body of academic research on the concept of health literacy is occurring in Finland. While most is reported as focusing on youth or in schools, other work is addressing health literacy in adult populations and attempting to develop a suitable measure of health literacy for the Finnish context, language, and culture. A participant noted that "there is a need for further research on health literacy in Finland. Even though, reading literacy in Finland is at high level, there are clear health inequalities between socio-economical groups. Health literacy research may help us to find methods for targeting health counselling to people with different needs."

EDUCATIONAL EFFORTS TARGETING HEALTH PROFESSIONALS

None reported.

HOW IS HEALTH LITERACY DEFINED IN FINLAND?

A recent scholarly publication reportedly defined health literacy as a learning outcome in schools, and described the learning conditions that are relevant for targeting health literacy (Paakkari and Paakkari, 2012).

Greece

GOVERNMENTAL POLICY

While participants indicated there has been no explicit health literacy policy in Greece to date, they did report that the National Organization for Medicines of Greece (EOF) (http://www.eof.gr) is the reviewing agency for pharmaceutical research, food and drug industry information, and generally has had a social marketing campaign about reducing the use of antibiotics. While this effort does not explicitly refer to health literacy, participants felt the effort sufficiently related to health literacy for inclusion.

The Hellenic Accreditation System (ESYD) (http://www.esyd.gr) was established in 2002 and succeeded the Hellenic Accreditation Council, which operated within the Ministry of Development after 1994. Participants describe ESYD as a private liability company operating in favor of the public interest with the responsibility of managing the accreditation system in Greece. The system focuses on food safety, organic certifying, laboratories, and environmental issues.

HEALTH LITERACY INITIATIVES (GOVERNMENTAL AND NONGOVERNMENTAL)

Greece was one of the participating countries in the recent HLS-EU health literacy survey (see the section of this paper focusing on the European Union for more details). In Greece, this effort was facilitated through the National School of Public Health with consultation from Hellenic American University.

The National School of Public Health and the University of Athens are reported to organize conferences where regulations, legislation, and plans of action are communicated to the public.

EDUCATIONAL EFFORTS TARGETING HEALTH PROFESSIONALS

Medical professional training is accomplished through the National School of Public Health (http://www.esdy.gr/nsph) in Greece, but health literacy is only considered at the master's level according to respondents. This effort trains health professionals how to help their patients become more health literate.

Other universities, such as the University of Athens, are reported to provide training for health professionals at all levels and to incorporate topics of health literacy. However, according to one participant, there is no specific class on the health literacy at public educational institutions in Greece at this time. Health literacy is said to be addressed within the context of other courses such as at the Hellenic American University where Health Psychology and Health Communication courses address health literacy.

HOW IS HEALTH LITERACY DEFINED IN GREECE?

None reported at this time. Efforts in general are reported to coalesce around health education rather than health literacy per se.

India

GOVERNMENTAL POLICY

The National Literacy Mission, launched in 1988, was aimed to attain a literacy rate of 75 percent by 2007 (National Literacy Mission, 2003). The effort, through the Total Literacy Campaign, attempts to bring literacy to non-literates. The Indian literacy rate reportedly increased to 74.04 percent in 2011 from 12 percent at the end of British rule in 1947. Although this was a greater than sixfold improvement, the level is well below the world average literacy rate of 84 percent (*Literacy in India*, 2012).

No governmental policies explicitly focusing on health literacy were reported. However, multiple government reports on health issues such as tobacco use, health equity, noncommunicable diseases, the state of urban health in Delhi, and the use of information technology for health refer to the importance of health literacy.

HEALTH LITERACY INITIATIVES
(GOVERNMENTAL AND NONGOVERNMENTAL)

Kalyani is an initiative of the Ministry of Health and Family Welfare of the Government of India and has been called the longest running public health campaign in the nation (http://www.ddindia.gov.in/devcom/Program+Column+1/Kalyani.htm). The program is broadcast over Doordarshan, National Public Television, in nine states of India, targeting approximately 50 percent of India's population. These nine states experience the poorest health indicators in the nation. Themes of the television program, reinforced by in community efforts, are Reproductive & Child Health, Malaria, tuberculosis, HIV/AIDS, Anti-Tobacco, Cancer, Water Borne Diseases, insulin-dependent diabetes (IDD), Blindness, and Leprosy and Food Safety. Knowledge of these areas among viewers of

Indian health literacy campaign.

the program compared to non-viewers is consistently higher. As of 2010, this effort is reported to have produced more than 7,000 programs in 3 languages and 14 dialects, visits to more than 4,500 villages by Kalyani teams, visits by physicians and Kalyani teams to more than 1,200 villages, more than 3,000 Kalyani health clubs, and more than 79,000 Kalyani health club volunteers.

Darpana Academy, based in Ahmdabad, India, uses Indian dance, puppetry, music, theatre, and television to educate, empower, and raise awareness about critical issues facing India today—health is one of the primary focus areas for their work (Darpna, 2012). Health issues that Darpana projects are reported to have addressed include family planning; diabetes; cervical cancer; maternal and infant mortality; HIV/AIDS; children's health; hygiene; sanitation; the medical and social impact of HIV/AIDS for at risk populations, including truck drivers, sex workers, and their clients and port labor; leprosy; and addictions.

The Public Health Foundation of India (PHFI) is a public–private initiative that is reported to have conducted community-based health literacy campaigns to effectively build engagement and facilitate action for improved health outcomes at the grassroots. The organization has conducted health literacy assessments, participatory action research projects on increasing health literacy at the grassroots relating to risk factors and symptoms of selected chronic disease prevention opportunities in three states in India. Campaigns conducted so far have reportedly used mass media through community and commercial radio, newspaper advertisements; participatory mid-level media using songs, health melas,[6] street plays, puppetry, public meetings, dance, and adapted board games as well as interpersonal communication through peer education via a cascade approach. The organization also runs the website http://www.healthy-india.org. That website, funded by the government of India, began in 2007 and has the goal of increasing health literacy through the provision of credible information.

Other particular projects related to health literacy conducted by the Public Health Foundation of India are reported to include

- "Maanavta Se Anmol Mann Tak" (2010–2012): Under the aegis of the National Mental Health Programme (NMHP), Ministry of Health and Family Welfare, Government of India, the PHFI completed the implementation of a pilot awareness generation campaign on Mental Health. This initiative was started with the objective of encouraging timely help-seeking behaviors by individuals and families through sharing information on available services

---

[6]*Mela* is a Sanskrit word meaning "gathering" or "to meet."

and initiating efforts in stigma reduction in 10 districts of Andhra Pradesh, Assam, Gujarat, Uttar Pradesh, and Delhi. A series of activities were conducted in partnership with civil society organizations and in close collaboration with the District Mental Health Programme teams; namely, development of information, education, and communication materials for dissemination, 20 mental health awareness and check-up camps, 20 Speakers' Bureau interactions with the public, university student sensitization workshops, and creation of student-led peer education and awareness activities, "Uniting Hearts and Minds"—a Festival of Creative Expressions on Mental Health and monitoring and evaluation. The findings of a survey and the experience of the pilot campaign are being used to create an up-scaled strategy and Behaviour Change Communication campaign on mental health, including key information and motivation to break the silence surrounding mental health illness.

• Health Literacy Project (2009–2010): A health literacy grassroots awareness project to enhance knowledge and awareness of risk factors and symptoms related to diabetes and cervix cancer among communities in Delhi, Gujarat, and Orissa. Participatory action research with communities has supported the creation of innovative, appropriate, and culturally acceptable media, such as nukkad natak, songs, health melas, adapted board games, community radio, and other cultural art forms. Thus, the project has developed a stronger understanding of community-led communication needs and requirements in partnership with Darpana for Development, South Orissa Voluntary Action and Deepalaya.

The Self-Employed Women's Association (SEWA) is a trade union of nearly a million self-employed women in Gujarat, India. The organization works to link health security to work security, which means that all economic activities at SEWA have a health component and all health action, in turn, is linked to producer's groups, workers' trade committees, and self-help groups and their economic activities (SEWA, 2009). SEWA has collectively organized health insurance to pay for health costs, organizes child care, centers for infants and young children, and campaigns with state and national level authorities for child care as an entitlement for all women workers (WHO, 2012). SEWA trains traditional midwives, so that they become the "barefoot doctors" of their communities/villages, promotes health and well-being by providing access to health information and health education, provides basic amenities like sanitation literacy and other developmental skills, and emphasizes self-reliance for women in economic terms and in terms of women themselves owning, controlling, and managing their own health activities (SEWA, 2009).

From Delhi, India, there are reports that Gender Resource Centers (GRCs) are "being implemented for overall empowerment of women in the areas of health literacy, legal awareness and skill development" (Ministry of Health and Family Welfare, 2007). There are efforts to achieve greater convergence of women welfare programs and activities of government and other agencies through single window information and facilitation centers for the community women to provide wider exposure to available services and better placement opportunities. At least four GRCs have been reported to exist now in Dakshinpuri, Kalyanpuri, Najafgarh, and Shahbad Daulatpur. More than 1,900 women are reported to have benefited from the health clinics, 1,130 women were provided free legal aid, and 1,207 women were assisted through skill development courses (Ministry of Health and Family Welfare, 2007).

See other activities ongoing in India in the Nongovernmental Organization section of this paper.

EDUCATIONAL EFFORTS TARGETING HEALTH PROFESSIONALS

The Public Health Foundation of India reports it conducted a program, Raising the discourse on the Arts and Public Health (2009). In an effort to strengthen innovative approaches to health promotion, a brainstorming was organized with experts and practitioners from the field to mine ideas for the creation of a common platform for national and international exchange of good practices in Public Health and the Arts. Enhancing the use of diverse art forms, sensitizing health professionals to use innovative approaches more often, and creation of new partnerships were part of the discussion.

HOW IS HEALTH LITERACY DEFINED IN INDIA?

One person reported that health literacy had been defined by some in India as implying the achievement of a level of knowledge, personal skills, and confidence to take action to improve personal and community health by changing personal lifestyles and living conditions. Thus, health literacy is meant to mean more than being able to read pamphlets and make appointments. By improving people's access to health information, and their capacity to use it effectively, health literacy is critical to empowerment in this definition. Health literacy is itself dependent upon more general levels of literacy.

Ireland

GOVERNMENTAL POLICY

According to participants, while the Department of Health does not have a health literacy policy in place, in recent years health literacy has been cited as a factor in a number of national health policy documents. Relevant governmental publications are reported to include

- Department of Health Statement of Strategy 2011–2014 (http://www.dohc.ie/publications/statement_of_strategy_2011_2014.html).
- Changing Cardiovascular Health National Cardiovascular Health Policy 2010–2019—which is reported to acknowledge health literacy as an issue (http://www.dohc.ie/publications/changing_cardiovascular_health.html).
- National Intercultural Health Strategy 2007–2012—which is reported to identify health literacy as an issue among minorities (http://www.hse.ie/eng/services/Publications/services/SocialInclusion/National_Intercultural_Health_Strategy_2007_-_2012.pdf).
- National Health Promotion Strategy 2000–2005 Department of Health (http://www.dohc.ie/publications/national_health_promotion_strategy.html).

HEALTH LITERACY INITIATIVES
(GOVERNMENTAL AND NONGOVERNMENTAL)

Ireland was one of the countries participating in the recent health literacy measurement effort coordinated by the European Union. (See the European Union section for more.) In Ireland, this effort was conducted by the Department of Health and the National Adult Literacy Agency (NALA) and involved 1,005 respondents. Of the respondents in Ireland, 10.3 percent were reported to have inadequate health literacy, 29.7 percent had problematic health literacy (these figures may be combined to give a limited health literacy rate of 40 percent), 38.7 percent had sufficient health literacy, and 21.3 percent had excellent health literacy (http://healthliteracy.ie/wp-content/uploads/2012/06/Executive-Summary.pdf).

NALA offers resources and conducts multiple activities related to health literacy. For example, there are health literacy exercises for students, activities to influence governmental policy related to health literacy, working with health organizations to make their efforts more health literate. These efforts include preparation and release of a 2002 report titled *Health Literacy, Policy and Strategy* (http://www. nala.ie/resources/health-literacy-policy-and-strategy-2002-research-report) and a 2009 Health Service Executive (HSE)/NALA publication, "Literacy Audit for Healthcare Settings" (http://health literacy.ie/wp-content/uploads/2010/11/NALA-Audit-Project-Nov-2010-report.pdf). HSE manages public health services in Ireland (http:// www.hse.ie).

Ireland is also home to the Merck Sharp & Dohme (MSD)/NALA Health Literacy Initiative (http://healthliteracy.ie) which is reported as a partnership between healthcare company MSD and NALA. The aim of the initiative is to increase awareness about the issue of health literacy in Ireland. A major activity of this initiative is the Crystal Clear Awards (http://healthliteracy.ie/crystal-awards) that recognizes individuals and organizations for their efforts to advance health literacy in Ireland.

Winners of this recognition in 2012 included the following. (The following information extracted from http://healthliteracy.ie/crystal-awards—previous year award winners and information describing all finalists can also be found at this website.)

Best Project in General Practice

- WINNER: DIT Student Health Centre, Dublin Institute of Technology (DIT). The *No Umbrella Campaign*. The *No Umbrella Campaign* was developed by Louise O'Donnell and Deirdre Adamson to make students aware of a new Sexually Transmitted Infection (STI) screening test for males that is simpler and easier than before. They also wanted to educate young males that, contrary to popular belief, STI screening no longer involves a painful and invasive test referred to as the "Umbrella Test." Research showed that there was an especially low uptake of STI testing amongst Northside Dublin males, who in turn became DIT's communication target. Louise and Deirdre developed a simple poster to dispel the myth and remove any fear associated with the test and increase uptake. They evaluated the success of the campaign by comparing attendance at 16 STI clinics before and after the launch of the campaign. Post launch, they found an increase of 73 percent in the number of students attending their STI clinic from their target group and an increase of 18 percent in the total number of students attending the STI clinic.

Best Project in a Hospital

- WINNER: National Cancer Control Programme Rapid Access Lung

Clinic Booklet Team. "NCCP Rapid Access Lung Clinic Patient Booklets." The National Cancer Control Programme (NCCP) developed the Rapid Access Lung Clinic patient booklet to provide information for patients about what to expect when they attend their Clinic. General practitioners (GPs) can refer patients with suspected lung cancer to a Rapid Access Lung Clinic. Early diagnosis of lung cancer increases the chance for a cure. The typical lung cancer patient is often from the lower socioeconomic groups, and therefore may have low literacy levels. The deliverable of this project was to produce and distribute the patient booklets to the eight designated cancer centres around the country. The core information in all eight booklets is standardized, and there is hospital specific information in the individual booklets. This was to ensure that clear information is available to all patients irrespective of which hospital they attend. As well as informing the patients about their visit to the clinic, they include health promotion information, in particular a focus on encouraging patients to quit smoking. The booklets have been awarded the Plain English mark by NALA. Pictures and diagrams were included to make the booklet easier to read.

Best Project in the Community or in a Social Setting

- WINNER: Arthritis Ireland. "My Health Organiser." Arthritis Ireland recognized that patients with arthritis could see up to 15 different health care professionals in a given year, and with no electronic record system in the country, and a lack of sharing patient files, patients were forced to give a full medical history every time they visited a health care professional. Arthritis Ireland developed My Health Organiser to encourage people with arthritis to take control and play an active part in their treatment. It also helps patients to actively engage in their health care management by providing them with somewhere to store all of their health records including diagnoses, medications and treatments in one place, literally putting the knowledge and information in their hands. The use of plain English throughout makes it easy to understand and fill out. The number of My Health Organiser booklets distributed to date is more than 6,500. The number of people calling the national helpline has doubled during the period of the campaign, resulting in an overall increased awareness of Arthritis Ireland among the public.

Best Health Promotion Project

- WINNER: Maeve Cusack and Laura Molloy, National Cancer Screening Service. "Bespoke cancer screening training for community health workers in the Traveller Community." The National Cancer Screening Service (NCSS) communications and screening promotion team aims to reduce barriers and enable eligible women from the Travelling community to participate in BreastCheck and CervicalCheck. The NCSS developed a bespoke, interactive training programme for community health workers (CHWs) that supports women with low literacy levels to understand complex messages about cancer and screening. The programme incorporates pictorial-led materials that support women with low literacy levels to understand often complex messages about cancer and screening. The overarching objective is to encourage women from the Travelling community to make informed choices about their cancer screening needs. The overwhelming response from 50 participants was that the training was enjoyable and participative. CHWs reported that the training challenged their fatalistic view of cancer. Many had never before seen the benefits of screening and getting early symptoms checked out. They are now actively sharing this positive message with their communities.

Best Health Communication Through Journalism

- WINNER: Nicoline Greer, Conor McGinnity, and Liam O'Brien, RTE Radio 1, "My Dad's Depression." RTE Radio 1, led by series producer Liam O'Brien and production supervisor Nicola Greer, put together a documentary on Conor McGinnity's personal story on how his father's depression has affected the whole family. The aim of the documentary is to give an insight into families who live with depression, but are not sufferers themselves. To that end they did not include any "expert" opinion—rather, they heard directly from the family at the centre of this issue. This documentary received an enormous response. On the weekend it was broadcast, it reached approximately 240,000 listeners. RTE Radio 1 was inundated with e-mails for a number of weeks after the documentary aired. It got sizeable online traffic (c. 30,000 podcasts/webpage visits). It was also picked up by Liveline the following Monday and became the kernel of that day's programming. Conor's family, including his father, was taken aback by the response they personally received—and still do to this day[7] (NALA, 2012).

EDUCATIONAL EFFORTS TARGETING HEALTH PROFESSIONALS

NALA reports offering a health literacy initiative for members of all sectors of the health profession as well as to members of the media who specialize in health promotion.

HOW IS HEALTH LITERACY DEFINED IN IRELAND?

The NALA report "Health Literacy Policy and Strategy" offered this definition: "Functional health literacy involves more than simply understanding written and oral communication about health. Functional health literacy is the ability to use written and oral material to function in health care settings and maintain one's health. It also includes the necessary skills to ask for clarification" (McCarthy and Lynch, 2002).

Israel

GOVERNMENTAL POLICY

A participant from Israel reported that there is a new governmental policy for Cultural and Linguistically Appropriate Health Services (available here in Hebrew: http://jer-icc.org/blog/wp-content/uploads/2011/02/hozermankalculturalcompetence-a3876_mk07_11.pdf). This effort is reported to create principles and standards for cultural accessibility in health care organizations and institutions on a national level in Israel. This includes translation services, education and training of medical staffs, and environmental adaptations of the institutions (Jerusalem Inter-Cultural Center, 2001). Additionally, quality assessment monitoring and auditing of primary care services is conducted by the Israel Ministry of Health that includes addressing health education materials in Hebrew, Arabic, and Russian as well as training of staff on cultural appropriateness. The Ministry of Health is also reportedly working to establish a national telephone translation service.

---

[7]Extracted from http://healthliteracy.ie/crystal-awards. Previous year award winners and information describing all finalists can also be found at this website.

HEALTH LITERACY INITIATIVES
(GOVERNMENTAL AND NONGOVERNMENTAL)

The Israel Ministry of Health is reported to be partnering with Clalit Health Services to provide cultural liaisons in primary care clinics that serve the Ethiopian immigrant population in Israel. Participants reported that Clalit Health Services has made the topic a priority by leading the National Health Literacy Survey in Israel, implementing policies and projects for culturally appropriate health information and education, and adding health literacy to treatment guidelines and conducting training for staff at different levels on health literacy. The Clalit hospitals are voluntarily undergoing The Joint Commission accreditation process, including patient education and culturally appropriate services and information. A particular effort described by the participant from Israel is the "Refuah Shlema" program that has sustained for more than 13 years cultural liaisons/mediators in Clalit primary care clinics that serve Ethiopian immigrant populations, in partnership with the Israel Ministry of Health. Also, the participant reported that Clalit maintains award-winning health websites in Hebrew, Arabic, Russian, French, and other languages with the opportunity to receive information, ask questions and get answers from experts in the person's preferred language and participate in discussion forums. Clalit also has adapted the "Ask Me 3" program from the United States into Hebrew, Arabic, and Russian. This participant reported that Clalit also conducts hundreds of activities each year to reach populations with special health literacy needs—all age groups, all levels of health behavior (prevention, early detection, self-care), and outreach programs in clinics, schools, hospitals, elderly clubs, and other settings. The health system also operates a call center that assists in navigation of the health care system and there is a telephone translation service for the entire system to serve the Amharic speaking population.

EDUCATIONAL EFFORTS TARGETING HEALTH PROFESSIONALS

A participant indicated that there is a new course from the Israel Ministry of Health for hospital representatives that coordinates culturally appropriate services and includes a unit on health literacy.

Health literacy is reported to be included in training of primary care staff at Clalit, particularly with regard to diabetes and treatment of chronic disease.

HOW IS HEALTH LITERACY DEFINED IN ISRAEL?

The participant reported the definition of health literacy used in Israel is that health literacy is the ability to gain access to, understand, and apply health information in a way that enables making positive decisions about health.

Japan

GOVERNMENTAL POLICY

None reported.

HEALTH LITERACY INITIATIVES (GOVERNMENTAL AND NONGOVERNMENTAL)

An effort sponsored in part by the Saint Luke's College of Nursing and Information Science in Tokyo, Japan, and reportedly supported by a research grant from the Japanese Ministry of Education, Science and Technology had produced a website, http://www.healthlitercy.jp, which is an attempt to provide health literate information to the Japanese population.

Further, the Saint Luke's College of Nursing World Health Organization Collaborating Centre for Nursing Development in Primary Health Care is reported to have embarked upon a "People-Centered Health Care" initiative based on the premise that peoples' participation is an essential part of reaching the Millennium Developmental Goals. The effort strives to help people to be empowered and strengthen their health literacy in order to control their own health. Toward that end, the effort has started health programs targeting elderly-, family-, and women-centered care, and with other people based on the people-centered care model.

EDUCATIONAL EFFORTS TARGETING HEALTH PROFESSIONALS

None reported.

HOW IS HEALTH LITERACY DEFINED IN JAPAN?

None reported.

BOX A-3
How Did You First Learn About Health Literacy?

"My personal story on how I first became aware of health literacy is quite difficult to describe as it was a dawning realisation of how disempowered and 'out of the information loop' most patients were, which was a stark contrast to the situation in much of the developed world in which patients were able to access unlimited health-related information via the internet. . . . My work in this area started with coming across the U.S. Pharmacopeial Convention pictograms years ago, thinking about their potential role in communicating health-related information to a population such as ours and then realising that many of the concepts and images used would probably be incomprehensible to our patients due to limited visual literacy, as well as cultural and lifestyle differences. During the huge number of interviews we have conducted over the years, the lack of knowledge, lack of awareness and disempowerment were glaringly apparent. What was interesting was investigating the visual literacy skills required in interpreting images and identifying the influence of culture and education in the ability to interpret them. . . . The two most important messages that continuously came through in every project, in every interview we conducted, were firstly to make no assumptions (e.g., that leaflet is SO simple, anyone will understand that, OR, but anyone can see that the picture is a person sitting on a toilet/rubbing cream on the skin etc.). The second message was to SIMPLIFY and take note of what patients actually want and need—which was NOT necessarily what the 'expert' nurse or doctor thought the patient needed to know. A huge challenge is to walk the thin line between 'enough' and 'too much' information and written text in a leaflet."

—South African participant

Kenya

GOVERNMENTAL POLICY

A participant reporting on health literacy in Kenya reported that the nation is guided by the WHO's 7th Global Conference on Health Promotion (which was held in Nairobi, Kenya) resolution on health literacy and health promotion. (One of the four tracks of this conference focused on health literacy and health behavior.) Further, a participant reported that the Kenyan constitution upholds the right to information access by citizens. In the Kenyan Ministry of Health, strategic documents such as the communication strategy and concepts like health literacy are reported to fall under the public education policy efforts. The overall aim reported is to transfer health care information to those otherwise marginalized and difficult to reach, including people living with disabilities.

HEALTH LITERACY INITIATIVES
(GOVERNMENTAL AND NONGOVERNMENTAL)

The Kenyan government is reported to have been rolling out an initiative, "Public Access to Health Information in Kenya." Communities in Kenya are reported to have embraced this effort that is working to translate health information materials into local languages to allow for easier access. Family Health Options Kenya (http://www.fhok.org) in partnership with the Ministry of Health is reported to have been in the forefront of this process. Through the Community Health Strategy, households are reached with health information in a language they can understand. The effort is also identifying health centers that have computers and appropriate technology so the community can visit and access health information in a language they can easily understand.

Another health literacy effort reported from Kenya is the creation of health information dialogues and reading tents where experts mingle with the community and discuss the prevailing health challenges within respective communities. These dialogues are reported to have developed suggestions better suited to alleviate health challenges and increase community ownerships of the activities.

At a 2009 conference on Health Literacy Capacities in East and Southern Africa, a participant reported on Rachuonyo Health Equity that is a Kenyan community-based organization reported to be working with people living with HIV/AIDS. The hope expressed for this effort is that

> health literacy will not only empower marginalized girls in Kenya with information and knowledge but to also act responsibly to improve their own health . . . the Health Literacy program will benefit the institution and communities in Kenya in many ways . . . increasing health literacy among these marginalized groups will make them more likely to create a sustainable healthy living, they will make more informed decisions about their health and more actively support their children to attend school and hopefully overcome similar barriers in future. (TARSC, 2009)

Several organizations in Kenya are reported to be conducting Magnet Theater efforts, particularly addressing HIV/AIDS. The methodology is called "Magnet Theater" due to its natural pulling power to draw audiences. Magnet theater performances are designed to get people talking about traditional attitudes and their role in health and public health. For example, PATH (an international nonprofit organization) has used Magnet Theater to encourage community dialogue around HIV and AIDS issues, consequences of early marriage, and tuberculosis (TB) prevention and treatment. REPACTED (Rapid Effective Participatory Action in Community Theater Education and Development) in Nakuru, Kenya, uses Magnet Theater to advance health literacy about HIV/AIDS, reproductive health issues, and applied the methodology to conflict resolution during the recent post election crisis.

EDUCATIONAL EFFORTS TARGETING HEALTH PROFESSIONALS

Kenya has health education programs within the Ministry of Health and also of Education. Various strategies are applied to educate and teach citizens on better health for quality health lives. Through health education programs, citizens at whatever level within the society are reported to be able to access health information.

HOW IS HEALTH LITERACY DEFINED IN KENYA?

None reported.

Liberia

See the International NGO section of this paper.

Malawi

GOVERNMENTAL POLICY

The government of Malawi is reported by a participant to have formulated policies that seek to address HIV/AIDS pandemic and maternal health problems, at least in part by addressing health literacy. According to this participant, the government established the National Aids Commission (NAC) to coordinate the HIV/AIDS programs in Malawi. The commission is responsible for formulating the National HIV/AIDS policy and its implementation, which includes educating the masses about the effects of HIV/AIDS on individuals and the society at large.

HEALTH LITERACY INITIATIVES
(GOVERNMENTAL AND NONGOVERNMENTAL)

A participant reported that the government of Malawi through the Presidential Initiative on Safe Motherhood has embarked on a campaign to sensitize the public on dangers that pregnant women and girls face with a focus on fistula. The government is encouraging pregnant women to seek help from antenatal clinics during and after pregnancy in order to reduce cases of fistula.

The participant from Malawi also reported initiatives by the United Nations to address problems of malaria and infant mortality in Africa are being supported by the European Union in Malawi. Also, the participant reported that some NGOs place programs on the radio to attempt to sensitize the public on malaria prevention and treatment.

According to a 2009 report on Health Literacy Capacities in East and Southern Africa (http://www.tarsc.org/publications/documents/HLregional%20meeting09.pdf), the Malawi Health Equity Network (MHEN) with support from the Training and Research Support Centre in Zimbabwe (TRSC) carried out a needs and capacity assessment for their health literacy program in 2007. The assessment was a build up to the country review meeting held in May 2007. Both exercises informed the content of a Malawi Health Literacy manual. The Malawi Health Literacy Materials were pre-tested in two districts and peer reviewed by a technical team in Malawi (TARSC, 2009). The effort also conducted a facilitators' training in four districts in Malawi, with 30 facilitators trained in 2008. Community Health Literacy work reportedly began in 2008. The report asserts that the Health Literacy program should also be viewed as a fundamental equity watchdog as it exposes unfair and unnecessary disparities at community level (TARSC, 2009).

EDUCATIONAL EFFORTS TARGETING HEALTH PROFESSIONALS

None reported.

HOW IS HEALTH LITERACY DEFINED IN MALAWI?

The effort supported by MHEN and TRSC defines health literacy as people's ability to obtain, interpret, and understand basic health information and health services, and to use such information and services in ways that promote their health (TARSC, 2009).

Mexico

GOVERNMENTAL POLICY

The main policy source related to health literacy in Mexico, according to participants, is the Secretaría de Salud (http://portal.salud.gob.mx). This governmental organization encourages citizens to obtain vaccinations, donate organs, and creates awareness through health risk campaigns and similar efforts according to participants. One participant suggests that health literacy is one of the few issues related to the uptake of science by the public where Mexico's governmental policies have been successful due to good quality health professionals and a strong medical tradition. A participant also indicates that there is a challenge in making clean distinctions between health, education, and health literacy policies and initiatives in Mexico.

A participant notes that top-down efforts in the form of governmental regulations such as a new law prohibiting selling "junk food" in schools and smoking in public places indicate a position in the government that may assume health literacy is not sufficient in and of itself, but that regulations are necessary to protect and improve health.

HEALTH LITERACY INITIATIVES (GOVERNMENTAL AND NONGOVERNMENTAL)

Successful examples of governmental efforts related to health literacy that participants reported in Mexico include the governmental led vaccination campaigns. Participants note that while many parents may vaccinate their children without fully understanding the immune system, saving children's lives has to be tackled efficiently and thus full health literacy regarding vaccinations is not always obtained or, it seems according to reports, necessary in order to meet the goal of vaccinating children. Another successful campaign that participants reported about focuses on birth control with a slogan "the small family lives better." An emerging national priority, according to participants, is to focus programs on obesity related to diabetes.

A participant also reported that the Instituto Mexicano de Seguro Social (http://www.imss.gob.mx) works as a public insurance institution, that they work on cancer, diabetes, obesity and nutrition, women's health, and "PrevinIMMS," which is an integrated health program focusing on prevention through education. Another governmental led effort participants reported on is at the Instituto de Seguridad y Servicios Sociales de los Trabajadores del Estado (http://www.issste.gob.mx/index2.html) that has a program, "PrevenISSTE" (http://www.prevenissste.gob.mx). This program is training health professionals across Mexico—especially nutritionists and fitness instructors—to be placed in medical clinics and hospitals in order to transform the health system from a focus on treatment into a comprehensive prevention effort. The effort has also created an online portal for health information to improve health literacy that includes modules on addictions, hypertension, cancer, heart health, diabetes, and influenza. A participant notes that challenges facing these sort of efforts in Mexico may be the number of people with access to the Internet and that the information seems designed for adults but not younger people or children.

Other challenges facing health literacy programs in Mexico that participants reported include addressing pre-existing cultural prejudices, especially in regard to preventing AIDS and teenage pregnancy given the Catholic church's strong stance against using condoms. One effort noted by participants is a radio campaign with the theme that if listeners would prefer to stay late and enjoy a party instead of taking care of a baby at home they should use a condom.

Health literacy–related efforts were also reported to be conducted by the Centro Nacional para la Salud de la Infancia y la Adolescencia (http://www.censia.salud.gob.mx) and many science centers around the country that can be identified through the Association of Mexican Science Centers (http://www.ammccyt.org.mx).

A participant, while noting a general shortage of projects or programs that explicitly focus on health literacy, did report that across the country social workers are addressing health literacy in their work in rural communities—for example, on vaccination or using medical services for prevention. Another participant reported that health professionals in Mexico continue to use very technical language to communicate with the public so often people do not understand or see the relevance of their efforts to communicate indicating a continuing need to further advance health literacy in the nation.

EDUCATIONAL EFFORTS TARGETING HEALTH PROFESSIONALS

Participants noted that many universities such as the Universidad Nacional Autónoma de México (http://www.unam.mx) have programs on health literacy.

HOW IS HEALTH LITERACY DEFINED IN MEXICO?

While no formal definitions were offered, one participant noted that the mission of the Secretaría de Salud has key elements that can be read to address and include health literacy. For example, the mission statement refers to promoting health as a social goal, providing universal access, meeting the needs and expectations of the population, and using honest, transparent, and efficient use of resources through broad citizen participation. In practice, one participant noted the efforts to meet that mission seem to be limited to radio and television campaigns. Other participants reported that while the exact official definition of health literacy was not known, the definition has to do with prevention that can only be achieved through addressing cultural attitudes.

Mozambique

GOVERNMENTAL POLICY

None reported.

HEALTH LITERACY INITIATIVES
(GOVERNMENTAL AND NONGOVERNMENTAL)

Massukos is a musical group that is said to be considered a national treasure in Mozambique, renowned both for their music and the humanitarian work that they perform (http://www.massukos.org). Feliciano dos Santos, the leader of Massukos, is also the director and founder of a nongovernmental organization named Estamos. Originating from Niassa in northern Mozambique, one of the poorest parts of Africa, Massukos uses their high profile to speak out against the hardships that have affected their lives and the nation. The band delivers simple life-saving messages—i.e., improves health literacy—about hygiene, sanitation, water, and HIV/AIDS through their music (PooP Creative, 2009). Estamos delivers public health programs that work to install latrines and clean water points as well as improve hygiene behaviors and provide HIV/AIDS education.

EDUCATIONAL EFFORTS TARGETING HEALTH PROFESSIONALS

None reported.

HOW IS HEALTH LITERACY DEFINED IN MOZAMBIQUE?

None reported.

Netherlands

GOVERNMENTAL POLICY

None reported.

HEALTH LITERACY INITIATIVES
(GOVERNMENTAL AND NONGOVERNMENTAL)

There has been research on health literacy conducted in the Netherlands. For example, scholar Alja Bosch performed a literature study to better understand and operationalize health literacy at the Netherlands

Institute for Health Promotion. That work (not in English), in 2005, concluded that health literacy is an almost unknown concept in Dutch health promotion efforts, but there was interest in the concept (http://essay.utwente.nl/57803/1/scriptie_Bosch.pdf).

EDUCATIONAL EFFORTS TARGETING HEALTH PROFESSIONALS

A workshop addressing health professionals was held in Finland in 2010 featuring multiple examples and speakers about health literacy (http://www.compriz.nl/nieuws/23).

HOW IS HEALTH LITERACY DEFINED IN THE NETHERLANDS?

The 2005 research mentioned above noted that there was no single operationalized definition of health literacy in the Netherlands, and that was an area that needed to be addressed in the future.

New Zealand

GOVERNMENTAL POLICY

New Zealand governmental policy is reported to address health literacy in many ways, but a participant noted that the government does not use the term/concept to organize policy. As a result, a participant noted that aspects of patient centered care and the country's health targets embed many aspects of health literacy without explicitly indicating a focus on health literacy.

Participants did report that regional health providers have received government funding to support research investigating health literacy in their regions, indicating at least some level of governmental policy support for health literacy. Others reported that they are not aware of formal governmental policies on health literacy per se, but one participant does note that New Zealand Ministry of Health Requests for Proposals for resources or projects that involve interventions are increasingly asking that health literacy be addressed. As a result, this participant suggests that more people in the health sector in New Zealand are becoming aware of and using health literacy in both policy and practice.

A search of the phrase "health literacy" on the New Zealand Ministry of Health's website produces multiple "hits," again indicating that there is some support within the governmental policy structure to support health literacy work.

HEALTH LITERACY INITIATIVES
(GOVERNMENTAL AND NONGOVERNMENTAL)

New Zealand is reported by participants to have joined the small number of nations in the world that has made the attempt to evaluate the level of health literacy of residents. The government sponsors a report on health literacy statistics in New Zealand, "Korero Marama," that is freely available online at http://www.health.govt.nz/publication/korero-marama-health-literacy-and-maori-results-2006-adult-literacy-and-life-skills-survey.

Participants reported that in producing this report, New Zealand has sufficiently sampled the indigenous population so that statistical analysis can make a valid distinction between Māori and non-Māori participants. The data collection process is based upon the 2006 Adult Literacy and Lifeskills Survey. The study found that "Māori have much poorer health literacy skills compared to non-Māori across all of the measured variables. Eighty per cent of Māori males and 75 per cent of Māori females were found to have poor health literacy skills. On average, New Zealanders have poor health literacy skills. The report presents findings by gender, rural and urban location, age, level of education, labour force status, and household income" (Ministry of Health, 2010).

In no small part as a result of this national data set, a respondent reported that there is an "increasing call for services—including health services—to empower people and their whānau[8] rather than see them as mere service users, the need to understand current levels of health literacy and how those might be improved is becoming even more important in New Zealand," according to one participant.

Participants reported that there are a large number of health literacy research projects going on at the University of Auckland. For example, one project (with the University of Waikato) investigated health literacy and palliative care for Māori. Another project (an international indigenous collaborative with Australia and Canada) is investigating health literacy about cardiovascular disease medicines among indigenous people. The New Zealand Ministry of Health is reported to also be currently sponsoring three health literacy projects at the University of Auckland that focus on the Māori population with specific foci on gout among older Māori men, skin infections for children under 14 years of age, and diabetes in pregnancy in mothers under age 25. Participants indicate that there are

---

[8]*Whānau*, according to multiple online sources, is a Māori-language word for *extended family*—comprised of the elders, the *pākeke* (senior adults such as parents, uncles, and aunts), and the sons and daughters, together with their spouses and children. Some report the word is now increasingly entering New Zealand English, particularly in official documents.

multiple other health literacy projects ongoing, for instance, one focusing on health literacy and caregivers for people living with disabilities.

A nonprofit organization—Health Navigator—promoting health literacy in New Zealand has developed a website at http://healthliteracy. org.nz. The site offers multiple resources and definitions of health literacy from around the world. The site also offers access to the Waipanu statement, which is a "brief paper encouraging health organisations, health professionals, patients, media and communities to take action about improving health literacy right across the health system" (Health Navigator New Zealand, 2011).

Another health literacy resource in New Zealand is Workbase (http:// www.workbase.org.nz). Workbase is a national, nonprofit organization working in partnership with business, the education sector, and government to raise the literacy, English, and numeracy skills of the New Zealand population (Anonymous, 2001). The organization includes a focus on health literacy (http://www.healthliteracy.org.nz) that includes definitions of health literacy, statistics on health literacy in New Zealand, resources for addressing health literacy, and health literacy consulting services.

BOX A-4
How Did You First Learn About Health Literacy?

"I am not aware how and when I became involved in health information literacy. I never thought about it, it just came in a natural way, as when you learn about caring for yourself, or use the personal computer. May this be an answer?"
—Italian participant

A participant reported this range of efforts is making inroads from a systems point of view.

A conference in May 2012 that featured U.S. health literacy scholar Rima Rudd as a keynote speaker is reported to have generated further interest in health literacy in New Zealand. Others reported that part of that growing success in informing governmental policy and practices in New Zealand is attributed to an Associate Minister of Health, Minister Tariana Turia, who is Māori and who understands that Māori have low levels of health literacy. So although most all of the projects funded by the government are reportedly focused on Māori and other Pacific peoples (also experiencing very low literacy and numeracy levels), there seems to be a shared understanding among some participants that interventions for Māori and Pacific people will also successfully inform interventions targeting other populations in New Zealand. Sir Peter Gluckman, the New Zealand Prime Minister's Chief Scientific Advisor, is also reported to be addressing health literacy.

Participants also reported that the New Zealand Health Quality and Safety Commission has initiated some projects on health literacy, but some also comment that those efforts are based upon a "limited understanding of health literacy." For example, participants asserted that within that organization the concept is solely related to patients' understanding and educational materials (http://www.hqsc.govt.nz/home/Search Form?Search=health+literacy+&Programme-clone=0&Programme=0). In September 2011, this governmental organization produced a report on an "environmental scan" of health literacy activities ongoing within the nation that is freely available at http://www.hqsc.govt.nz/assets/Consumer-Engagement/Publications/FINAL-NZGG-HQSC-Health-literacy-environmental-scan.pdf. That report on health literacy efforts, appropriately, reports on more specific efforts within New Zealand than is contained within this summary of efforts within the nation.

The New Zealand Ministry of Health is also reported to have published a revised version of its guide to developing health education materials titled "Rauemi Atawhai: A Guide to Developing Health Education Resources in New Zealand" that includes a section on health literacy. The full report is available at http://www.health.govt.nz/publication/rauemi-atawhai-guide-developing-health-education-resources-new-zealand.

Health Workforce New Zealand (http://www.healthworkforce.govt.nz) is reported to have commissioned a health literacy literature review, but that project is not yet published.

EDUCATIONAL EFFORTS TARGETING HEALTH PROFESSIONALS

The New Zealand Ministry of Health via Health Workforce New Zealand has launched an online cultural competency tool that includes a basic module on health literacy that can be seen at http://www.health workforce.govt.nz/news/2012/06/20/minister-releases-online-cultural-competency-training.

HOW IS HEALTH LITERACY DEFINED IN NEW ZEALAND?

Health literacy in New Zealand, some participants note, is a widely used term that encompasses a range of ideas and definitions.

The New Zealand Ministry of Health on its website and in reports such as "Korero Marama" defines health literacy "as the ability to obtain, process and understand basic health information and services in order to make informed and appropriate health decisions" (Ministry of Health, 2010). The Ministry also expresses that knowing and understanding the extent to which people are able to read and comprehend health instructions and messages is an important part of tailoring appropriate population and personal health services (Ministry of Health, 2010).

The Health Navigator New Zealand website defines health literacy as "the ability to read, understand and effectively use basic medical instructions and information." Their website adds that "For health providers, health literacy includes the capacity of professionals and institutions to: communicate effectively so that community members can make informed decisions and take appropriate actions to protect and promote their health" (Health Navigator New Zealand, 2012).

The New Zealand Tertiary Education Commission is reported to define literacy as the "written and oral language people use in their everyday life and work; it includes reading, writing, speaking and listening" (Ministry of Health, 2010). Thus, literacy is the skills people need in order to function at an optimal level in society.

Participants add that the approach to health literacy in New Zealand acknowledges that health literacy operates within a complex group of reading, listening, analytical, and decision-making skills and is dependent upon a person's ability to apply these skills to health situations. Health literacy, one participant added, is essentially the skills people need to find their way to the right place in hospital, fill out medical and insurance forms, and communicate with their health providers.

One participant reported that the understanding of health literacy within the New Zealand health sector seems to this person to be limited to conceptualizing health literacy as solely being about the educational process and that health literacy is a problem solely of individuals versus a health system and larger societal issue. This participant reported that efforts to broaden that limited conceptualization of health literacy are occurring within the health sector in New Zealand.

Finally, another respondent summed up what seems to reflect a consensus: that health literacy is generally defined either by the WHO definition or the definition from the Ministry of Health in New Zealand reported above, but that there is not a truly standardized definition of health literacy in New Zealand.

Pakistan

GOVERNMENTAL POLICY

The government of Pakistan's health policy is reported to be almost silent about health literacy. There are multiple reports that the government of Pakistan has abolished the national Ministry of Health, handing off those services to individual provinces versus a national agency (Nishtar and Mehboob, 2011).

HEALTH LITERACY INITIATIVES
(GOVERNMENTAL AND NONGOVERNMENTAL)

A participant from Pakistan notes that occasionally there are government led immunization promotions, family planning promotions, and responses to epidemics like the dengue virus but that there is not a formal or regular program focusing on health literacy. Another participant who works as a social worker reported that "I receive a lot of people from the rural areas with health issues. Some cases get complicated only due to lack of awareness. Timely help is not sought and patients end up in precarious condition and even death. We tried to run a lot of awareness and treatment camps in rural areas, but the challenge was too big to be physically everywhere. With the advent of the technological revolution that we are experiencing, my approach changed. I am now developing all kinds of mass communication tools and content to convey to the unserved and under-served. It's a slow process but I feel that over a decade things will definitely be different. A lot of pain will be reduced and a lot of lives will be saved."

See the Business section of the forthcoming report for other efforts in Pakistan.

EDUCATIONAL EFFORTS TARGETING HEALTH PROFESSIONALS

A participant reported that international NGOs do fund the government to promote awareness in relation to specific health issues, but that there is not a long-term methodical plan for health literacy education and training.

HOW IS HEALTH LITERACY DEFINED IN PAKISTAN?

In the Pakistan National Health Policy, there is not a definition for health literacy at either the patient or public level according to a participant. Another participant reported that NGOs define health literacy as providing information on personal hygiene, diseases of different ages and geographies, different sexes and ages, chronic diseases, and epidemics.

Peru

GOVERNMENTAL POLICY

None reported.

HEALTH LITERACY INITIATIVES
(GOVERNMENTAL AND NONGOVERNMENTAL)

In Peru, a participant reported, there is a group called Iniciativa Contra la Desnutricion Infantil (Initiative Against Child Malnutrition) that is made up of NGOs and international agencies that has the purpose of informing and influencing public policy on the subject of infant malnutrition, including stunting and anemia. The group shares information and attempts to present a coherent interpretation and messages in relation to the main nutrition and health problems facing the country (http://www.iniciativacontradesnutricion.org.pe). Peru also has a program to provide health insurance for all children—Seguro Integral de Salud that a participant reported is being expanded to include all members of the poorest families.

Another organization, "La Mesa de Concertación para la Lucha contra la Pobreza" (The Board for Consensus Building in the Fight Against Poverty), is organized to reduce poverty in Peru. Reflecting health literacy, two of the group's aims are to enhance participation of citizens in the design, decision making, and oversight of government policy; and to maximize transparency in programs addressing poverty.

Another participant from Peru reported that there are many projects and programs in Peru that address health literacy. The "Arts for Behavior Change" program is a study that evaluates an arts intervention to improve home hygiene practices in a peri-urban area of Lima. This project in Peru is created by Canyon Ranch Institute, implemented in Peru by local partners Instituto de Investigacion Nutricional and KALLPA. The program developed and tested a new methodology, Theater for the Arts, which improved household hygiene behaviors in the participating community. The Clorox Company funded the program that also included partners from Boston University College of Fine Arts and the University of Arizona's Mel and Enid Zuckerman College of Public Health. For more information on this effort see the International Nongovernmental Organization section of this report.

EDUCATIONAL EFFORTS TARGETING HEALTH PROFESSIONALS

None reported.

HOW IS HEALTH LITERACY DEFINED IN PERU?

The Arts for Behavior Change program in Peru is based on a definition of health literacy based on the Calgary Charter that defines health literacy as allowing "the public and personnel working in all health-related contexts to find, understand, evaluate, communicate, and use information. Health literacy is the use of a wide range of skills that improve the ability of people to act on information in order to live healthier lives. These skills include reading, writing, listening, speaking, numeracy, and critical analysis, as well as communication and interaction skills" (Coleman et al., 2008). In addition, the Charter fairly uniquely suggests that health literacy applies to both individuals and to health systems, explaining that a system is health literate when it provides equal, easy to use, and shame-free access to and delivery of health care and health information.

Singapore

GOVERNMENTAL POLICY

A participant reported that the Singapore government has only recently begun efforts to promote health literacy by recognizing its importance in promoting the health of the nation. Reportedly, the government through the Health Promotion Board is implementing plain language guidelines to ensure that all material produced are health literate.

HEALTH LITERACY INITIATIVES
(GOVERNMENTAL AND NONGOVERNMENTAL)

The government is reported to be embarking on an effort to establish a baseline of the levels of health literacy in Singapore by administering an adapted and validated version of the S-TOFHLA (Short Test of Functional Health Literacy in Adults).

EDUCATIONAL EFFORTS TARGETING HEALTH PROFESSIONALS

The Health Promotion Board of the Singapore government is spearheading all health literacy efforts in the nation. This organization is reported to be undertaking a capacity building effort targeting health care professionals, and nursing and pharmacy students, and other allied health professionals. The Health Promotion Board is also reported to be working with educational institutions—schools of medicine, pharmacy, and nursing—to introduce health literacy into their curriculum.

HOW IS HEALTH LITERACY DEFINED IN SINGAPORE?

None reported.

Slovenia

GOVERNMENTAL POLICY

None reported.

HEALTH LITERACY INITIATIVES (GOVERNMENTAL AND NONGOVERNMENTAL)

A participant reported working on a Slovenian Chemical Safety Literacy project with the Slovenian government to raise the health literacy of the public and professionals related to chemical safety. The government is reported to have declared a chemical safety week and the project's method to stimulate action on the local level was to train "catalysts" to create awareness raising events through a training course for national and local government officials, NGOs, academics, and private-sector communication people on advocacy.

EDUCATIONAL EFFORTS TARGETING HEALTH PROFESSIONALS

None reported.

HOW IS HEALTH LITERACY DEFINED IN SLOVENIA?

None reported.

South Africa

GOVERNMENTAL POLICY

Participants note that while the South African government does have a variety of health programs, they are not aware of any governmental policies or programs explicitly focused on health literacy or health com-

munication. The *National Drug Policy for South Africa* (The National Depar-
ment of Health, 1996) is an example of a policy, published 2 years after
the first democratic elections, when the new government was beginning
to address changes in the health care system. A respondent reported that
a section on rational drug use that includes making literature understandable to the public but nothing is said about "health literacy," but the
policy does indicate an awareness that much effort is required to facilitate
understanding by patients. The National Department of Health (2011)
has a *Policy on Language Services* that stipulates that the responsibility lies
with the provider to ensure the availability of information and documentation in at least two of the official languages. This is critically important
in South Africa, a nation with 11 official languages, a respondent noted.

The Constitution of South Africa does include guarantees for access
to health care services and sufficient food and water as well as the right
to a basic education, including adult basic education (South African Government, 2009). Other relevant rights addressed within the South African
constitution include the right to use the language and to participate in the
cultural life of their choice, the right of access to information held by the
state, and that people belonging to a cultural, religious or linguistic community may not be denied the right to enjoy their culture, practice their
religion and use their language; and to form, join, and maintain cultural,
religious, and linguistic associations and other organs of civil society
(South African Government, 2009).

HEALTH LITERACY INTERVENTIONS
(GOVERNMENTAL AND NONGOVERNMENTAL)

To help set the stage for an understanding of health literacy efforts in
South Africa, a respondent noted that "the real literacy problems in South
Africa—and hence health literacy problems—have been a constant issue
in the healthcare landscape here forever, and apply to the majority of the
population, rather than the 'ethnic minorities' so often reported about as
lacking literacy and health literacy in the literature from Britain, U.S.A., or
Europe." Reportedly, about 18 percent of South Africans have no school-
ing, 41 percent have only primary school (including the 18 percent), 31
percent have some secondary school, and only 20 percent have completed
secondary school. South Africa is reported to consistently perform near
the bottom of all international benchmark literacy tests, for example, in
the 2006 Progress in International Reading Literacy Study (PIRLS), South
Africa was ranked 40 out of 40 countries (Mullis et al., 2007).

According to participants, the one disease that has had a vast influence on the way patients are treated in South Africa is HIV/AIDS. One
participant reported that "Healthcare in South Africa, as a result, has

definitely shifted from having focused on a purely biomedical approach
to a much more all-inclusive biopsychosocial approach where the patient
is acknowledged as being part of a particular community and social structure. Interestingly, though, the term health literacy has still not become a
prominent one. In a way, 'health literacy' is tacitly acknowledged as being
a component of every consultation, as all health care providers are aware
of the lack of relevant background knowledge required to fully comprehend complex health conditions, e.g., a knowledge of the workings of the
body, what a heart is, what lungs are, the way food is digested. One of our
rural asthma patients declared, 'I knew that sheep and cows have lungs,
but I did not know I had them!'"

Other participants reported that some of the best known HIV/health
communication campaigns in South Africa such as LoveLife (http://www.
lovelife.org.za) and Soul City (http://www.soulcity.org.za) address health
literacy according to a participant. These efforts are reported to have some
government involvement (via individuals), but they are not government-
funded programs or a government initiative. A participant reported that
the edutainment program Soul City was developed specifically for the
highest target market on South Africa's Broadcasting Corporation (SABC)
television channel 2 (viewers aged 15 and older), explores themes related
to health, including gender-based violence, alcohol use, HIV/AIDS, and
stigma to improve the health literacy of viewers through the dramatic
series. Soul City's work is evidence-based, pre-tested, and evaluated after
every series. Another series aimed at children called Soul Buddyz has the
same objectives for children (http://www.soulcity.org.za).

A participant reported that perhaps the most useful application of
the health literacy work done over the years in South Africa in terms
of developing and testing pictograms is currently being applied on the
Phelophepa Healthcare Train (see http://www.transnetfoundation.co.za/
CSIPortfolios/Pages/Health.aspx#aboutphelophepa or http://www.
trainofhope.org). The two trains travel around the rural areas of South
Africa that are the poorest most underserved areas, offering a diverse
range of primary health care. There is also a dispensary on the train. Ros
Dowse, a lecturer in Pharmaceutics at the Faculty of Pharmacy, Rhodes
University, South Africa, reported that "a couple of years I met up with
the pharmacists on the Train and offered the use of the materials I had
developed. As the Train travels around all areas of the country, patients
speaking a huge variety of languages are tended to. A selection of our
pictograms are now used as stickers which are attached to the medicine boxes or bottles and which provide a valuable communication tool,
facilitating the interaction between provider and patient. It is extremely
rewarding to see the outcome of many years of research impacting positively on patient care."

Another participant notes that there are national, provincial, and district health promotion and education programs focusing on healthy lifestyles, HIV and AIDS, nutrition, child and maternal health, and youth health, among other issues, but this individual did not report on any specifically based on or addressing health literacy. For example, a participant reported that the government offers health services at provincial hospitals and local clinics—and may hand out information pamphlets from time to time—but this individual was not aware of any efforts specifically focusing on health literacy.

EDUCATIONAL EFFORTS TARGETING HEALTH PROFESSIONALS

None reported.

HOW IS HEALTH LITERACY DEFINED IN SOUTH AFRICA?

Participants reported that they are not aware of health literacy being formally defined as a public policy issue in South Africa. A participant reported that the term "health literacy" is not a commonly used term in South Africa. The expectation in the public health care system is that the vast majority of patients will be able to comprehend only very basic health information. Thus, this participant reported that there is almost no point in measuring health literacy, because no test exists that is simple enough to differentiate between the low levels of health literacy seen in South Africa.

Spain

GOVERNMENTAL POLICY

None reported.

HEALTH LITERACY INITIATIVES
(GOVERNMENTAL AND NONGOVERNMENTAL)

The AIDS Research Institute IrsiCaixa is reported by participants to work with countries all over the world regarding research, but in regard to the field of health literacy the organization is only active in Spain. IrsiCaixa and the La Caixa Foundation conduct the Scientific Dissemination and Prevention Programme on AIDS. This program is reported to include multimedia tools offered via the IrsiCaixa Outreach website (http://www.irsicaixa.es/outreach), participative dissemination and reflection workshops, experiment workshops where youngsters can perform real research experiments, and scientific updating sessions for teachers at the museums CosmoCaixa Barcelona and CaixaForums in other cities of Catalonia. Youth are encouraged to actively participate in the program, producing their own communication tools and/or disseminating the information using social networking, as well as in local communities within their environment.

Proyecto LIS España (http://lisic.isciii.es) is a search engine focused on providing health information that is selected through established quality criteria. The initiative is the result of technical cooperation between the National Library of Health Sciences of Spain and the Latin American and Caribbean Center on Health Sciences which is an agency of the Pan American Health Organization/WoHO.

EDUCATIONAL EFFORTS TARGETING HEALTH PROFESSIONALS

SIPES (Sistema de Información de Promoción y Educación para la Salud) is an effort to enhance communication between professionals and health institutions related to health promotion and education. Key objectives of the network include the exchange of information and experiences between professionals and various government institutions, organizations, social groups, and organizations working on issues related to health promotion and education; facilitating management initiatives and demands of existing health education to improve decision making in health promotion; providing evidence-based information on health promotion, accessible and professional schools, including implications for health services, education, and social services system; and improving the quality and accessibility of health information aimed at the general public, professionals, social groups, and organizations (http://sipes.msps.es/sipes2/indexAction.do).

HOW IS HEALTH LITERACY DEFINED IN SPAIN?

None reported.

Switzerland

GOVERNMENTAL POLICY

None reported.

HEALTH LITERACY INITIATIVES
(GOVERNMENTAL AND NONGOVERNMENTAL)

The network of Swiss Public Health, Health Promotion Switzerland, the Careum Foundation, the Swiss Medical Association FMH, and MSD created Alliance Compétences en matière de santé. The goal of this organization is to significantly increase the health literacy of Swiss citizens and enable them to positively influence the determinants of health, risk assessment, and move independently within the health system. The organization has completed an assessment of health literacy in 22 of the 26 cantons of Switzerland. This report is available, in French, at http://www.alliance-competences-en-sante.ch/logicio/client/allianz/file/Projekte/20120222_Competences_en_sante_F_FINAL-001.pdf. The report found that health literacy was generally known, but not a public health priority. The organization also offered a prize for the most innovative projects in health literacy.

(See the Business section of the forthcoming report for other efforts in Switzerland.)

EDUCATIONAL EFFORTS TARGETING HEALTH PROFESSIONALS

One training session in the Swiss Master of Public Health training was reported to be on the topic of health literacy. No further information was provided or available.

HOW IS HEALTH LITERACY DEFINED IN SWITZERLAND?

The Alliance Compétences en matière de santé defines health literacy as the ability to make decisions with a positive impact on health in everyday life. The organization states that health literacy is, among other things, knowledge and skills that allow an individual to behave favorable to health. The concept of "health literacy" has many facets. It is not only the case of the health system. Skills development in health is a cross-cutting theme that should include not only health insurance, medical, patient organizations but also the education sector, the food industry, and sport as well as retailers (http://www.alliance-competences-en-sante.ch/logicio/pmws/indexDOM.php?client_id=allianz&page_id=home&lang_iso639=fr).

Turkey

GOVERNMENTAL POLICY

A participant from Turkey noted that "First, I wanted to participate to your study and then I declined because in fact nothing has been done in terms of health literacy in Turkey. The efforts of the Turkish Ministry of Health in this field could not be named as health literacy but as health education and public awareness programs." This participant noted that in Turkey illiteracy is an important social problem and around 5,000,000 cannot read and write. Among them 4,500,000 are women.

HEALTH LITERACY INITIATIVES
(GOVERNMENTAL AND NONGOVERNMENTAL)

While not specifically targeting or based on health literacy, a participant reported that in the 1980s, together with the Johns Hopkins University Center for Communication Programs and School of Public Health, the Turkish Ministry of Health launched a campaign for family planning based on the Enter Education approach; this was followed by efforts focusing on use of oral rehydration salts, vaccination against preventable communicable diseases, and AIDS prevention. In the 1990s, campaigns for public awareness against smoking, washing hands, preventing the flu were conducted. In the 2000s, antismoking campaigns are still occurring along with campaigns targeting obesity and the importance of physical exercise. All these campaigns were performed by showing short films and awareness spots on television, distributing pamphlets and posters, and through face-to-face interviews between health care providers and people.

EDUCATIONAL EFFORTS TARGETING HEALTH PROFESSIONALS

None reported.

HOW IS HEALTH LITERACY DEFINED IN TURKEY?

None reported.

United Kingdom (Great Britain, Scotland, Wales, and Northern Ireland)

GOVERNMENTAL POLICY

Participants agreed that health literacy appears only in policy at the national level; there is not a United Kingdom wide policy on health literacy.

According to participants, the most developed strategy is that of Scotland. A participant from Scotland reported that while there is no national policy addressing health literacy, a scoping exercise was conducted with funding through the Health Improvement Strategy Division of the Scottish Government to assess the effects of poor health literacy on accessing local support and managing long-term conditions (http://www.scotland.gov.uk/Resource/Doc/296717/0092261.pdf). This report, released in 2009, states that

> There is no appetite for, or requirement for a "health literacy strategy" for Scotland. This is mainly because the ideas underpinning health literacy are complex and diffuse. Pursuing a separate policy on health literacy would be counterproductive, and would not achieve the aim of improving health literacy across the population of Scotland. (The Scottish Government, 2009)

Instead, the recommendation is to "focus on the practical integration of the ideas underpinning health literacy into existing programmes, projects and initiatives." Another participant reported that health literacy now has a prominent role in health policy development in regard to the Scottish government's Person Centred Health and Care Program. This participant reported that the Scottish government has developed a national health literacy action group that brings together policy, practice, research, and education sectors to develop a National Health Literacy Action Plan (http://nhlag.wordpress.com).

In England, participants reported that health literacy is part of the health inequalities strategy report, *Health Inequalities: Progress and Next Steps*, available at http://www.dh.gov.uk/en/Publicationsandstatistics/Publications/PublicationsPolicyAndGuidance/DH_085307. However, a participant noted that the government has changed since the publication of this report and health literacy does not appear in current government documents or reports.

Another participant noted that current government policy on the National Health Service is reflected in the report, *Equity and Excellence: Liberating the NHS* (http://www.dh.gov.uk/en/Publicationsandstatistics/Publications/PublicationsPolicyAndGuidance/DH_117353). In particular, health literacy–related references in this policy document include entries on shared decision making. These sections report that "we want the principle of 'shared decision-making' to become the norm: *no decision about me without me*" (Department of Health, 2010). Also, that the "new NHS Commissioning Board will champion patient and carer involvement, and the Secretary of State will hold it to account for progress. In the meantime, the Department will work with patients, carers and professional groups, to bring forward proposals about transforming care through shared decision-making" (Department of Health, 2010).

In Wales, health literacy is reported to be a part of the public health strategy, Our Healthy Future, a strategic action plan for reducing health inequity. As part of that strategy, the report *Fairer Health Outcomes for All: Reducing Inequities in Health Strategic Action Plan* directly addresses health literacy (http://wales.gov.uk/docs/phhs/publications/110329working2en.pdf). Health literacy is one of the seven action areas indicated in this report.

There is no report of a health literacy policy in Northern Ireland.

HEALTH LITERACY INITIATIVES
(GOVERNMENTAL AND NONGOVERNMENTAL)

Health Literacy Group UK is a Special Interest Group of the Society for Academic Primary Care that participants reported is committed to raising the profile of health literacy as a remediable cause of health inequalities in England, and to developing and undertaking research to achieve that. The group allows membership for individuals outside of the United Kingdom as well (http://www.healthliteracy.org.uk).

Reflecting the level of policy involvement noted above, the Scottish government is reported by participants to have funded several health literacy projects. Education Scotland maintains a database of these efforts at http://www.educationscotland.gov.uk/communitylearning anddevelopment/adultlearning/adultliteracies/adultliteraciesin practice/health.asp. This includes many examples of partnerships in Scotland between adult-learning providers and the health sector and also features a Communities of Practice forum, a segment of which is focused on health literacy efforts.

In England, participants reported that the Skilled for Health (SfH) program is the national learning program that embeds Skills for Life learning into health improvement topics. SfH courses and workshops address both the low skills and health inequalities prevalent within traditionally disadvantaged communities. This program uses an embedded approach to add to our understanding of how these issues can be addressed (http://www.continyou.org.uk/what_we_do/skilled_health). This approach is reflected in the use of an innovative national partnership to run the program, consisting of the Department of Health, the Department for Business, Innovation and Skills (formerly the Department for Innovation, Universities and Skills) and the learning and health charity ContinYou, which has overseen SfH since its inception (ContinYou, 2011b). ContinYou is one of the United Kingdom's leading education charities that provide services in partnership with schools for children and young people across the country, particularly those from the most disadvantaged communities (ContinYou, 2011a).

Another national project in health literacy in England reported by participants included a national curriculum focusing on personal, social, health, and economic education in the school system (http://www.education.gov.uk/schools/teachingandlearning/curriculum/secondary/b00198880/pshee).

The "Expert Patients Programme" (EPP) is a self-management effort for people who are living with a chronic (long-term) condition. The aim is to support people by increasing their confidence, improving their quality of life, and helping them manage their condition more effectively (NHS, 2012). An expert patient is described as an individual who, "feels confident and in control of their life, aims to manage their condition and its treatment in partnership with healthcare professionals, communicates effectively with professionals and is willing to share responsibility for treatment, is realistic about how their condition affects them and their family, and uses their skills and knowledge to lead a full life" (NHS, 2012).

The Welsh Government, a participant reported, has commissioned work on developing a strategic approach to health literacy in Wales from Public Health Wales, which is the national organization that leads on public health. Participants reported the policy efforts in Wales draw on an effort, produced in 2010, *Health Literacy in Wales: A Scoping Document for Wales*. This report provides context on the health literacy situation and activities in Wales and is available at http://www.google.co.uk/url?sa=t&rct=j&q=wales%20health%20literacy%20osborne&source=web&cd=1&ved=0CFIQFjAA&url=http%3A%2F%2Fwww2.nphs.wales.nhs.uk%3A8080%2Fcommunicationsgroupdocs.nsf%2F61c1e930f9121fd080256f2a004937ed%2Fa2588bc62b678a5b802578c70032b10e%2F%24FILE%2FHealth%2520Literacy%2520Scoping%2520Document%2520FINAL%2520Sarah%2520Puntoni.pdf&ei=FJPfT5iJNsTOtAbB4viDCQ&usg=AFQjCNHjju67ttRRPdCJzXkQrXgbHKy46w.

Participants reported that ongoing work in Wales includes efforts to create a program of work related to raising awareness of functional health literacy and health, including guidelines and standards for public health information and translation and validation of measurement tools for use in the Welsh language.

EDUCATIONAL EFFORTS TARGETING HEALTH PROFESSIONALS

In Wales, a participant reported that aspects of health literacy are included within the Personal and Social Education Curriculum and the Skills Development Curriculum (http://wales.gov.uk/topics/education andskills/schoolshome/curriculuminwales/arevisedcurriculum forwales/pse/?lang=en) and that the Welsh Government also supports self management programs for those with chronic conditions (http://www.eppwales.org).

Participants note that the Scottish Government funded several projects on health and numeracy, many concentrating on drug calculation for nurses and others focusing on raising awareness within health sector staff (http://www.educationscotland.gov.uk/communitylearningand development/adultlearning/adultliteracies/adultliteraciesinpractice/health.asp).

BOX A-5
How Did You First Learn About Health Literacy?

"Several years ago I got a call for papers [in an] e-mail from a scientific journal concerning studies about health literacy. This was the first time that I heard the term of health literacy and I searched for the meaning. I read many scholarly articles about health literacy and most of them were from USA. Together with my colleagues we planned to perform a study on this subject and we did."
—Participant from Turkey

The Patient Information Forum (http://www.pifonline.org.uk) is a membership organization for consumer health information producers and providers in the United Kingdom. The organization is reported to campaign to ensure that health information is central to high-quality, patient-centered care and helps producers and providers to develop high-quality information for their patients and the public. The organization offers health literacy resources, meetings and seminars, reports, and group sessions.

HOW IS HEALTH LITERACY DEFINED
IN THE UNITED KINGDOM?

One participant reported that health literacy is defined in the United Kingdom as representing "the cognitive and social skills which determine the motivation and ability of individuals to gain access to, understand,

and use information in ways which promote and maintain good health. Health literacy means more than being able to read pamphlets and successfully make appointments. By improving people's access to health information and their capacity to use it effectively, health literacy is critical to empowerment."

On a rather similar note, the Department of Health in England's report on Health Inequalities defines health literacy as "the cognitive and social skills that determine the motivation and ability of individuals to gain access to, understand and use information in ways that promote and maintain good health. This means much more than transmitting information and developing skills to undertake basic tasks. It is also necessary to improve people's access to, and understanding of, health information and their capacity to use it effectively supports improved health."

Another participant reported that health literacy is operationalized in the United Kingdom mainly in terms of health care, shared decision making, and successful management of long-term conditions.

In Wales, according to multiple participants, health literacy has been recently defined as "the ability and motivation level of an individual to access, understand, communicate, and evaluate both narrative and numeric information to promote, manage, and improve their health status throughout their lifetime." Participants note that this is a modification of a definition prepared by a Canadian Expert panel in order to demonstrate the role of both narrative and numeracy abilities and to reflect a motivational dimension to health literacy.

Participants reported that in Scotland, multiple definitions are stated in policy documents and no single definition is widely accepted or used.

Zimbabwe

GOVERNMENTAL POLICY

The Ministry of Health and Child Welfare in Zimbabwe reported that the government has shown commitment to increasing health literacy levels through supporting health promotion activities over the past several years. The Ministry points to a decline in HIV prevalence as evidence that individuals are translating their HIV literacy into action (Ministry of Health and Child Welfare, 2009).

The 2009 Assessment Survey of Primary Health Care in Zimbabwe ("Health where it matters most") found that information is fundamental in disease prevention and control. The assessment found that people in Zimbabwe "have a reasonable knowledge of common health conditions, but lack the specific knowledge needed to act in an informed way to promote and protect their health (such as how to make and use sugar salt solution (SSS) to manage dehydration)" (Ministry of Health and Child Welfare, 2009).

The Ministry reports that the assessment data is supporting efforts to ensure that communities to have consistent, regular, specific information flows and recommends that ad hoc and one-off information to communities needs to be integrated into a more comprehensive health literacy program, as is currently being implemented in the districts supported by the Community Working Group on Health (CWGH). Support for the functioning of Village Health Workers and other community-based health workers, person-to-person health information and mass media also provide a means to improved health information flows (Ministry of Health and Child Welfare, 2009).

HEALTH LITERACY INITIATIVES
(GOVERNMENTAL AND NONGOVERNMENTAL)

The CWGH is a network of approximately 30 civic/community-based organizations that aim to collectively enhance community participation in health in Zimbabwe. The CWGH was formed in early 1998 to take up health issues of common concern and was registered as a trust in 2002 (http://www.cwgh.co.zw).

Health literacy is one of the four programmatic areas of the CWGH, the other being adolescent reproductive health, advocacy and lobbying, and community home-based care.

The Health Literacy program is reported to have grown out of a civic education on health program that, in turn, arose out of concern about the deterioration of key social indicators during the 1990s. Demand for information and participation from civic groups in 1998 on a range of public health, health systems, and organizational issues saw the birth of this program. The Health Literacy Program aims to consolidate the work done through the Civic Education program, identifying and filling gaps, as well as to introduce innovative processes and concepts into the work. It is a regional program of work in East and Southern Africa being coordinated by TARSC Zimbabwe.

The health literacy effort is reported to be operating in Zimbabwe, Malawi, and Botswana to support the development and use of participatory health education materials for health civil society. Health facilities are realizing the importance of health literacy and are starting to develop health literacy programs to address the difficulties that patients have in obtaining and understanding health information, to equip civil societies in selected communities with the skills they need to assess quality of service delivery at their health institutions. For example, the effort is reported to have partnered with the Zimbabwe Association of Church-related Hospitals (ZACH) to build health literacy in health centre committees in clinics in two ZACH districts. This program hopes to increase level of knowledge of communities around health facilities on quality health services responsive to their needs. The work also facilitates and supports the establishment of mechanisms of community participation, such as Health Centre Committees, district chapters and Health Advisory Boards. The effort is reported to have trained a total of 60 facilitators from the Northern and Southern Regions of Zimbabwe that are implementing health literacy community programs in 20 districts in Zimbabwe.

The CWGH Zimbabwe has also started work around resuscitating community health committees in districts through reviving the Health Centre Committees and linking them with the Health Literacy facilitators in the districts under the program "Strengthening Health Centre Committees: Enhancing Community Participation in Health." Health Centre Committees are vehicles through which communities can participate in primary health care and district health systems. The work being done under the health literacy program facilitates and supports the establishment of mechanisms of community participation. Health literacy campaigns have been held at both the district and national level while the community health literacy trainings have reportedly reached more than 3,500 people and have the capacity to multiply. CWGH has campaigned for health literacy as a means to attaining some of the Millennium Development Goals, in improving primary health care, and in organizing people's power for health at the CWGH 15th annual conference held in October 2008 (CWGH, 2012).

EDUCATIONAL EFFORTS TARGETING HEALTH PROFESSIONALS

The CWGH efforts described above include specific components targeting Village Health Workers and other community-based health workers.

HOW IS HEALTH LITERACY DEFINED IN ZIMBABWE?

The CWGH defines literacy as an individual's ability to read and write and the degree to which a person can apply these skills to function in society, learn and achieve goals. Health literacy specifically refers to one's ability to obtain, process, and understand health information and services to make appropriate health decisions (CWGH, 2012).

European Union (EU)

EU POLICY

The white paper "Together for Health: A Strategic Approach for the EU 2008–2013" puts forth, first, a justification for policy efforts at the EU level. "Member States have the main responsibility for health policy and provision of healthcare to European citizens. The EC's role is not to mirror or duplicate their work. However, there are areas where Member States cannot act alone effectively and where cooperative action at Community level is indispensable. These include major health threats and issues with a cross-border or international impact, such as pandemics and bioterrorism, as well as those relating to free movement of goods, services and people" (Commission of the European Communities, 2007). The document continues by laying out core values held by members of the European community related to health policy. These core values are, in part, extrapolated from the report *Council Conclusions on Common Values and Principles in European Union Health Systems* (http://eur-lex.europa. eu/LexUriServ/site/en/oj/2006/c_146/c_14620060622en00010003.pdf). That report states, for example, that "The overarching values of universality, access to good quality care, equity, and solidarity have been widely accepted in the work of the different EU institutions," and that "All health systems in the EU aim to make provision, which is patient-centred and responsive to individual need" (The Council of the European Union, 2006). Building upon that basis, the White Paper identified a core value of "Citizen's Empowerment." This value is described as meaning that "Community health policy must take citizens' and patients' rights as a key starting point. This includes participation in and influence on decision-making, as well as competences needed for wellbeing, including 'health literacy'" (Commission of the European Communities, 2007).

EU HEALTH LITERACY INITIATIVES

Health literacy efforts seem to be increasing in number across the European Union. Perhaps most often reported is the European Health Literacy Survey (HLS-EU). The objectives of the initial effort, from 2009 to 2011, were to

- establish a European Health Literacy Network;
- adapt a model instrument for measuring health literacy in Europe;
- generate first-time data on health literacy in European countries, providing indicators for national and EU monitoring;

- make comparative assessment of health literacy in European countries; and
- create National Advisory Boards in countries participating in the survey and to document different strategies to establish an economic basis for health literacy efforts in differing national structures and priorities (Maastricht University, 2011).

The effort has successfully conducted a health literacy assessment in eight countries—Austria, Bulgaria, Germany, Greece, Ireland, the Netherlands, Poland, and Spain. Initial results collected during the summer of 2011 provide first-time data on health literacy across eight European countries (http://www.health-literacy.eu). The results of the HLS-EU were first reported at the European Health Literacy Conference in November 2011. The event, held in Brussels, attracted more than 150 participants from more than 20 countries (http://www.maastrichtuniversity.nl/web/Institutes/FHML/FHML/DepartmentsCAPHRI/InternationalHealth/ResearchINTHEALTH/Projects/HealthLiteracyHLSEU/Events.htm).

Although health literacy is not mentioned specifically in the EU 2020 strategy, the European Commission has launched the program "Health for Growth" in the context of the EU2020 strategy to increase productivity and to meet the challenges of an aging population and chronic diseases (http://ec.europa.eu/health/programme/docs/prop_prog2014_en.pdf). Health literacy, however, is not explicitly mentioned as part of the effort.

A respondent reported that growing interest in health literacy across the European Union is, in part, due to a panel discussion held as part of the 8th European Health Forum Gastein (2005) where a panel of international experts discussed health literacy and its importance and impact on Europeans. The report *Navigating Health: The Role of Health Literacy* is reported to have laid the foundation for EU recognition of health literacy as a critical empowerment strategy for European citizens and a pillar of both health and lifelong learning (http://www.emhf.org/resource_images/NavigatingHealth_FINAL.pdf).

More recently, The Collaborative Venture on Health Literacy is one of the priority initiatives of Enterprise 2020 of CSR Europe (http://www.csreurope.org). The effort was launched in 2010 and is jointly led by Edenred, Microsoft, MSD, Nestlé, Maastricht University, and Business in the Community UK with the support of CSR Europe. The effort produced a report, "Blueprint for Action on Health Literacy: Creating Value for Employees, Businesses and Indirectly the Wider Communities." This report essentially provides a toolbox for businesses to strengthen the health literacy of their employees by laying out the business case for health literacy and the justification for health literacy as the basis for corporate social responsibility activities (http://www.csreurope.org/data/

files/HL_Blueprint_/Final_Draft_HL_Blueprint_14_March_2012_FINAL. pdf).

A participant also reported on an EU project "Xplore Health" which targets youth from 15 to 18 years old with the aim to improve health literacy, to inspire future researchers in this area, and to bridge the gap between biomedical research and education (http://www.xplorehealth. eu). The initiative is reported to be an educational portal on cutting-edge health research that offers innovative multimedia and hands-on experiences to young people through the Internet, schools and science centers and museums (XploreHealth, 2010). The portal offers videos, computer games, virtual experiments, card games to promote dialogues on ethical, legal, and social aspects, and protocols of experiments linked to current research and activities for the classroom.

A brief roundup of health literacy efforts and policies across EU is offered at EurActiv.com where the issue is framed as moving forward as, "The first half of 2012 is set to see the Council and Parliament debate the Commission's new proposals for updating the directive on information to patients on medicines. The debate will take place against a backdrop of statistics showing that almost half of Europe's patients are 'health illiterates'" (*Health Literacy: Helping Patients Help Themselves*, 2012).

EU EDUCATIONAL EFFORTS TARGETING HEALTH PROFESSIONALS

None reported.

HOW IS HEALTH LITERACY DEFINED BY THE EUROPEAN UNION?

Respondents reported that health literacy is defined as the ability to make sound health decisions in the context of everyday life, at home, in the community, at the workplace, in the health care system, the market place, and the political arena. It is a critical empowerment strategy to increase people's control over their health, their ability to seek out information and their ability to take responsibility. Others reported that health literacy is defined as the ability to read, filter, and understand health information in order to form sound judgments.

The European Health Literacy Survey (HLS-EU) effort is reported to have adopted an integrated definition of health literacy, which was developed from a review of more than 15 definitions found in scientific literature. This approach posits that health literacy is based on general literacy and entails people's knowledge, motivation, and competences to access, understand, appraise, and apply health information to make judgments and take decisions in terms of health care, disease prevention, and health promotion in order to maintain and improve quality of life throughout the life course (Sørensen et al., 2012).

As reported from several nations, other respondents reported that they are not able to accurately offer a single definition of health literacy in the European Union, as there is variation within the member states.

United Nations (UN)

UN POLICY

In 2011, the UN General Assembly adopted the Political Declaration of the High-level Meeting of the General Assembly on the Prevention and Control of Non-communicable Diseases. In part, this resolution asserts that in order to reduce the risk of noncommunicable diseases and create health promoting environments, measures shall be taken to "Develop, strengthen and implement, as appropriate, multisectoral public policies and action plans to promote health education and health literacy, including through evidence-based education and information strategies and programmes in and out of schools, and through public awareness campaigns, as important factors in furthering the prevention and control of non-communicable diseases, recognizing that a strong focus on health literacy is at an early stage in many countries" (UN, 2011).

Also in 2011, the WHO Regional Office for Europe released a report, "Patient Engagement in Reducing Safety Risks in Health Care," which explicitly "aims to improve patient safety by enhancing patient empowerment and health literacy" (WHO, 2011). The same WHO office produced an earlier report in 2010, "Patient safety and rights: Developing tools to support consumer health literacy." In particular, this report asserts that "Both the topics of patient safety and patient rights are high on the health agendas of countries in the European region. This project aims to bridge the two approaches by trying to look at the links between patient rights and patient safety and more particular at means to improve patient safety by enhancing patient empowerment and health literacy." Specific foci of the project include blood transfusion, hospital infections/hand hygiene, and communication during patient handovers (WHO, 2010).

Earlier, in July of 2009, the UN Economic and Social Council (ECOSOC) issued a Ministerial Declaration that paid explicit attention to health literacy, which was "seen as an important factor in ensuring significant health outcomes," and included a call for appropriate action plans to promote health literacy (WHO, 2009).

More recently, in 2001 the United Nations Educational, Scientific and Cultural Organization (UNESCO) hosted the International Conference on Women's Literacy for Inclusive and Sustainable Development. While the conference highlighted the role of literacy, no explicit mention was made of health literacy (http://portal.unesco.org/geography/en/files/14476/13190177885Outcome_Document.pdf/Outcome%2BDocument.pdf).

In the UN Convention on Rights of People with Disability of 2006, Article 2 described the breadth of communication modes, Article 9 addresses issues of accessibility, and Article 21 addresses issues related to freedom of expression and opinion and access to information. Further discussion can be found in Basterfield (2009).

UN HEALTH LITERACY INITIATIVES

The WHO's 7th Global Conference on Health Promotion in 2009, held in Nairobi, Kenya, featured a specific track focusing on health literacy. A working document on health literacy was prepared to inform the discussion on health literacy, available at http://www.who.int/health promotion/conferences/7gchp/Track1_Inner.pdf.

Another member of the UN family of organizations, UNESCO, held a 2009 Regional Ministerial meeting on "Promoting Health Literacy" in Beijing, China. A summary report of the meeting is available at http://www.un.org/Docs/journal/asp/ws.asp?m=E/2009/104.

The WHO Healthy Cities Network includes efforts in more than 1,000 cities around the world and in every WHO region. The effort is reported to undertake a wide variety of projects addressing health literacy, health promotion, social marketing, and education (http://www.who.int/healthy_settings/types/cities/en).

The UNESCO Institute for Education produced a report on the follow-up to the Fifth International Conference on Adult Education (CONFINTEA V), held in Hamburg in 1997. The report specifically highlights health literacy as a tool for policy development and that it is necessary to identify indicators for the health literacy of individuals and society. Additionally, the report recommends that strategies to increase health literacy need to be developed (UNESCO, 1999).

An article in the UN Chronicle links health literacy with sustainable development. The article specifically relates information on UN projects ongoing in Angola, Mexico, Moldova, and Vietnam (http://www.un.org/wcm/content/site/chronicle/home/archive/issues2009/wemustdisarm/healthliteracyandsustainabledevelopment).

United Nations Children's Fund (UNICEF) is also reported to conduct health literacy–related efforts around the world. For example, the 2010 UNICEF annual report on efforts in China reports that the organization's

Health and Nutrition program will follow a health systems approach to reach the overall objective to support China's health sector reform so that "poor and vulnerable children and women will enjoy a better health and nutrition status, and protection from disease and impoverishment due to ill health, in line with 2011–2015 United Nations Development Assistance Framework (UNDAF) outcome two" (UNICEF, 2010). Objectively improving levels of health literacy among leaders and beneficiaries is a key expected result of that outcome.

Other efforts reported by participants to be related to health literacy at the UN level include

- Global partnership for girls and Women's Education: http://www.unesco.org/new/en/education/themes/education-building-blocks/literacy/single-view/news/unesco_global_partnership_for_girls_and_womens_education_enters_its_second_year
- Public-Private Partnerships in Education: Evidence-Based Approach: http://www.unesco.org/new/en/education/themes/education-building-blocks/literacy/single-view/news/public_private_partnerships_in_education_evidence_based_approach
- Innovative financing for education in Africa which is gathering data on educational systems using mobile media: http://www.iiep.unesco.org/no-cache/en/news/single-view.html?tx_ttnews%5Btt_news%5D=1019&tx_ttnews%5BbackPid%5D=262
- Yoza cellphone stories: Getting South African teenagers reading: http://www.unesco.org/new/en/unesco/themes/icts/single-view/news/yoza_cellphone_stories_getting_south_african_teenagers_reading

UN EDUCATIONAL EFFORTS TARGETING
HEALTH PROFESSIONALS

UNESCO is reported to have provided training for health care providers in Africa on doctor patient communication. No other information was reported.

HOW IS HEALTH LITERACY DEFINED
BY THE UNITED NATIONS?

In 1998, the *WHO Health Promotion Glossary* defined health literacy as, "The cognitive and social skills which determine the motivation and ability of individuals to gain access to, understand and use information in ways which promote and maintain good health" (WHO, 1998).

The UNESCO 2009 meeting discussed above defined health literacy as "the ability to gain access to, understand and use health information for promoting and maintaining good health" (UNESCO, 1999).

WHO is also reported to have defined health literacy as "the achievement of a level of knowledge, personal skills, and confidence to take action to improve personal and community health by changing personal lifestyles and living conditions. Thus, health literacy means more than being able to read pamphlets and make appointments. By improving people's access to health information, and their capacity to use it effectively, health literacy is critical to empowerment. Health literacy is itself dependent upon more general levels of literacy. Poor literacy can affect people's health directly by limiting their personal, social and cultural development, as well as hindering the development of health literacy" (European Health Management Association, 2008).

International Nongovernmental Organizations (in alphabetical order)

Participants in the data-gathering process that helped create these reports on health literacy efforts around the world identified several NGOs that are conducting efforts in more than one nation. In this section, those health literacy efforts conducted by NGOs working in multiple countries are reported in alphabetical order.

The Asia-Europe Foundation—Health on Stage Program

The Asia-Europe Foundation program (http://www.asef.org/index.php/projects/themes/public-health/1987-10th-asia-europe-young-volunteers-exchange-health-on-stage). This program aimed to involve young people in tackling key global public health issues. Twenty-seven young participants from 14 countries in Asia and Europe gathered in three cities in India: Bangalore, Chennai, and Mysore. They identified crucial health issues in these areas and put together a series of plays from August to October 2011, which reached out to more than 3,000 people from the local communities. The forum theatre format was chosen as it allowed interaction and engagement between the audience and volunteers and thereby created opportunities for a meaningful dialogue on cultural and health issues (Wongjarin, 2012). *Health on Stage* aimed to enhance cultural competencies and creative thinking of young volunteers in fostering dialogue on public health, focusing on water-related health issues. The initiative was a response to the recommendations of the Connecting Civil Society Conference 4 (CCS4), an official side-event of the 8th Asia-Europe

Meeting Heads of State and Government Summit, which took place in Brussels, Belgium, in 2010. At the Summit, the role of youth in promoting public health was emphasized.

Canyon Ranch Institute

Canyon Ranch Institute (http://www.canyonranchinstitute.org) is a 501(c)3 nonprofit public charity based in the United States and has, to date, conducted health literacy programs in Peru and the United States. In Peru, the organization developed the "Arts for Behavior Change" program, a study that developed and tested a new methodology, "Theater for Health," that used the arts to advance health literacy and, as a result, improved knowledge, home hygiene behaviors, and reduced microbiological risk factors among residents of a low-income community in Lima, Peru. In the United States, the organization has 14 active partnerships with a broad range of organizations in business, education, health care, and policy. The partnerships range from focusing on improving health policy to creating active community-based health literacy efforts like the Canyon Ranch Institute Life Enhancement Program and Time to Talk CARDIO.

European Patients Forum

The European Patients Forum (EPF) is based in Brussels and works European-wide. A participant reported that the EPF holds health literacy high on the agenda in terms of patients' rights and safety. The group organized a conference with health literacy as a theme in 2008 and partner on the issue in European Union matters as they strive to raise awareness of health literacy and integrate it into policies (http://www.eu-patient.eu).

BOX A-6
How Did You First Learn About Health Literacy?

"I believe that the first time I learned about health literacy was in 1989 when I had dinner with Scott Ratzan in Toronto after he had done a presentation for the Health Communication Unit which was part of the Centre for Heath Promotion at the University of Toronto that I directed at the time.

That encounter led me to be invited to a meeting on health literacy in Washington sponsored by Pfizer. A subsequent meeting with Rima Rudd when I joined the Institute of Medicine Board on Health Promotion cemented my interest in the topic and ultimately led me to do research using this concept and to participate in the Institute of Medicine Committee on Health Literacy and Co-Chair the Canadian Expert Panel on Health Literacy."

—Canadian participant

International Union of Health Promotion and Education (IUHPE)

The IUHPE established a Global Working Group on Health Literacy in 2011 (http://iuhpe.org/index.html?page=661&lang=en). The group has established a 3-year work plan for promoting healthy literacy policy, practice, and research. Members of the working group are from different regions of the world. IUHPE has designated health literacy as one of the central topics for sub-plenary sessions in the upcoming world conference and a priority area. Multiple presentations and workshops on health literacy have been organized at previous international conferences.

Sisters of Mercy of the Americas

Sisters of Mercy of the Americas is reported by a participant to have been carrying out their mission in the following eight countries (year efforts started in each nation are in parenthesis): Argentina (1856), Belize (1883), Chile (1965), Guatemala (1971), Guyana (1894), Honduras (1959), Panama (1959), and Peru (1962). Ministries in the eight countries range from formal education and health care to empowerment of women, care of children, aid to those suffering from poverty, literacy education, and pastoral responses to spiritual and temporal hungers. The participant reported that the organization's tradition of formal education is continuing at Colegio Santa Ethnea in Argentina, Muffles Junior College and St. Catherine Academy in Belize as well as Instituto Maria Regina in Honduras. Literacy and alternative educational programs are ongoing in Argentina, Guyana, Panama, and Peru. All the educational endeavors give particular attention to women and children suffering from poverty (http://www.sistersofmercy.org).

The What to Expect Foundation

On June 14, 2012, U.S. Secretary of State Hillary Clinton announced what is perhaps the newest health literacy initiative that will be ongoing in multiple nations—specifically in Bangladesh, Brazil, and Liberia. The U.S. Office of Global Women's Issues is partnered with The What to Expect Foundation (http://www.whattoexpect.org) to implement their Baby Basics Program in these three nations. The Women's Health Innovation Program will expand the Foundation's work to the international arena, and will be piloted in Bangladesh, Brazil, and Liberia. Building on more than 10 years of successful implementation across the United States, the international program aims to empower vulnerable and expectant mothers with evidence-based, culturally appropriate pregnancy information, education, and social support, in an effort to improve maternal and child health and literacy. The Foundation will develop innovative materials inspired and informed by their Baby Basics book and prenatal health literacy program. Work will be implemented with local partners and government agencies. The partnership will support and coordinate the work of front-line health care providers and policy makers by fostering collaboration, increasing capacity and ensuring that health information is accurate, comprehensive and readily available and accessible. The goals of the program are

- To provide evidence-based, culturally appropriate pregnancy and parenting materials to underserved families that are attractive, comprehensive and easy to read, and serve as a catalyst for learning and family literacy;
- To empower and educate low-income expecting women so they have the skills and the support they need to advocate for themselves, their babies, families and communities;
- To teach health care providers, educators and communities how to respectfully engage, communicate and educate low-income mothers during their pregnancy and childbirth; and
- To build initiatives to bring communities together to support pregnant and new mothers' learning, and ensure families receive compassionate information and timely care.

A small grants component will be awarded to local grassroots organizations to implement the program using the country-specific Baby Basics tools and curriculum.

World University Network (WUN)

The WUN held a Global Public Health Conference held in May 2012, where their Health Literacy Network held their first workshop to generate ideas about collaborative projects. This initial meeting resulted in five working research groups, centered on the following themes (http://www. wun.ac.uk/research/wun-global-health-literacy-network):

- Health literacy conceptual and priority issues
- Health literacy in an age of digital communication
- Health literacy and health inequalities
- Integrating health literacy into health professional training
- Participatory approaches to health literacy research

PRELIMINARY SUMMARY AND CONCLUSIONS

This discussion paper details the responses received regarding health literacy efforts outside of the United States as well as efforts reported in the European Union and the United Nations. A forthcoming paper will detail responses about health literacy efforts occurring within the United States. That forthcoming paper will also report on efforts sponsored by the business community around the world. Additionally, that forthcoming paper will include information on what participants in this process suggest as the best next steps for the field of health literacy and their quantitative assessments of the state of the field of health literacy.

Essentially, these two planned discussion papers make up two parts of a larger whole. The decision to separate the information was based on a desire to not create an appearance that health literacy efforts in the United States were any more advanced than in other nations. The amount of data from one nation compared to another or several nations is simply an indication of quantity, not necessarily quality. Additionally, given the vast amount of information collected in this effort, combining the information into one document would have produced a discussion paper that was quite simply impractical in length. Thus, given the amount of information to come in the forthcoming report, the conclusions and recommendations in this initial paper on health literacy activities occurring outside of the United States are necessarily preliminary and constrained.

Much of these data could perhaps have been subsumed in analysis versus reported, but there is a certain obligation to participants in such an effort to report their data as accurately and completely as possible from a non-critical perspective. The central aspiration is that this and the forthcoming discussion paper on efforts in the United States will provide a baseline that can and should be used for future study and comparison. The hope is that this effort uncovered a sufficient sample of activities to give an adequate—though incomplete—"taste" of how health literacy is being put to use and diffusing around the world. Clearly, however, the population of interest remains under-sampled—especially in nations where English is not the primary language.

Turning to analysis of the information that was gathered and reported, several points seem worth highlighting. First, the reports received from many nations clearly indicate the vital importance of leadership within a governmental structure. When leadership clearly adopts health literacy as an important factor, the results are significant. The vast body of evidence about health literacy supports the active promotion of health literacy by governmental, social, and cultural leaders, but nonetheless uptake among policy makers around the world seems delayed in many—but certainly not all—instances. To those policy makers remaining on the edge of the field as spectators, hopefully this key finding will suggest the presence of a clear opportunity. You will create a positive effect if health literacy is made central to your platform.

Second, the importance of engaging broad-based multidisciplinary partnerships is equally clear across the spectrum of information and sources that this effort encountered. A best practice of health literacy is to involve people early and often in order to better engage with their entire life. That inherently requires an integrative approach to be successful, and that is something many health care organizations are just coming to appreciate and embrace. Often, health care facilities may not have the personnel on hand to create an integrative, multidisciplinary effort—but rarely is it the case that an entire community does not have the resources to do so. Thus, creating partnerships across organizations may well be a critically important key to successful health literacy policy and practice efforts. Embracing both those approaches—adopting health literacy at the highest levels of leadership and creating multidisciplinary partnerships between organizations—seems likely to produce even greater progress in addressing health disparities around the world.

Several other lessons to policy makers and advocates should be clear as a result of this discussion paper. First, there is more than sufficient technical knowledge in the world to resolve many of the health issues that continue to plague the human population. What has been lacking is the means to effectively translate that knowledge into universal and precautionary action. The primary challenges seem to lie in how robust health literacy is conceptualized and the ability and willingness to engage a diverse group of stakeholders.

Next, it seems increasingly clear as a result of this data collection and reporting process that when governments have collected data on the status of health literacy among the populations they serve, they have also created health literacy policies and intervention projects. This project's design is limited in its ability to determine whether the data collection prompts policy development, or whether policy development causes data collection efforts, but a relationship clearly exists. A long history of research into health policy and efforts to inform practice with evidence confirms the importance of robust data to support the policy creation processes. Still, that remains a complex relationship that is neither unidirectional nor unidimensional. The causality, effectiveness, and outcomes of that relationship will, and should, be subject to continuing analysis. For example, a very promising area for future analysis of this relationship for the field of health literacy is to observe the outcomes to the recently completed survey of health literacy in eight European nations. Many of those nations are not among the leaders in creating health literacy policy to date, according to the results of this effort. The future outcomes of that effort shall help the field discover the direction and strength of the relationship between empirical data collection and policy activity in a variety of geopolitical and social contexts, but only if adequate resources are directed to the evaluation of the outcomes of that measurement effort.

Some, however, may question if an emphasis on policy making is warranted in a field that focuses so strongly on empowering individuals and communities to take action. Ironically, an emphasis on individual empowerment could lead to a logical fallacy that health literacy is not a policy-related field, as "top-down" efforts are not the primary or initial goal. However, a primary goal of empowering individuals and communities through advancing their health literacy is, in fact, to change or develop policies that produce healthier outcomes for all people. Thus, a monitoring of policy progress is a key indicator of the effectiveness of the field of health literacy and should remain a consideration of those designing health literacy interventions.

The information gathered in this effort does point out a critically important area for reflection and a strategic choice that faces the field of health literacy. Health literacy efforts are likely under way in every nation around the world. However, many may not have adopted the phrase "health literacy." An open-ended definition of the concept that accepts all comers has certainly helped the field of health literacy to rapidly grow. This discussion paper makes that growth increasingly clear. However, this effort has also found indications of cracks at the foundation to the field— especially as efforts to introduce health literacy into governmental policy move forward. Despite multiple policy initiatives, there remains to date a lack of a clear and effective approach to incorporating health literacy into policy that moves beyond rhetoric and into regulation that requires health literacy as a universal precaution. The one possible exception that may be emerging is plain language requirements, but those seem to be often either voluntary or not stringently enforced. Further, plain language in and of itself is unlikely to reach the level of effect that can be achieved through a focus on a more robust conceptualization of health literacy.

Health literacy, even more clearly as a result of this data collection process, is a socially constructed concept that nearly everyone agrees is important. However, very few seem to agree on what the concept actually represents. The risk to continuing that situation seems clear. If there is not a broadly shared consensus about the definition of health literacy, then the measurement and identification of health literacy remain problematic— and that puts into risk the adoption and effectiveness of policy formulations addressing health literacy.

Health literacy may well be a field on the verge of needing to make a major, collective decision. One path is to continue with the current status quo that does not demand a certain level of consensus or rigor regarding what is or is not health literacy. This approach, as demonstrated in this discussion paper, has attracted a broad range of interest and activity. A second path is to collectively agree on a core definition of health literacy that makes a distinction between a health literacy effort and, for example, efforts in health education or health communication. Those efforts are certainly not unrelated, but a core definition of the constructs can be delineated, measured, evaluated, and formulated into policy constructs if the will to do so is present.

One possible approach to making that distinction, should the field decide to move in that direction, is by defining health literacy as a theoretical cause of behavior change that produces positive health outcomes. That path would necessitate that studies of health literacy not stop data collection efforts at documenting the acquisition of knowledge or at the change of attitudes. Those outcomes have been historically true of much of health communication and health education—and much of health literacy to date. A more rigorous approach would demand that to be truly health literacy, efforts must demonstrate that the health literacy intervention caused behavior changes that produced health effects. In that sense, health literacy could use strategies from health communication and health education, but in many instances those strategies (or theories) would in and of themselves be insufficient to be identified as health literacy. That, in fact, is a very high bar that may even be unattainable. For instance, if this effort had initiated criteria for inclusion such that the collection and reporting of data about changes in health behavior and health status were requisite, at least half—if not vastly more—of the initiatives reported in this and the forthcoming discussion paper would likely have been excluded. Such criteria would have also demanded a nearly universal exclusion of the policy efforts reported around the world as they, by and large, have not been evaluated for outcomes.

Looking forward to the completion and distribution of the forthcoming discussion paper, it is important to note in closing that there should be much room for optimism given the clear expansion of health literacy that is documented in this initial discussion paper and will continue in the forthcoming paper. Awareness of and use of health literacy has diffused into some of the most remote regions of the world. Health literacy has also diffused into the heart of many of the most populous and connected locations on earth. Both are locations where people can and do experience some of the greatest inequities in health and where a rigorous application of health literacy's best practices—which we continue to develop—can have a tremendous and positive effect. That reality and the growing awareness of health literacy around the world are outcomes that clearly should be celebrated.

REFERENCES

Anonymous. 2001. IRA literacy award winner boosts workplace literacy. *Reading Today* 19(2):15.

Australian Bureau of Statistics. 2006. *Health literacy Australia.* Canberra, ACT: Australian Bureau of Statistics.

Australian Government Department of Health and Ageing. 2009. *Primary health care reform in Australia: Report to support Australia's first national primary health care strategy.* Canberra, ACT: Department of Health and Ageing.

CAST (China Association for Science and Technology). 2011. *The objectives and tasks of CAST.* http://english.cast.org.cn/n1181872/n1257426/n1263419/47292.html (accessed September 11, 2012).

Chinese Government. 2012. *Law of the People's Republic of China on popularization of science and technology (order of the president no. 71).* http://english.gov.cn/laws/2005-10/08/content_75055.htm (accessed September 11, 2012).

Coleman, C., S. Kurtz-Rossi, J. McKinney, A. Pleasant, I. Rootman, and L. Shohet. 2008. *The Calgary charter on health literacy: Rationale and core principles for the development of health literacy curricula.* Montreal: The Centre for Literacy.

Commission of the European Communities. 2007. *Together for health: A strategic approach for the EU 2008-2013.* Brussels: Commission of the European Communities.

ContinYou. 2011a. *About us.* http://www.continyou.org.uk/about_us (accessed September 11, 2012).

ContinYou. 2011b. *What is skilled for health?* http://www.continyou.org.uk/archive/skilled_health/what_skilled_health (accessed April 26, 2012).

The Council of the European Union. 2006. Council conclusions on common values and principles in European Union health systems. *Official Journal of the European Union* 49(C146).

CWGH (Community Working Group on Health). 2012. *Health literacy.* http://www.cwgh.co.zw/programmes/health-literacy (accessed September 11, 2012).

Darpna. 2012. *Welcome to the world of Darpna.* http://www.darpana.com/about_us.php (accessed September 11, 2012).

Department of Health. 2010. *Equity and excellence: Liberating the NHS.* Department of Health, United Kingdom.

Department of Health and Human Services Tasmania. 2011. *Bridging the communication gap. Communication and health literacy action plan 1 July 2011-June 2013.* Hobart, Tasmania: Department of Health and Human Services Tasmania.

Department of Health Government of Western Australia. 2012. *Patient first program.* http://www.safetyandquality.health.wa.gov.au/involving_patient/patient_1st.cfm (accessed September 11, 2012).

Duncan, G., L. Emmerton, J. Hughes, P. Darzins, K. Stewart, B. Chaar, T. Kairuz, R. Ostini, K. Williams, S. Hussainy, K. McNamara, K. Hoti, R. Bush, F. Boyle, M. Jiwa, B. Suen, and G. Swinburne. 2012. *Development of a health literacy education package for community pharmacists and pharmacy staff in Australia.* Paper presented at Institute for Healthcare Advancement Health Literacy Conference, Irvine, CA, May 9.

European Health Management Association. 2008. *Quality in and equity of access to healthcare services.* Brussels: European Health Management Association.

Faugier, J., and M. Sargenat. 1997. Sampling hard to reach populations. *Journal of Advanced Nursing* 26:790-797.

Health Canada. 2011. *About Health Canada.* http://www.hc-sc.gc.ca/ahc-asc/index-eng.php (accessed September 11, 2012).

Health Issues Center. 2012. *Create meaningful and sustainable participation within your organisation.* http://www.hic.infoxchange.net.au/home.shtml (accessed September 11, 2012).

Health Literacy: Helping Patients Help Themselves. 2012. http://www.euractiv.com/health/
health-literacy-helping-patients-linksdossier-496951 (accessed September 12, 2012).

Health Navigator New Zealand. 2011. *Waipuna statement 2011.* http://www.healthnaviga-
tor.org.nz/centre-for-clinical-excellence/health-literacy/waipuna-statement (accessed
September 11, 2012).

Health Navigator New Zealand. 2012. *Health literacy—Health Navigator NZ.* http://www.
healthnavigator.org.nz/centre-for-clinical-excellence/health-literacy (accessed September 11, 2012).

IOM (Institute of Medicine). 2004. *Health literacy: A prescription to end confusion.* Washington,
DC: The National Academies Press.

IOM. 2009. *Toward health equity and patient-centeredness: Integrating health litearcy, disparities
reduction, and quality improvement.* Washington, DC: The National Academies Press.

IOM. 2011a. *Innovations in health literacy research: Workshop summary.* Washington, DC: The
National Academies Press.

IOM. 2011b. *Promoting health literacy to encourage prevention and wellness: Workshop summary.*
Washington, DC: The National Academies Press.

Jerusalem Inter-Cultural Center. 2001. *The official directive of the Israeli Ministry of Health on
cultural competence is now formal!* http://jer-icc.org/blog/?p=857 (accessed September
11, 2012).

Jorm, A. F., A. E. Korten, P. A. Jacomb, H. Christensen, B. Rodgers, and P. Pollitt. 1997. Mental
health literacy: A survey of the public's ability to recognise mental disorders and their
beliefs about the effectiveness of treatment. *Medical Journal of Australia* 166(4):182-186.

Literacy in India. 2012. http://medlibrary.org/medwiki/Literacy_in_India (accessed September 11, 2012).

Maastricht University. 2011. *Health literacy (HLS-EU).* http://www.maastrichtuniversity.
nl/web/institutes/fhml/fhml/departmentscaphri/internationalhealth/
researchinthealth/projects/healthliteracyhlseu/healthliteracyhlseu.htm (accessed
September 11, 2012).

McCarthy, A., and J. Lynch. 2002. *Health literacy policy and strategy: Research report for national
adult literacy agency.* Dublin: National Adult Literacy Agency.

Ministry of Health. 2010. *Korero marama: Health literacy and Maori—results from the 2006 adult
literacy and life skills survey.* Wellington: Ministry of Health.

Ministry of Health and Child Welfare. 2009. *National health strategy, 2009-2013 for Zimbabwe:
Equity and quality in health—a people's right.* Harare: Ministry of Health and Child Welfare, Zimbabwe.

Ministry of Health and Family Welfare. 2007. *State of urban health in Delhi.* Delhi: Ministry
of Health and Family Welfare.

Mitic, W., and I. Rootman. 2012. *Approach for improving health literacy for Canadians.* Victoria,
BC: Public Health Association of British Columbia.

Mullis, I. V. S., M. O. Martin, A. M. Kennedy, and P. Foy. 2007. *PIRLS 2006 international report:
IEA's progress in international reading literacy study in primary schools in 40 countries.* Boston: International Association for the Evaluation of Educational Achievement.

NALA (National Adult Literacy Agency). 2012. *CrystalClear awards—previous winners.*
http://www.healthliteracy.ie/crystal-awards/previous-winners (accessed September
11, 2012).

The National Department of Health. 1996. *National drug policy for South Africa.* Pretoria: The
National Department of Health, Republic of South Africa.

The National Department of Health. 2011. *Policy on language services for the National Department of Health.* Pretoria: The National Department of Health, Republic of South Africa.

National Literacy Mission. 2003. *NLM goals.* http://www.nlm.nic.in/nlmgoals_nlm.htm
(accessed September 11, 2012).

NHS (National Health Service). 2012. *The expert patients programme (EPP).* http://www.nhs. uk/NHSEngland/AboutNHSservices/doctors/Pages/expert-patients-programme. aspx (accessed September 11, 2012).

Nishtar, S., and A. B. Mehboob. 2011. Pakistan prepares to abolish Ministry of Health. *Lancet* 378(9792):648-649.

Paakkari, L., and O. Paakkari. 2012. Health literacy as a learning outcome in schools. *Health Education* 112(2):133-152.

Pleasant, A. 2011. Health literacy: An opportunity to improve individual, community, and global health. *Adult Education for Health and Wellness* 130(Summer 2011):43-54.

PooP Creative. 2009. *Massukos.* http://www.poopcreative.org/music/massukos/massukos. html (accessed September 12, 2012).

Rootman, I., and D. Gordon-El-Bihbety. 2008. *Executive summary, a vision for a health literate Canada: Report of the Expert Panel on Health Literacy.* Ottawa: Canadian Public Health Association.

Rushforth, J., P. Arbo, J. Puukka, and J. Vestergaard. 2006. *Supporting the contribution of higher education institutions to regional development: Peer review report, Jutland-Funen in Denmark.* Washington, DC: Organisation for Economic Co-operation and Development, Directorate for Education, Education Management and Infrastructure Division, Programme on Institutional Management of Higher Education.

The Scottish Government. 2009. *Health literacy—a scoping study: Final report.* Glasgow: The Scottish Government.

SEWA (Self Employed Women's Association). 2009. *Part B social security.* http://www.sewa. org/Annual_Report2004_Part_B_Social_Security.asp (accessed September 11, 2012).

Simonds, S. K. 1974. Health education as social policy. *Health Education Monographs* 2(Supplement 1):1-10.

Sørensen, K., S. Van den Broucke, J. Fullam, G. Doyle, J. Pelikan, Z. Slonska, and H. Brand. 2012. Health literacy and public health: A systematic review and integration of definitions and models. *BMC Public Health* 12(1):80.

South African Government. 2009. *Constitution—1996—Chapter 2—Bill of Rights.* http://www. info.gov.za/documents/constitution/1996/96cons2.htm (accessed September 11, 2012).

TARSC (Training and Research Support Centre). 2009. *Building health literacy capacities in East and Southern Africa: Regional meeting.* Munyonyo, Uganda: Training and Research Support Centre.

UN (United Nations). 2011. *Political declaration of the high-level meeting of the General Assembly on the prevention and control of non-communicable diseases.* New York: United Nations.

UNESCO (United Nations Educational, Scientific and Cultural Organization). 1999. *6b health education for adults.* Hamburg: United Nations Educational, Scientific and Cultural Organization.

UNICEF (United Nations Children's Fund). 2010. *UNICEF annual report for China.* Washington, DC: United Nations Children's Fund.

Victorian Government. 2011. *Victorian health priorities framework 2012-2022: Metropolitan health plan.* Melbourne: Department of Health, Victoria.

WAHO (West African Health Organization). 2009. *Programme—promotion and dissemination of best practices.* http://www.wahooas.org/spip.php?article308 (accessed September 11, 2012).

WHO (World Health Organization). 1998. *The WHO health promotion glossary.* Geneva: World Health Organization.

WHO. 2009. *7th global conference on health promotion primer.* http://www.who.int/health promotion/conferences/7gchp/Primer_Inner.pdf (accessed September 12, 2012).

WHO. 2010. *Patient safety and rights: Developing tools to support consumer health literacy.* Copenhagen: World Health Organization Regional Office for Europe.

WHO. 2011. *Patient engagement in reducing safety risks in health care: Report of the meeting on patient safety and rights Copenhagen.* Copenhagen: World Health Organization Regional Office for Europe.

WHO. 2012. *Track 1: Community empowerment.* http://www.who.int/healthpromotion/conferences/7gchp/track1/en (accessed September 11, 2012).

Wongjarin, S. 2012. *Health on stage: A life-changing experience.* http://culture360.org/magazine/health-on-stage-%E2%80%93-a-life-changing-experience (accessed September 11, 2012).

XploreHealth. 2010. *About us.* http://www.xplorehealth.eu/en/about-us (accessed September 11, 2011).

Appendix B

Speaker Biosketches

Franklin Apfel, M.D., is the managing director and founding partner of World Health Communication Associates Ltd. His current work focuses on health literacy, mHealth, scorecard and checklist development, and building public health communication networks to counter hazard merchants, to brand health initiatives, and to make healthier choices easier. Previously, he has worked as head of communications for the World Health Organization Regional Office for Europe (Copenhagen), as Primary Health Care Fellow of the King's Fund (London), as regional director for Central and Eastern Europe Project HOPE (Bratislava), and as a general practitioner and medical director/CEO of California Health Leadership Inc. (Ukiah).

Cynthia Baur, Ph.D., is the senior advisor for health literacy, Office of the Associate Director for Communication, Centers for Disease Control and Prevention (CDC), U.S. Department of Health and Human Services (HHS). She chairs the CDC Health Literacy Council and manages the CDC health literacy website and blog. Also, she was one of the developers of CDC's online health literacy training for health professionals. From 2006 to 2010, she was the director, Division of Health Communication and Marketing, National Center for Health Marketing, CDC. She is a co-chair of the *Healthy People 2020* Health Communication and Health Information Technology Workgroup and a co-chair of the HHS workgroup on health literacy. She is the lead author of the National Action Plan to Improve Health Literacy. Dr. Baur holds a Ph.D. in communication from the University of California, San Diego.

Jo Ivey Boufford, M.D., is president of the New York Academy of Medicine. Dr. Boufford is professor of public service, health policy and management at the Robert F. Wagner Graduate School of Public Service, and clinical professor of pediatrics at New York University School of Medicine. She served as dean of the Robert F. Wagner Graduate School of Public Service at New York University from June 1997 to November 2002. Prior to that, she served as principal deputy assistant secretary for health in the U.S. Department of Health and Human Services (HHS) from November 1993 to January 1997, and as acting assistant secretary from January 1997 to May 1997. While at HHS, she served as the U.S. representative on the Executive Board of the World Health Organization from 1994 to 1997.

From May 1991 to September 1993, Dr. Boufford served as director of the King's Fund College, London, England. The King's Fund is a royal charity dedicated to the support of health and social services in London and the United Kingdom. She served as president of the New York City Health and Hospitals Corporation, the largest municipal system in the United States, from December 1985 until October 1989.

Dr. Boufford was awarded a Robert Wood Johnson Health Policy Fellowship at the Institute of Medicine (IOM) in Washington, DC, for 1979–1980. She served as a member of the National Council on Graduate Medical Education and the National Advisory Council for the Agency for Healthcare Research and Quality from 1997 to 2002. She currently serves on the boards of the United Hospital Fund, the Primary Care Development Corporation, and Public Health Solutions (formerly MHRA). She was president of the National Association of Schools of Public Affairs and Administration in 2002–2003. She was elected to membership in the IOM in 1992 and is a member of its Executive Council, Board on Global Health, and Board on African Science Academy Development. She was elected to serve a second 4-year term as the foreign secretary of the IOM beginning July 1, 2010. She received an honorary doctorate of science degree from the State University of New York, Brooklyn, in May 1992, and the New York Medical College in May 2007. She was elected a fellow of the National Academy of Public Administration in 2005. She has been a fellow of the New York Academy of Medicine since 1988 and a trustee since 2004.

Dr. Boufford attended Wellesley College for 2 years and received her B.A. (psychology) magna cum laude from the University of Michigan, and her M.D., with distinction, from the University of Michigan Medical School. She is board-certified in pediatrics.

Jennifer Cabe, M.A., leads strategic and operations functions for Canyon Ranch Institute, a 501(c)3 nonprofit public charity. Canyon Ranch Institute catalyzes the possibility of optimal health for all people by translating the best practices of Canyon Ranch and its partners to help educate, inspire, and empower every person to prevent disease and choose a life of wellness. Its partners include The Clorox Company, George Washington University, LIVESTRONG, and the University of Arizona. Ms. Cabe joined Canyon Ranch Institute in 2007, and was elected to the Board of Directors in 2011.

Ms. Cabe previously served in the Office of the Surgeon General as communications director and speechwriter for U.S. Surgeon General Richard H. Carmona. In that capacity, she developed health literacy initiatives with advocacy groups, community leaders, health professionals, policy makers, and the public. In 2005, Ms. Cabe was awarded the Surgeon General's Medallion, which is the highest honor the U.S. Surgeon General can confer. Ms. Cabe also received the prestigious U.S. Department of Health and Human Services Honor Award for her role in developing the "U.S. Surgeon General's Family History Initiative." In 2006, Ms. Cabe was awarded the National Institutes of Health Team Merit Award for her work on the Cancer Genome Atlas, a collaboration of the National Cancer Institute and the National Human Genome Research Institute. Prior to joining the Office of the Surgeon General, Ms. Cabe was communications officer at the Fogarty International Center at the National Institutes of Health.

Ms. Cabe is currently a member of the faculty of the Ohio State University College of Nursing. She is also chair of the National Call to Action on Cancer Prevention and Survivorship Council of Experts and serves on the advisory board of the Partnership to Fight Chronic Disease. Ms. Cabe also serves on the advisory board for Time to Talk CARDIO, an online health literacy program that received the Institute for Healthcare Advancement's Health Literacy Innovation Award in 2010.

Ms. Cabe earned a B.A. in English and communication at Trinity University in San Antonio, Texas, and an M.A. in public communication at American University in Washington, DC.

Nicola Dunbar, Ph.D., is a program manager at the Australian Commission on Safety and Quality in Health Care with responsibility for a range of program areas, including the deteriorating patient, primary health care, and patient-centered care. Dr. Dunbar has a background in health research, program management, and policy development and has worked for government, universities, and nongovernment organizations at local, state, and national levels. She has a Ph.D. in neuropsychology and HIV infection, and a master's in policy.

Federica Gazzotti, Ph.D., completed her doctorate in sociology with an emphasis on communication, following a degree in Oriental Languages.

She joined the Local Health Authority of Reggio Emilia, Italy, in 1998, focusing on public health communication. Dr. Gazzotti is responsible for the communication staff activities, which include front office and citizens welcome, public relations, press releases, Web communication management (internal and public website), and conference/training organization. She coordinates the Health Literacy Panel for the Emilia-Romagna Region, which facilitates and oversees health literacy projects in all the local health units of the region.

Steven J. Hoffman is an assistant professor of clinical epidemiology and biostatistics at McMaster University in Canada, and serves as a fellow in the executive office of United Nations Secretary-General Ban Ki-moon, where he offers strategic and technical input on a range of global health issues. A lawyer by training, Mr. Hoffman previously worked as a cross-border intellectual property litigator and held several positions with the World Health Organization (WHO). He continues to advise WHO on the development of a global strategy for health systems research. In the area of health literacy, Steven chairs an academic advisory committee on health and science, reporting for Canada's only national weekly current affairs magazine.

Fikry W. Isaac, M.D., M.P.H., FACOEM, is vice president, global health services, Johnson & Johnson. Dr. Isaac leads the development of health and wellness strategies, policies, guidelines, and services worldwide (Occupational Medicine, Employee Assistance Program and Wellness). Dr. Isaac has been with Johnson & Johnson since 1989, and for the past 10 years, he has been driving the comprehensive Total Health programs that have reduced the company's health care costs and improved the health of employees. He also serves as the chief medical officer for Wellness & Prevention, Inc., a Johnson & Johnson company. In this role, he provides health management expertise and strategic direction and supports customer acquisition and lead generation. In addition to his M.D., he received his master of public health degree in occupational medicine from the Medical College of Wisconsin in May 2001. He is a fellow of the American College of Occupational and Environmental Medicine, where he chairs the Pharmaceutical Section and the Corporate Health Achievement Award. Dr. Isaac is the industry co-chair of the Life Science and Innovation Forum–APEC. He also serves on several boards, including the Partnership for Prevention, the Global Health & Benefits Institute, and the Health Enhancement Research Organization.

Ilona Kickbusch, Ph.D., is the director of the Global Health Programme at the Graduate Institute of International and Development Studies, Geneva.

She is the chair of Global Health Europe, a platform for European Commitment to Global Health and of the Consortium on Global Health Diplomacy. In Switzerland, she serves on the executive board of the Careum Foundation and is the chairperson of the World Demography and Ageing Congress, St. Gallen. She is senior advisor to the regional director of the World Health Organization (WHO) Regional Office for Europe.

She advises organizations, government agencies, and the private sector on policies and strategies to promote health at the national, European, and international levels. She has published widely and is a member of a number of advisory boards in both the academic and the health policy arena. She has received many awards. In 2007, she was appointed as the Adelaide Thinker in Residence for the subject area "Healthy Societies" at the invitation of the premier of South Australia and continues to be involved in a range of projects in South Australia, in particular as regards Health in All Policies.

Her key areas of interest are Health in All Policies, the health society and health literacy, global health governance, and global health diplomacy. She has had a distinguished career with WHO at both the regional and the global level. She then joined Yale University as the head of the global health division, where she contributed to shaping the field of global health and headed a major Fulbright program. She is a political scientist with a Ph.D. from the University of Konstanz, Germany. Details can be found on her website: http://www.ilonakickbusch.com.

Jacob Kumaresan, M.D., Dr.P.H., is currently executive director, World Health Organization (WHO) Office at the United Nations in New York. Earlier, he was director at the WHO Centre for Health Development in Kobe, Japan, from 2008 to 2011, and president of the International Trachoma Initiative, a nonprofit organization dedicated to eliminating the leading cause of preventable blindness, from 2003 to 2007. He joined WHO headquarters in Geneva in 1992, where he eventually headed the Stop TB Partnership, expanding efforts to meet the global targets to stop tuberculosis. He has widespread public health experience and worked with the governments of Zimbabwe and Botswana during the 1980s.

Diane Levin-Zamir, Ph.D., M.P.H., MCHES, is director of the National Department of Health Education and Promotion of Clalit, Israel's largest health service organization, and lecturer in health promotion in the Schools of Public Health in Haifa, Tel Aviv, and Hebrew Universities. Dr. Levin-Zamir is a summa cum laude graduate of Tufts University in Boston, and earned a M.P.H. and Ph.D. from the Braun School of Public Health of Hadassah Hospital and Hebrew University's Faculty of Medicine in Jerusalem.

Dr. Levin-Zamir specializes in action research in health promotion in community primary care, hospital and media settings, media health literacy, and measuring health literacy, and she currently leads the Israel Health Literacy Survey. She has specialized in health promotion among special groups—children and adolescents, the elderly, and people with chronic conditions—and health promotion in multicultural settings. She is active in promoting comprehensive and sustainable health promotion implementation on national and local levels. She teaches health promotion planning, evaluation, and health literacy in medical, public health, and health professional training frameworks. Dr. Levin-Zamir has published extensively on various aspects of health literacy and health promotion. She is one of the founding members of the Israel Association of Health Promoters and Educators and is an active member of the National Council for Health Promotion of Israel's Ministry of Health.

Dr. Levin-Zamir has fulfilled a number of leadership roles in the International Union of Health Education and Promotion, is chairperson of the Global Working Group on Health Literacy, serves on the editorial board of the *Global Health Promotion Journal*, and is editor of the HP-Source.com for building capacity in health promotion.

Jennifer Lynch, M.A., is projects coordinator at the National Adult Literacy Agency (NALA). She is responsible for health literacy project initiatives. Jennifer joined NALA in 1997 as their first communications officer. Ms. Lynch, who holds a diploma in Plain English, introduced Plain English to the agency and other government agencies. She has been responsible for commissioning and managing IT projects such as www.literacytools.ie. She has an M.A. in sociology University College Cork and a postgraduate diploma in public relations Dublin Institute of Technology.

Don Nutbeam, Ph.D., FFPH, is vice-chancellor of the University of Southampton, a position he has held since 2009. His career has spanned positions in universities, government, health services, and an independent research institute. From 2003 to 2009, he was in senior academic roles in the University of Sydney, Australia, and prior to this he was head of public health in the UK Department of Health. His research interests have included social and behavioral interventions in schools and communities as well as studies of health literacy and adolescent health behavior. He is author of more than 100 publications in peer-reviewed journals as well as two popular public health textbooks. He remains active in research (within the constraints of his current role) through funded projects and Ph.D. student supervision. Dr. Nutbeam has substantial international experience in both developing and developed countries, working as an advisor and consultant for the World Health Organization over a 20-year period, and as consultant and team leader in projects for the World Bank.

Jürgen M. Pelikan, D.Phil., is a trained sociologist and psychologist (at the Universities of Berlin, Hamburg, Vienna, London School of Economics, and Columbia University) specializing in teaching and research in sociological systems theory, health promotion and health literacy, sociology of health and health care, and sociology of organizations (with a focus on organizational change), based in Vienna, Austria. At present he is professor emeritus of sociology at Vienna University, key researcher and director of World Health Organization Collaborating Center (WHO-CC) for Health Promotion in Hospitals and Health Care at the Ludwig Boltzmann Institute Health Promotion Research, Vienna, Austria, and adjunct professor at Griffith University in Brisbane, Australia.

In the last two decades, he has focused his basic and applied research on reform of health care (psychiatric care, medical education, quality in health care) and development of health promotion in theory and practice (theory of health, settings approach, health promoting hospitals). In these areas, he has directed several European and Austrian research projects and has supported the International Network of Health Promoting Hospitals and Health Services from its beginning in 1990 in his capacity as director of a corresponding WHO-CC.

He has done research on health literacy since 2001, being the project director of the European Project on Migrant Friendly Hospitals (2002–2005), whose three subprojects (interpreting in clinical communication, training and information in mother and child care, and cultural competence training for staff) had a strong focus on health literacy. Following this project, he was involved in workshops on health literacy at the European Health Forum in Gastein, Austria, and in European conferences on public health. He belonged to a group of European researchers initiating the European Health Literacy Survey (2009–2012) supported by European Commission, DG Sanco. In this project, he was a member of the project steering group, responsible for the Austrian part of the study and the report on overall and comparative analysis of health literacy data of the European project (WP 6). Currently, he also is directing the analysis for a specific report on health literacy in Austria and its regions and an additional Austrian study on health literacy of 15-year-old adolescents. Within the International Union of Health Promotion and Education (IUHPE), where he is a member of the board of trustees, he has together with colleagues initiated a working group on health literacy. He was jointly responsible for a stream on health literacy at the 20th IUHPE World Conference, 2010, in Geneva, and is planning one for the 21st IUPHE World Conference, 2013, in Pattaya. At present he also is working as co-editor and contributor on a WHO publication *Solid Facts of Health Literacy*. He will be a principal investigator in a EU-FP 7 project on diabetes literacy.

Scott C. Ratzan, M.D., M.P.A., is vice president, global health, Johnson & Johnson (J&J), and editor-in-chief of the *Journal of Health Communication: International Perspectives.* Dr. Ratzan is co-chair of the United Nations (UN) Secretary-General's Innovation Working Group on Women and Children's Health. He presented the "Framework for Action for the Prevention and Control of Non-Communicable Diseases" at the UN General Assembly interactive hearing in June 2011 as chair of the International Federation of Pharmaceutical Manufacturers & Associations NCD Taskforce. He currently serves on the World Economic Forum Global Agenda Council on health and well-being.

Dr. Ratzan continues research in health literacy, as he is the co-author of the definition that serves as the basis for U.S. efforts in this area. He currently is a member of the Institute of Medicine's Roundtable on Health Literacy. In 2010, he testified before the U.S. Congressional Committee on Achieving the United Nations Millennium Development Goals: Progress Through Partnerships. In 2009, he was selected by Research!America as an ambassador for global health research.

Dr. Ratzan initially joined J&J in 2002 as vice president for European Government Affairs and Policy based in Brussels. From 2005 to 2008, he served as the industry representative on the European Union High Level Pharmaceutical Forum Working Group on Information to Patients. Prior to joining J&J, he was senior technical adviser in the Bureau of Global Health at the U.S. Agency for International Development, where he developed the global health communication strategy for U.S.-funded efforts. He spent a decade in Boston (1988–1998) in academia as founder and director of the Emerson-Tufts Program in Health Communication, a joint master's degree program between Emerson College and Tufts University School of Medicine. In 1998, he moved to Washington, where he worked at the Academy for Educational Development on domestic and global health policy and innovation. He currently maintains faculty appointments at Tufts University School of Medicine and George Washington University Medical Center, and the University of Cambridge, Judge Business School.

His books include *The Mad Cow Crisis: Health and the Public Good, Attaining Global Health: Challenges and Opportunities*, and *AIDS: Effective Health Communication for the 90s*. He also has delivered many presentations, including the Leiter Lecture on Quality Health Communication for the National Library of Medicine and an address on risk communication for the National Cancer Institute which was selected in *Vital Speeches of the Day*. Dr. Ratzan has appeared on *Good Morning America* and *Nightline* and has published articles in the *New York Times*, *Wall Street Journal*, and

Financial Times and in academic journals, including *JAMA* and the *Lancet.*
Dr. Ratzan drafted "Maxims for Effective Communication on Health and
Risk Issues," which was published as part of a World Health Organization
Consultation in 1998.

He received an M.D. from the University of Southern California, an
M.P.A. from the John F. Kennedy School of Government, Harvard University, and an M.A. (communication) from Emerson College.

Michael Rosenblatt, M.D., scientist, educator, and hospital and global
health care company executive, is executive vice president and chief medical officer at Merck & Co., Inc. He represents the voice of the patient and
medicine inside Merck and is the company's primary external advocate
on medical issues.

He is the first person to serve in this role for Merck. Previously, he
served as dean of Tufts University School of Medicine. Prior to that,
he held the appointment of George R. Minot Professor of Medicine at
Harvard Medical School and chief of the Division of Bone and Mineral
Metabolism Research at Beth Israel Deaconess Medical Center (BIDMC).
He served as the president of BIDMC from 1999 to 2001. Previously, he
was the Harvard faculty dean and senior vice president for academic
programs at CareGroup and BIDMC and a founder of the Carl J. Shapiro
Institute for Education and Research at Harvard Medical School and
BIDMC, a joint venture whose mission is to manage the academic enterprise and promote academic innovation.

Prior to that, he served as director of the Harvard–Massachusetts
Institute of Technology (MIT) Division of Health Sciences and Technology, during which time he led a medical education organization for M.D.,
Ph.D., and M.D.-Ph.D. training jointly sponsored by Harvard and MIT.
And earlier, he was senior vice president for research at Merck Sharp &
Dohme Research Laboratories, where he co-led the worldwide development team for alendronate (FOSAMAX), Merck's bisphosphonate for
osteoporosis and bone disorders. In addition, he directed drug discovery efforts in molecular biology, bone biology and calcium metabolism,
virology, cancer research, lipid metabolism, and cardiovascular research
in the United States, Japan, and Italy. In leading most of Merck's international research efforts, he established two major basic research institutes,
one in Tsukuba, Japan, and one near Rome, Italy. He also headed Merck
Research's worldwide University and Industry Relations Department.

He is the recipient of the Fuller Albright Award for his work on parathyroid hormone and the Vincent du Vigneaud Award in peptide chemistry and biology, and the Chairman's Award from Merck. His research is in
the field of hormonal regulation of calcium metabolism, osteoporosis, and
cancer metastasis to bone. His major research projects are in the design

of peptide hormone antagonists for parathyroid hormone and the tumor-secreted parathyroid hormone-like protein, isolation/characterization of receptors and mapping hormone—receptor interactions, elucidating the mechanisms by which breast cancer "homes" to bone, and osteoporosis and bone biology.

He has been an active participant in the biotechnology industry, serving on the board of directors and scientific advisory boards of several biotech companies. He was a scientific founder of ProScript, the company that discovered bortezomib (Velcade), now Millennium Pharmaceutical's drug for multiple myeloma and other malignancies. He was a member of the Board of Scientific Counselors of the National Institute of Diabetes and Digestive and Kidney Diseases of the National Institutes of Health. He has been elected to the American Society of Clinical Investigation, the Association of American Physicians, to fellowship in the American Association for the Advancement of Science and the American College of Physicians, and the presidency of the American Society of Bone and Mineral Research. He has testified before a Senate hearing on U.S. biomedical research priorities in 1997, and in 2011 as a consultant to the U.S. President's Council of Advisors on Science and Technology.

From 1981 to 1984, he served as chief of the endocrine unit, Massachusetts General Hospital. He received his undergraduate degree summa cum laude from Columbia University and his M.D. magna cum laude from Harvard University. His internship, residency, and endocrinology training were all at the Massachusetts General Hospital.

Kristine Sørensen is researcher and project coordinator for the European Health Literacy Project hosted by the Department of International Health at Maastricht University in the Netherlands. She is the focal point for Health Literacy Europe, the European health literacy network. Ms. Sørensen is also engaged in other related projects such as the Joint Venture on Health Literacy with CSR Europe, which integrates health literacy into business action and corporate social responsibility, and the study on health literacy and the right to access to health in collaboration with the Council of Europe. In addition, she works closely with members of the European Parliament, the European Commission (DG Sanco), and the World Health Organization Regional Office for Europe to establish health literacy on the European health agenda.

Since 2007, she has been involved in the bachelor and master of European Public Health programs at the Maastricht University in various functions. Furthermore, she is a visiting lecturer at Centre for European Studies in Maastricht and the National School of Public Health in Lisbon, and she collaborates closely with Copenhagen and Aarhus University in Denmark.

Being Danish of origin her educational background is in medicine and public health with a bachelor's/master's degree in public health science from Copenhagen University. At present she is finalizing her Ph.D. studies at the research school CAPHRI/Maastricht University on the topic of health literacy in Europe.

Ms. Sørensen has held several organizational honorary positions at national, regional, and international levels. Currently, she is a member of the program committee in CaRe, Netherlands, Research School on Primary Care, and the board of commissioners in Kindante—an umbrella organization of 50 primary schools in the Limburg region of the Netherlands embracing more than 1,000 staff members and 10,000 pupils.

Suzanne Thompson, M.S., vice president for R&D, The Clorox Company, currently leads the Global Stewardship and Innovation group. In this role, she leads technology, design, corporate innovation, product stewardship, and regulatory issues. Prior to her current role, Ms. Thompson led the Cleaning Division R&D group starting in 2008. She has been working in the consumer packaged goods industry at The Clorox Company for the last 26 years in R&D. She has had experience in process, product, and packaging development for divisions such as Kingsford Charcoal, laundry, home care, auto, foods, litter, and professional products.

A native of Missouri, Ms. Thompson holds a master's degree in chemical engineering from the University of California, Berkeley, and a bachelor's degree in chemical engineering from the Massachusetts Institute of Technology, Cambridge, Massachusetts.

Sandra Vamos, Ed.D., Ed.S., M.S., is a senior advisor on health education and health literacy for the Centre for Chronic Disease Prevention and Control at the Public Health Agency of Canada (PHAC). Dr. Vamos joined PHAC from the faculty of education at Simon Fraser University in Vancouver, British Columbia, as an associate professor of health education and graduate coordinator. Her expertise, developed through her experiences in Canada, Australia, and the United States, includes health-promoting schools, health literacy, curriculum development, and teacher preparation. Her government work focuses on providing leadership and collaboration with key stakeholders such as academics, public health practitioners, and policy makers on knowledge development, dissemination, exchange, and translation of innovative health literacy interventions. Dr. Vamos provides strategic agency direction and contribution to the development and implementation of frameworks, approaches, tools, and products to build internal and external capacity for building health literacy awareness and the application of concepts into public health practices and programs. Her higher education work focused on both creating and restructuring university-level health education programs and improvements in school health education (K–12) to enhance health literacy through curricular and programmatic innovations emphasizing partnerships, including families, schools, communities and local, state/provincial, national and international organizations, associations, and institutions.

Dr. Vamos previously served as a faculty member in the Department of Exercise Science, School Health Education Master of Science program at Southern Connecticut State University. In Connecticut, she participated as a state trainer in the National Health Education Assessment Project initiative designed to direct improvements in health education planning and delivery to promote health literacy by aligning curriculum, instruction, and assessment. She also served as a faculty member and program coordinator at Canisius College in Buffalo, New York, where she developed both undergraduate and graduate health education programs.